PENGUIN ACADEMICS

CONSTRUCTING WORLDS TOGETHER

INTERPERSONAL COMMUNICATION AS RELATIONAL PROCESS

Kenneth J. Gergen

Swarthmore College

Stuart M. Schrader

Indiana University, Indianapolis

Mary Gergen

Penn State University, Brandywine

PEARSON

Boston   New York   San Francisco
Mexico City   Montreal   Toronto   London   Madrid   Munich   Paris
Hong Kong   Singapore   Tokyo   Cape Town   Sydney

Acquisitions Editor: Jeanne Zalesky
Series Editorial Assistant: Megan Lentz
Marketing Manager: Suzan Czajkowski
Production Editor: Karen Mason
Editorial Production Service: GGS Connie Strassburg
Manufacturing Buyer: JoAnne Sweeney
Electronic Composition: GGS Book Services-PMG
Cover Administrator: Kristina Mose-Libon

For related titles and support materials, visit our online catalog at www.
pearsonhighered.com.

To obtain permission(s) to use material from this work, please submit a written
request to Pearson Higher Education, Rights and Contracts Department, 501 Boylston
Street, Suite 900, Boston, MA 02116, or fax your request to 617-671-3447.

Between the time website information is gathered and then published, it is not
unusual for some sites to have closed. Also, the transcription of URLs can result in
typographical errors. The publisher would appreciate notification where these errors
occur so that they may be corrected in subsequent editions.

Library of Congress Cataloging-in-Publication Data

Constructing worlds together : interpersonal communication as relational
process / [edited by] Kenneth Gergen & Stuart M. Schrader & Mary Gergen.
     p. cm.
  ISBN-13: 978-0-205-38205-7
  ISBN-10: 0-205-38205-3
   1. Interpersonal communication—Study and teaching. 2. Oral communication—
Study and teaching. I. Gergen, Kenneth J. II. Schrader, Stuart M. III. Gergen, Mary M.

  BF637.C45C677 2009
  153.6—dc22   2008020268

Printed in the United States of America

10 9 8 7 6 5 4 3 2 1   12 11 10 09 08

Credits appear on page 293, which constitutes an extension of the copyright page.

To our families, friends, colleagues, and students
with affection and appreciation

contents

PART 2 The Relational Self 41

Introduction 41

CONTENTS

In this book, we take the view that interpersonal communication is at the very center of all that we take to be real, rational, and valuable in life. As we propose, it is within the process of interpersonal communication that the world becomes significant to us. This view, called *social constructionist*, stresses the major significance of relationships in our lives. It is in our relationships with parents, friends, neighbors, intimates, and even enemies that we become who we are, and plant the seeds of who we become. These views grow out of the past several decades of scholarship, not only in Communication, but in neighboring fields such as Philosophy, Literature, Political Science, Sociology, and the social and humanistic studies of science. It is our hope that the excitement surrounding this emerging view of communication can be shared with students in interpersonal communication classes throughout this country and abroad. Our wish is that the ideas contained in this book will not only be intellectually stimulating, but even more importantly, that they will enter the daily lives of students in ways that are both inspiring and practical.

The design of this book is uniquely suited to its purposes. A constructionist view of communication is crucially concerned with practices of relationship. Rather than simply presenting a standardized set of materials that students must master, we invite students into an active relationship with the authors represented in the text—and hopefully with each other and with their teachers. To be sure, there are many important concepts illuminated in the readings we have selected. However, we are far less interested in whether students can recite and regurgitate than we are in the enrichment resulting from engaging in dialogue about the ideas. Where most introductions to interpersonal communication are filled to capacity with the voices of authority—leaving the student with little room for participation—we attempt to reverse the emphasis.

As you will find, we present relevant readings in a brief form, and open a major space for students to engage the challenging ideas. We invite students to apply these ideas about interpersonal communication to their personal lives. While we may sacrifice coverage of "all the available concepts," we do so in the interest of creating a lively and personally meaningful educational experience.

In effect, this book asks students to be vigorous participants in an interactive, experiential learning encounter. Students are invited to take an embodied, physical, emotional, caring, and critical perspective in exploring the book's offerings.

They will encounter ideas that encourage them to reconstruct, reframe, and transform common patterns of living in ways that offer enriching possibilities for change. The reader will find special emphasis given to:

- How we mutually affect each other's lives.
- The importance of shifting from an individual centered view of meaning to a relational orientation to meaning.
- Our joint responsibility for the outcome(s) of our interactions.
- How our well-being as persons is crucially related to our relationships with each other.
- How we routinely act spontaneously and yet how spontaneity is routine.
- The significance of how the cultural, ethnic, racial and gendered group(s) in which we participate influence our understanding of the "taken for granted worlds" in which we live.
- The enriching capacity of exploring multiple truths and rationalities.
- The recognition of plural worlds of values and morality, and the importance of respectful encounters with these differences.
- The importance of dialogic practice in addressing plural worlds.

This book is about all of these issues and the possibilities they afford us for relational, familial, and social change. Our intent is to expand our common ways of understanding perception, verbal and nonverbal communication, listening, friendships, families, romantic partnerships, cultural identities, conflicts, and the ways in which we use and are affected by technologies.

Creating this text was an adventure for all of us. It is our fondest hope that by engaging with it, the experience will be transformative for students as well.

acknowledgments

As authors and editors of this work, we are enormously indebted to the many who have contributed to its design, development and production. We are all most grateful for the assistance provided to us by the helpful team of editing professionals at Allyn and Bacon. We especially wish to thank Karon Bowers for believing in the unique qualities and characteristics of this project and in supporting its development and design throughout. We also offer special thanks for the advocacy and continued support from Jeanne Zalesky. The volume has benefited as well from the good services of Karen Mason, Annie Pickert, Robert Tonner, Sarah Bylund, Jenell Forschler, and especially Connie Strassburg, Production Editor, GGS Book Services. We would also like to thank the many dedicated, helpful and thoughtful reviewers for this book: Robert Bookwalter, Marshall University; Bryan Crow, Southern Illinois University; Dennis Doyle, Central College; Doug Hurst, St. Louis Community College; Karta Jensen, Nebraska Wesleyan; Stephen A. Kilen, Augustana College; Sheila McNamee, University of New Hampshire; Patricia Sotirin, Michigan Technological University; and Shannon Valdivia, Mt. Hood Community College.

In terms of personal thanks, **Stuart Schrader** wishes to acknowledge the following:

First and foremost I give my sincerest and most heartfelt thanks to Ken and Mary Gergen. They have both graciously and most kindly taken me into their professional and personal lives by repeatedly inviting me to meet with them in their home so that we could create and recreate the text before you. I have found both Ken and Mary to be the rarest of colleagues in that they embody the genuine everyday performance of constructionist principles. They live life in a vibrant, giving and caring fashion. I am most respectfully grateful for their commitment, steadfastness and enormous effort and energy in collaborating on this book.

I am also grateful to my Communication colleagues both at IUPUI and throughout the discipline of Communication for supporting this book. I wish to thank my school, my department, and my current colleagues for all of their support. Additionally, I wish to thank several others for their generous support and insights: Kim White-Mills, Indiana University Purdue University, Indianapolis; Subah Packer, Indiana University, Indianapolis; Steve Fox, Indiana University Purdue University, Indianapolis; Len Assante, Volunteer State College; Bill Babler, Indiana University, Indianapolis; and Kathy Zoppi, Indiana University, Indianapolis.

Most importantly, this book would not have been completed without the technical administrative support and the diligent commitment to details of the following people: David Zahl, Mark McCleerey, Cindy Budyn, Janie McCammon, and Deb Komlanc.

Ultimately, it is the personal relations in my life that make the professional even possible. Without the support and engaged stimulation from my family and friends, my work on this project would not be possible. I owe many thanks to my spouse, Catherine A. Dobris, my colleague at Indiana University Purdue University, Indianapolis who is without question the most dedicated and principled teacher and educator I have ever known. She consistently provided routine editing, critical reflections, and unwavering support. I also wish to thank my three children: Jeremy, Alexandra, and Daniel and our close family friend Leslie Newland, who was and remains there for all of us whenever we need her. Finally, I want to thank my family, especially my parents, stepparents, in-laws and my sister, Ruth, in addition to all of the past mentors and educators who have influenced my decision to carry this book idea forward and whose teachings have greatly influenced my own communicative processes and practices.

Indianapolis, Indiana   August, 2008

Kenneth and Mary Gergen wish to acknowledge the following:

First we wish to express our deepest gratitude to our co-editor, Stuart Schrader, without whose invitation, we would never have become involved in this challenging project. Perhaps the three of us should also acknowledge the Café du Monde in New Orleans, famous for beignets and coffee, where under the spell of its indulgent atmosphere, we all decided to move ahead in the creation of the book. Since that fateful day, Stuart has been our creative and courageous companion, colleague and collaborator throughout the process. We have spent many days together with Stuart in working on this volume, and he has been delightful and supportive company throughout.

We also wish to thank the many scholars in the field of communication who have been such stimulating companions and loyal supporters over the years. We particularly wish to thank Art Bochner, Vernon Cronen, Carolyn Ellis, Jack Lannamann, Sheila McNamee, Barbara Montgomery, Barnett and Kim Pearce, Linda Putnam, William Rawlins, Jonathan Shailor, and John Shotter, many of whom are our close friends as well as colleagues.

The morning on which the three of us agreed to embark on this journey, New Orleans was in its classic form, undisturbed by the turmoil and tragedy that was to befall it. We look forward to a reunion there someday soon to celebrate not only the resilience of the city, but the final realization of our collective dreams.

Wallingford, Pennsylvania   August, 2008

about the editors

Kenneth J. Gergen is a Senior Research Professor at Swarthmore College, an Affiliate Professor at Tilburg University, and an Honorary Professor at the University of Buenos Aires. He is also the President of the Board of the Taos Institute, a non-profit organization devoted to relating social constructionist theory with social practices. Professor Gergen received his undergraduate degree at Yale University, and his PhD in social psychology at Duke University. Prior to taking the position as Chair of the Department of Psychology at Swarthmore, he taught at Harvard, and served there as the Chairman of the Board of Tutors and Advisors in the Department of Social Relations. He has also taught courses at the University of North Carolina, the University of Colorado, Marburg University, and Heidelberg University.

Professor Gergen has published hundreds of scholarly articles over his professional career and has written or edited over 20 books. Among his most significant books are *Toward Transformation in Social Knowledge* (Sage Ltd), *Realities and Relationships* (Harvard University Press), *The Saturated Self* (Basic Books), and *An Invitation to Social Construction* (Sage Ltd.). His forthcoming work, *Relational Being,*

Beyond the Individual and Community, is being published by Oxford University Press. Central to Gergen's writings are concerns with the self, communication, reality construction, cultural change, technology, conflict, and the nature of knowledge. Gergen has received numerous awards for his contributions, including fellowships from the Guggenheim Foundation, the Fulbright Foundation, and the Alexander von Humboldt Foundation. He has also been awarded honorary degrees in the United States, the Netherlands, and in Greece. Professor Gergen lives happily with his wife, closest friend, colleague, and joint editor of the present work, Mary Gergen.

Stuart M. Schrader is a Clinical Assistant Professor of Behavioral Sciences at the Indiana University School of Dentistry in Indianapolis. He is also an Adjunct Clinical Assistant Professor in Communication Studies at Indiana University Purdue University, Indianapolis and an Adjunct Clinical Assistant Professor in Family Medicine at the Indiana University School of Medicine. He has also taught at Ithaca College, Bloomsburg University and DePauw College. Since completing his Bachelor of Arts in Psychology from Humboldt State University, a Master of Arts in Communication from Western Kentucky University and a Ph.D. in Health Communication from the State University of New York (SUNY) at Buffalo, he has conducted research and presented extensively about issues pertaining to communication, interpersonal communication, scholarship of teaching and learning, and relationship-centered health care.

Professor Schrader has presented at over 50 scholarly conferences, reviewed numerous textbooks, published in national and international communication and teaching journals and has authored a custom edited textbook which introduced readers to a culturally sensitive approach to understanding interpersonal communication. He has been a highly effective course director for seven years of a large multi-section Interpersonal Communication course reaching approximately 500 students per semester. He has also received 5 teaching awards and one national mentorship award.

Professor Schrader lives with his spouse, Dr. Catherine A. Dobris, who is an associate professor of Communication Studies at Indiana University Purdue University Indianapolis and their 3 highly expressive children: Jeremy, Alexandra, and Daniel. When not teaching and writing, Professor Schrader enjoys traveling, cooking, cycling, and spending quality time with family, friends, colleagues, and students.

Mary Gergen is Professor Emerita at Penn State University Brandywine in the departments of Psychology and Women's Studies. She is also an advisor in the PhD program in Applied Social Sciences sponsored by the Taos Institute and Tilburg University, The Netherlands. Her educational background includes a Bachelor's degree from the University of Minnesota, as well as a Master's degree. Her PhD in social psychology is from Temple University. She has worked as a researcher at Harvard University, in Social Relations and the School of Business Administration, and at Swarthmore College. She has also taught at Widener University. During her sabbatical years she has been involved in research activities at Kyoto University, Japan; the Sorbonne in Paris; University of Heidelberg, Germany; the Max Plank Institute in Berlin; and as a research scholar at the Netherlands Institute of Advanced Study.

Professor Gergen has presented at numerous scholarly conferences, and has been an invited speaker at the Western Communication Conference and the National Communication Conference in Chicago, in 2008. She has been on the board of various journals, including *Feminism & Psychology*, and has recently been a co-editor of a special issue on performative studies in the electronic journal, *Forum for Qualitative Research*. Dr. Gergen has published widely in journals and edited volumes, and has authored or edited several scholarly books, including *Feminist Reconstructions in Psychology: Narrative, Gender & Performance*, as well as several textbooks. Her special interest has been in feminist theory and social constructionist ideas.

She has been a prize-winning educator at Penn State, and has always viewed her role in the classroom as a facilitator of each student's development.

Ken and Mary Gergen live in Wallingford, Pennsylvania, along with their dog, Julian. Their home is a center of intellectual activity and family fun, especially when their children, grandchildren, their significant others, and friends gather around the table for festivities and food. They travel a great deal, especially in Europe, and are torn between the generosity of foreign hospitality and the comforts of home. Tennis, golf, and exploring cultural venues engage them, at home and abroad.

Communication as Social Construction

You may think that you are beginning to read just another academic book, perhaps to fulfill another requirement. Ho, hum . . . business as usual. But think again! We have not put this book together because it "does a good job covering the field," or it is "proper education." Actually, such goals are not very exciting for us. Rather, it is our belief that if you truly understand what is in this book it could change your life. It will illuminate the world so that you will never see it in quite the same way again. Moreover, this illumination will be coupled with an enormous increase in freedom, an invitation to unlimited creativity and the deepest appreciation for human relationships. Yes, these are big words and lofty aspirations, but they reflect the way these ideas have had an impact our own lives. Moreover, they reflect the views of countless scholars and practitioners, not only in the field of communication but in numerous other fields—and across the globe.

We are not saying that you will agree with every reading. On the contrary, you may sometimes feel skeptical. However, if you find yourself resisting the arguments as they unfold, you will not be alone. Many of the readings in this book stir controversy, some of it heated. For example, some readings throw into question the concepts of truth and objectivity. Some raise questions about the idea of a basic, true, or real self. Other readings focus on the traditional understandings of moral values. There will be plenty of material for engaging discussions. As the editors of this work we find ourselves part of an educational system that generally defines the world in simplistic terms of true and false and right and wrong. For most of the important issues confronting humankind, it is important to be able to understand many sides of an issue, and then enter into and enrich the dialogue. It is not the final answer that counts in communicating with someone, but the continuing process of deliberation.

You are free, of course, to reject all that you find here. But before you do, please realize that we are not attempting to "sell a point of view." The important question is not whether you come to accept or reject these ideas, but rather, what you might be able to do with them. Think of these readings as resources for living in the world. Just like a pair of shoes or a winter coat, you may not need them all the time. At certain times and in certain places, however, they may be indispensable.

The social constructionist approach to communication will allow you to do things with words and actions that might otherwise be impossible. Regardless of how much you take from these readings, there is one conclusion that should be loud and clear: *It is in the process of communication that the world is born for us.* These words are a fitting welcome to the major theme of these readings.

Communication as Social Construction

Let us begin simply. When you look about you, what do you see? Perhaps there are some trees, several buildings, students, and a couple of cars . . . no big deal. But let's take little Julie, a one-year-old, out for a walk. Her gaze seems to move past the trees, buildings, and cars without notice; she does not seem to distinguish one person from another. William James once said that the world of a child is a "booming, buzzing confusion." Whether you agree with him or not, Julie's world doesn't seem to be the kind of world we live in as adults. Unlike Julie, we notice that autumn leaves turn from green to gold, that the house on our left is Victorian, that the car in the driveway is a BMW, or that what appears to be a male student is actually a female student. Julie doesn't stare with appreciation at the autumn leaves, she doesn't consider how much more attractive Victorian houses are than modern ones, and the price of the BMW is utterly irrelevant to her. Our world as adults is alive with interesting objects and entities; they have significance for us; we seek them out or avoid them; we place value on some and see others as dangerous or evil. Meanwhile, Julie seems to be staring at a speck on the side of her stroller.

How is it that our world becomes so full, so rich, and so saturated with value? The answer we find most compelling is that we achieve these "meaning-full" worlds primarily through human communication. If Julie were raised without human company—like the few feral children who have been found over the years—she would never look forward to a swim in a pool, a chance to play on a championship team, a beautiful wedding, a promising career, or a more just society. It is when we as human beings get together, and begin to coordinate our words and actions, that our worlds begin to take on shape and value. And, when her parents and friends begin to play with Julie, she will begin to call this figure a "boy," and this a "girl," this one a "momma," and another a "daddy." When she first hears her mother say "I love you," she may be utterly puzzled. By the age of 2, she may repeat "I love you" without understanding the words. By 3 or 4, she may find comfort and reassurance in hearing and repeating them in turn. At 16, she may be delirious with joy that a special person has spoken these words to her. Her joy is the result of her immersion in communicative relationships.

It is through communication that we construct our worlds. We begin to differentiate, for example, between men and women, Catholics and Protestants, stars and planets, east and west, and good and evil. Most groups want to declare that their way of constructing things is the right one—true, accurate, or objective. Newspapers strive to be objective, courts of law strive to locate the truth, and scientists want to draw accurate conclusions about the nature of reality. In the same way, many groups want to declare that their constructions reflect what is good, moral, or just. For example, religious struggles in the world today can be traced in part to disagreements about the nature of good and evil.

Proofs are often offered for why one construction is true and another is false. To suggest that all statements of belief are simply "ways of constructing the world," and not the real or right way, is upsetting if not antagonizing to many people. We suggest you consider that what we take to be true and good is "always created in human communication."

In these readings, evidence is generated and arguments are given as to why one position is better than another. We must realize, however, that evidence and reason are also generated within one's relationships. The physicist offers evidence that is compatible with the understandings and values within the field of physics; whereas the religious fundamentalist will offer evidence compatible with her or his spiritual beliefs. The physicist would not try to convince you of the reality of atoms by quoting the Bible, and the lay religious person will not try to prove that God exists through a laboratory experiment. However, it is our communicative relations that create the seemingly unshakeable and undeniable realities of physics and religious fundamentalism.

To illustrate this point, we ask that you consider what an objective or accurate description of yourself might look like. Imagine a group of people, drawn from all walks of life and regions of the world. Each member of the group may perceive particular "objective facts" about you, depending on their own background. It might go like this:

Biologist	A mammal
Hairdresser	Last year's style
Teacher	Promising
Gay man	Straight
Fundamentalist Christian	A sinner
Your father	Surprisingly successful
Your mother	Not devoted enough
Artist	Renoir body
Psychologist	Slightly neurotic
Physicist	An atomic composition
Banker	A future customer
Doctor	A hypochondriac
Hindu	Imperfect state of Atman
Your best friend	A loving, wonderful person
An Ifalukian	Filled with liget

If we removed all traditional conventions of communicating, then who would you be? Would you be anything at all? Each group has a different reality because of a history of communicative relationships. Each has learned a separate vocabulary of what is important about you from within a particular group's standpoint.

Your skeptical voice might respond, "You mean that death, or my body, or the sun, or this chair are all not real?" We must be clear on this point. Whenever people define what "reality" is or claim to have the objective facts, they are speaking from some tradition of communication. Whatever may exist outside our capacity to communicate is unknown to us because we cannot communicate about it. *Something* in our world happens, but the moment we begin to describe what "it" is, we do so from a particular tradition of communication.

Why is this line of reasoning important? First, it invites us to be curious and open to multiple points of view and values—even those which are contradictory. We do not have to fight over who has the *real truth*, the *right reasons*, or the *best way to live*. Rather, we are invited to see all truths, reasons, and ways of life as plausible in themselves. This gives us reason to explore alternatives and not be stuck in any one way of understanding.

Consider, for example, the seemingly obvious and simple fact of death. When we say "her father died" we are usually speaking from a biological standpoint. We are constructing the event as the termination of certain bodily functioning. Within the traditional communicative language of biology this may certainly be true. However, from other religious or spiritual traditions we might also say "He has gone to heaven," "He will live forever in her heart," "This is the beginning of a new cycle of his reincarnation," "His burden has been eased," "He lives in his legacy of good works," or "In his three children, his life goes on." In the reality of conventional biological communication there is only termination. He is gone, and that's it. In other traditions the same event is constructed in ways that offer hope, consolation, and a continuation of the person. These are valuable resources in times of crisis. We need not compare biological truth with these other traditions. Each offers something different to us as we live our lives together.

Further, when there are antagonisms among conflicting realities, truths, or conceptions of good, constructionist ideas work against tendencies to annihilate the opposition. There is little point in fighting it out. All constructions are legitimate within their own tradition. Rather than a fight to the finish, we invite you to seek new ways of communicating with each other. If it is through communication that we have created differences, then it is through communication that we can best resolve them.

Constructionist ideas are also important because they liberate us from "taken-for-granted moments." As long as we remain in our familiar traditions of speaking, we do not need to ask questions about what we mean by life or death. Things continue as usual. As long as we make the familiar distinctions, for example, between men and women, the rich and the poor, or the educated and the uneducated, our understanding of life remains relatively predictable. Yet, if we are oppressed by these traditional ways of expression, a constructionist orientation invites us to ask questions about these so-called realities. For example, "problems" don't exist in the world for all to see. Rather, we construct worlds of "what is good" and declare those events that stand in the way of achieving what we value as "good" to be "the problem." For example, in 1962 Betty Friedan wrote *The Feminine Mystique*, in part to explore how women were unfulfilled in their roles as housewives and mothers. She called this condition "the problem with no name." Her book created a major upheaval among women, and was virtually a bible for those who created the contemporary feminist movement. Without Friedan and other prominent feminists to identify this condition as a problem, the day-to-day life of U.S. women might have continued without question.

In addition to liberating us from the taken-for-granted, constructionist ideas alert us to the continuous possibility of creating new realities and values. For example, problems can also be reconstructed as opportunities. In the case of the feminist movement women began to move from the predominance of only advocating a critical stance to developing new visions of the ideal woman. By the same token we could construct together other worlds in which there are three genders or in which men are "the weaker sex."

It is at this point that you can begin to appreciate the enormous potential of the communication process. As we become aware of constructed worlds, our actions need not be constrained by anything traditionally accepted as true, rational, or right. Standing before us is a vast spectrum of possibilities and an endless invitation to innovation. This is not to say that we should abandon all that we value, but that the chains of either history or traditions of communication do not ultimately bind us. As we speak together, listen to new voices, raise questions, ponder alternative metaphors, and play at the edges of the taken-for-granted, we cross the threshold into new worlds of meaning. The future is ours—together—to create.

Key Constructions

- We create our worlds through communication
- We live and communicate within traditions of communication
- A constructionist invites us to
  - feel liberated, not needing to fight over what is ultimately "right," "real," or "absolute"
  - creatively explore the taken-for-granted
  - be curious about multiple views, positions, and values
  - search for new ways of talking that lead to alternative possibilities

Organization of the Book

This book is divided into five parts. They may be read in order, but it is not essential to do so. Once you have grasped the central ideas presented in Parts I and II you can go on to any other part without difficulty. Readings are selected with many different ends in mind. Some are from major contributions to contemporary thought and practice, whereas other readings bring up timely or fascinating issues relevant to interpersonal relationships. Still others are designed to create lively discussions. Wherever possible we have tried to select readings that are accessible, though you will find some may be easier to grasp than others.

At the beginning of each part you will find an introduction to the readings in that section. In addition, Parts III, IV, and V are broken down into sections that address specific topics, and each includes introductory text as well. These introductions will give you an overview of what is important in the section. In turn, each reading is introduced. These introductions are essential for locating important messages in the readings. At the end of each reading you will find a set of Explorations and a list of Key Constructions. The Explorations are especially designed to bring the readings and their importance to life and make them more relevant to you, the reader. We have created challenging questions that invite you to reflect on your own life, communication, and relationships in light of the issues raised by the reading. The Explorations will enable you to see the world and yourself in interesting and useful ways. The list of Key Constructions will help you keep major concepts in focus. Finally, we have provided photographs, cartoons, poems, and other inserts to give further life and dimension to these ideas.

PART ONE

Communication and World Construction: Making Worlds Together

Introduction

The readings in Part I are intended to bring to life some central ideas about communication and world construction. If you master these basic ideas, you should find it much easier to grasp and appreciate the offerings in the later parts of the book.

We begin with Reading 1, an excerpt from one of the most important philosophical writings of the 20th century, Ludwig Wittgenstein's *Philosophical Investigations*. We include only a single page of this work, but it contains a simple image of profound significance: *using language is like playing a game together*. Like a game, there are rules—typically unspoken—about how we talk and act with each other. This is obvious in the case of grammar. We are not supposed to say "he throwed ball." We would correct an English-speaking child who spoke this way. Other language rules are also present throughout our daily interchange. If someone thanks you for a favor, you are playing by the rules in mainstream American culture if you say something like "you're welcome," or "no problem." If you respond by saying "what's it to you?" or "you idiot!" you would not be playing by or within the rules. Not only would you make no sense, but you might be looked at as weird by your "teammates" in the game.

Although this seems reasonable enough, the implications of Wittgenstein's images are far reaching. Is it possible that most of our lives are guided by such rules? Whereas relations seem to be spontaneous and fluid, is there not always a form or structure that guides or invites us to move in relation to another? Consider, for example, an intense emotional situation in which you feel virtually out of control. You will typically play by the rules. You cannot, for example, shout angrily in the middle of a kiss, or yell at the clouds that you stub your toe. Emotional expressions must "make sense" in our particular culture. Wittgenstein's writing makes us wonder if we can ever escape the games of language.

The vision of the language game suggests that the communities in which we participate largely govern the way we describe the world. Thus, on a simple level, the world as described by a newspaper with Democratic leanings will be different from one with Republican beliefs. Or more profoundly, the world described by a scientist will differ from that of the poet or the religious fundamentalist. Each reality is constructed from within a community's tradition. In Reading 2, by David Morris, we extend this proposal to consider the way we experience our own bodies, and particularly what we call *pain*. We typically treat pain as a natural and objective given; when pain receptors are stimulated, we all feel pain. This is a natural fact of the world, and not subject to community standards. This reading asks us to reconsider this commonsense view. Is it possible that because of the communities in which we live, we will experience and thereby communicate about pain differently? Or more radically, is it possible that an experience constructed as pain in one community tradition would be considered pleasure within another? This reading opens these issues for exploration.

Reading 3 by David Rosenhan is also a classic. However, it begins to demonstrate the shortcomings of our constructed worlds. We owe to our rule-based conventions of communication our sense of what is real and good, our sense of a stable and reasonable world, and much that gives us pleasure and pain. But there are costs. One of them is a certain blindness or inflexibility in the face of change. Once we are participating in a certain convention of speaking and acting, we tend to understand everything in these terms, and to rely on our standard repertoire of communication. We can become blind to complexities and the kinds of novel actions required to relate successfully in new situations. In this reading, Rosenhan demonstrates that once mental health professionals have classified someone as mentally ill, the patient can scarcely escape the naming and labeling of this reality. Even when a person is behaving in the most normal way, he or she will continue to be treated as ill.

Reading 4 illustrates the rules of the game in everyday life. Here we offer a brief excerpt from the groundbreaking work of Harold Garfinkel. From Garfinkel's perspective, humans can scarcely function without rules governing the way we talk and act toward each other. Life would be nonsensical. There would be nothing we call "common sense," "reasonable," or "good." To demonstrate the profound significance of the unspoken rules governing everyday life, Garfinkel asked his students to go out and try to break the rules. What happens when we violate the common patterns of understanding we have constructed? The results are fascinating.

As we find out in Reading 5 by Christopher L. Bodily, the straight jacket of convention is scarcely limited to mental health professionals. All of us tend to live within the limits of our constructions. For example, we distinguish between men and women and between heterosexuals and gay people, without a second thought. And to be sure, there are certain practical reasons for dividing up the world in this way. But when you stop to consider all the various sizes and shapes of bodies, and all the various activities in which people find physical pleasure together, you quickly realize how limiting these terms might be in describing possibilities lying outside of our taken-for-granted constructions about sexual orientation. If a male and female have sex it doesn't necessarily make them heterosexual. Is a woman who has only one sexual encounter with another woman a lesbian? How do we decide who "is" heterosexual, homosexual or bisexual? Are these communication conventions too limiting? Do we need more or less language to describe our actions together? In this reading, Bodily shows us how our conventions of defining ourselves as "old" begin to reduce the richness of our lives—and possibly bring about an early death. What does it mean to be old, elderly, a senior? How do we define, use, and reuse this language?

In the final reading of Part I, Reading 6 by David Alexander, we take up the possibility of resistance. That is, once we understand that we live within conventions of talk and action, we open the door to possible reconstruction. On a simple level we can ask, "Is this the best way to define things?" "Is there another way we could talk about this that would bring about better results?" or, "Do we have to argue with each other like this?" We have a choice in how we define the glass as "half empty" as opposed to "half full."

The challenge becomes greater, however, when we confront good-old common sense, or challenge concepts that "everyone knows" are supposedly "true." To challenge is often to alienate, and creating alternative constructions is difficult and at times risky. Even more difficult is to raise questions about authoritative knowledge. Recall that even the most rigorous sciences do not tell us the "truth"; scientists too are parts of communities with conventional languages that construct worlds for specific purposes. In reading 6 we introduce an excerpt from the account of an ex-mental patient, David Alexander. He has been treated and named by mental health professionals as "diseased." Here he struggles with ways to transform this definition and to find a more promising form of self-construction.

Language Games

We typically treat language as a picture of the world. When scientists tell us about the world, we expect their words to be an accurate *portrayal* of their observations. In the same way we search for news reports that give an accurate *depiction* of events. We are skeptical of politicians whose words don't seem to match reality.

Although this picture theory of language is common enough, think again. Take the simple process of naming. There is Frank, Sally, Ben, and Sascha. Now these individuals were scarcely born into the world with nametags. The names were assigned by their parents, and in this sense they are arbitrary. For example, Frank could have been named Ben, Robert, or Yong Su. But why were they given names in the first place? The most important reason is practicality. For example, parents want to talk about Sally's welfare: Is she eating properly? Does her diaper need changing? Is her brother Frank jealous of her? In effect, the parents require the name to carry out practices of good parenting; and later they will need the name for other practical purposes, like enrolling her in school, and asking why she is out so late. More broadly, the words we use—just like the names we give to each other—are used to carry out relationships. They are not static pictures of the world, with singular meanings, but *practical actions*. More formally, we say that the words serve *pragmatic* functions. They are useful to us in carrying out relationships.

This is easy enough to understand in the case of words and phrases such as "Stop," "Danger!" or "Throw me the ball." All are useful in coordinating our actions. You can begin to see how our use of common names is socially useful. However, it is less obvious in the case of news reports, scientific accounts, or telling someone about your day. Here the words do seem to function like pictures; we can prove through observation that they are either true or false. But consider this again: Whether a description of an event is accepted as "accurate" will depend on a communal tradition. For example, whether we think someone is telling the truth depends on whether she or he uses language the same way we do. Is his or her tradition of description the same as ours? As you can quickly see, this means that our descriptions of the world always carry with them certain values, namely the values of our traditions. This is easy to see in cases of opposing teams or nations. What is "good aggressive play" from one side of the hockey rink will be called "brutal bullying" from the other. A "terrorist" in one country is a "hero" in another. Description and evaluation walk hand in hand.

In Reading 1, Wittgenstein suggests that we replace the image of words as a picture of the world with the image of a *language game*. To illustrate, you see a friend and say "Hey, what's up?" This is one move in the game. The friend responds "Nothing much." This is a second move in the game. And you both played by the commonly understood rules. If your friend had said "bird in sky" or "blub blub," you would be surprised, perhaps wondering "what's going on?" In effect, your friend stopped playing by the rules of the ordinary game of carrying out a greeting. If we are at a wedding, we will use a different vocabulary and the rules will be different than if we are attending a funeral or a sporting event.

It is also important to realize, however, that the concept of the language game extends beyond words alone. Our words are typically embedded in patterns of action. If you play by the rules you can't say "Hey, what's up?" and be looking up at the sky or down at your shoes.

To play by the rules means that your actions are patterned in special ways. Consider the game of baseball. Not only are there rules of talk, as in "strike one," or "stealing home," but the way we talk is associated with certain actions, like swinging the bat and missing the ball, or running in a certain direction. Our talk is also linked to objects such as bats, balls, and bases. Wittgenstein calls the collective relationship among "talk," "action," and "objects" a *form of life*. In this sense, weddings and funerals and baseball games are all forms of life. So, for example, students in classrooms also exhibit a way of talking, acting, and using objects differently than in other forms of life.

The following are a few passages from Wittgenstein's original formulation of the language game in 1953.

Reading 1   LUDWIG WITTGENSTEIN

Let us imagine a language . . . meant to serve for communication between a builder A and an assistant B. A is building with building-stones: There are blocks, pillars, slabs, and beams. B has to pass the stones, of the type and in the order in which A needs them. For this purpose they use a language consisting of the words "block," "pillar," "slab," "beam." A calls them out; B brings the stone which he has learnt to bring at such-and-such a call. Conceive this as a complete primitive language.

An important part of the training will consist in the [builder's] pointing to the objects, directing the [assistant's] attention to them, and at the same time, uttering a word; for instance, the word "slab" as he points to that shape. . . . This ostensive teaching of words can be said to establish an association between the word and the thing. But what does this mean? Well, it may mean various things; but one very likely thinks first of all that a picture of the object comes before the assistant's mind when he hears the word. . . . But now, if this does happen—is it the purpose of the word? . . . In the language [of the builder and the assistant] it is *not* the purpose of the words to evoke images. . . . Don't you understand the call "Slab" if you act upon it in such-and-such a way?

In the practice of the use of language one party calls out the words, the other acts on them. In instruction in the language the following process will occur: the learner *names* the objects; that is, he utters the word when the teacher points to the stone. And there will be this still simpler exercise: the pupil repeats the words after the teacher and both of these [are] processes resembling language.

We can also think of the whole process of using words as one of those games by means of which children learn their native language. I will call these games "language-games" and will sometimes speak of a primitive language as a language-game.

And the processes of naming the stones and of repeating words after someone might also be called language-games. Think of much of the use of words in games like [ring-around-the-roses].

I shall also call the whole, consisting of language and the actions, into which it is woven, the "language-game."

. . . Think of the tools in a tool-box: there is a hammer, pliers, a saw, a screwdriver, a rule, a glue-pot, glue, nails and screws. The functions of words are as diverse as the functions of these objects.

It is easy to imagine a language consisting only of orders and reports in battle. Or a language consisting only of questions and expressions for answering yes and no. And innumerable others. And to imagine a language means to imagine a form of life.

Explorations

1. Following are a series of sentence beginnings. Complete the sentences in three ways that would illustrate "playing by the ordinary rules of the game."

    Then try to disrupt or disobey these rules.

    Example: As she waved goodbye to me, with tears in her eyes, I began . . .

    a. Playing by the rules:

      to feel very sad.
      to cry.
      to feel relieved she was finally going.

    b. Violating the rules:

      to scream at her.
      laughing—heh, heh, heh.
      to tickle her.

    My father was angry with me, so I . . .

    a. Playing by the rules:

    _____

    _____

    _____

b. Violating the rules:

_____

_____

_____

I felt deeply moved by the expression of love, so I responded . . .

a. Playing by the rules:

_____

_____

_____

b. Violating the rules:

_____

_____

_____

I was unjustly accused of lying, so I told my romantic partner . . .

a. Playing by the rules:

_____

_____

_____

b. Violating the rules:

_____

_____

_____

2. Every language game creates a different world of reality and importance. Each new language game provides new possibilities and opportunities for understanding and acting in the world. Following is a list of several groups of people, each of which shares a specialized language game. In each case, write down several words commonly used to depict their reality. Consider how these words contribute to a "form of life."

Example: Dentists: teeth, cavities, drills, fillings, braces

Doctors: _____

Hairdressers: _____

Basketball players: _____

Priests: _____

3. When we understand language use as playing by the rules of a particular community, we also see that we "do things with words." We accomplish something pragmatically important within the community. In the following cases indicate what the parties accomplish in their exchange.

Example:

You say:	You hurt my feelings.
I respond:	I am really sorry, I didn't mean to.
The accomplishment:	You feel better.

a. You say: I would like to see a movie tonight.

   I respond: That would be great.

   The accomplishment: _____

b. You say: Can you tell me the time?

   I respond: My watch says 3:20.

   The accomplishment: _____

c. You say: I think I really screwed up my exam.

   I respond: I doubt it; you usually get a good grade.

   The accomplishment: _____

d. You say: I have a real problem with my parents

   I respond: You know, I feel the same way.

   The accomplishment: _____

Key Constructions

- Form of life
- Language game
- Language as pragmatic
- Picture theory of language
- Playing by the rules

The Culture of Pain

To say that we construct our realities through communication is easier to see in some cases than others. For example, most of us can agree that our conceptions of justice, good behavior, heroism, or love are constructed within various cultural settings. It is more difficult, however, to believe that the concept of gravity, the earth being round, or that chemical elements are each constructed by various groups of people (e.g., natural scientists) who share particular sets of values, standards, and language games.

One of the most challenging and yet fascinating cases of how we construct our worlds is that of physical pain. It seems so clear that we naturally feel pain from a blow to the head, a wound from a knife, or a sharp stone on bare feet. These reactions seem built into the physical system, or hard wired, as they say. Yet, constructionist ideas invite us to consider carefully assumptions that anything we do as taken-for-granted, is a natural hard-wired occurrence. In Reading 2 by David Morris, we are asked to consider the meanings attached to the physical experience.

Yes, blows to the body are among the events that place our body in discomfort. But such events must always be interpreted, and our interpretations grow from our relationships. Thus, the same blow to the head would be interpreted differently by a boxer than a pedestrian on the street. The former might sneer at his opponent; the latter might sue his assailant for the chronic pain he has inflicted. Do they both feel and experience the same pain? It is doubtful. As you read this account, try to consider how the process of communication and interpretation might function in altering our understanding of physical experiences.

Reading 2   DAVID MORRIS

Anyone who has endured a period of intense pain has probably asked, silently or openly, the following incessant questions: Why me? Why is this happening? Why won't it stop? Suddenly we simply do not possess the knowledge we need. The combination of doubt and fear can loosen an avalanche of related questions. How will I earn a living if I can't go back to work? Will my sex drive ever return? Am I doomed to spend the rest of my life in pain? To be in pain is often to be in a state of crisis. It is a state in which we experience far more than physical discomfort. Pain has not simply interrupted our normal feeling of health. It has opened a huge fault or fissure in our world. We need answers. We want to know what all this torment in our bones—the disarrangement of our personal cosmos—adds up to. What does it mean?

Today, of course, we seek the meaning of pain at the doctor's office. Sometimes, mercifully, the answer is straightforward. The pain you feel is caused by a ruptured disk or an infected ear. An operation or a course of antibiotics will set you right and eliminate your questions. But suppose that a successful operation still leaves you with constant pain. Suppose x-rays and lab tests reveal no hidden organic cause. Suddenly the questions multiply and seem more urgent. Your doctor refers you to a specialist, who finds nothing and refers you to another specialist, who also finds nothing wrong, but still the pain continues. The meaning of pain seems a nonissue as long as medicine can provide its reassuring explanations and magical cures. When cures repeatedly fail, however, or when the explanations patently fall flat, we must confront once again with renewed seriousness, even desperation—the ever-implicit question of meaning.

Ivan Ilych was an ordinary man: intelligent, cheerful, capable, sociable, good-natured. After his graduation from law school, he became a successful magistrate, performing his duties with honesty and exactness. He made a good salary, married an attractive young woman, and settled down to a life of domestic comfort. In due course, several children arrived. Soon he was promoted to Assistant Public Prosecutor and—after experiencing a slight but unpleasant friction in his marriage—thereafter he redoubled his application to the law. His greatest pleasure was playing bridge. A life so pleasant and so industrious brought further rewards. Before long he and his wife, who now got along better, moved into the house of their dreams.

It was in climbing a ladder (the metaphor is almost too common) while decorating the new house that Ivan Ilych slipped and fell, bruising his side. The bruise was painful, but the pain quickly passed. Soon, however, he noticed a queer taste that lingered in his mouth and an uncomfortable pressure where the bruise had subsided. He grew worried, uncharacteristically irritable, and at times quarreled openly with his wife. Eventually he developed in his side a dull, gnawing ache that never left him. He saw a doctor, got a prescription, consulted new doctors, got new prescriptions. There was no improvement. The pain in his side was like a slow poison relentlessly destroying his sense of satisfaction with life. He felt changed, alone, as if on the edge of a precipice.

The physical change in his appearance shocked him. At length even his family recognized that something was terribly wrong. It occurred to Ivan Ilych that he was dying, but the thought was impossible to grasp or understand. All the ordinary events at home and at work now seemed a sham or falsehood. He could not concentrate on them. His pain alone occupied his mind. His pain alone seemed real. It grew worse and worse still because his family (wishing to encourage him) steadfastly maintained the pretense that he was not dying. As his pain increased, Ivan Ilych began to wonder whether his entire life had been a lie: a carefully maintained structure of fraud and self deception. When the crisis finally came, he began to scream, and he screamed continuously for three days. It is said that one could not hear the screaming through two closed doors without feeling horror.

Tolstoy's spare, parable-like story *The Death of Ivan Ilych* (1886) provides a useful beginning because it introduces us so clearly to what specialists might want to call the hermeneutics of pain. Borrowing its name from Hermes, the Greek messenger-god who presided over dreams and rites of divination, hermeneutics concerns the art or science of interpretation. The Greeks and Romans seldom took important actions—an invasion, say, or a long journey—without the support of a favorable omen, but dreams and sacrificial rites were often full of ambiguous images (snakes killing eagles, discolored intestines, strange patterns in the rising smoke). Someone in a position of authority, usually a priest, was needed to interpret the omen. Pain, while perhaps less eloquent than a discolored intestine, is something that almost intrinsically calls for interpretation. . . .

Pain, whatever else philosophy or biomedical science can tell us about it, is almost always the occasion for an encounter with meaning. It not only invites interpretation: like an insult or an outrageous act, it seems to *require* an explanation. As David Bakan writes:

> To attempt to understand the nature of pain, to seek to find its meaning, is already to respond to an imperative of pain itself. No experience demands and insists upon interpretation in the same way. Pain forces the question of its meaning, and especially of its cause, insofar as cause is an important part of its meaning. In those instances in which pain is intense and intractable and in which its causes are obscure, its demand for interpretation is most naked, manifested in the sufferer asking, "Why?"'

Generally, of course, the explanations we expect today center on questions of medicine, and Bakan is especially useful in reminding us that such medical diagnoses constitute an interpretation. They implicitly help us to make sense of pain: to give it a meaning.

The interpretation of pain, however, has not always centered so exclusively on questions of medicine. The impulse to phone our local physician, which seems now almost instinctive and certainly belongs to the domain of absolute common sense, has required over the centuries significant learning and unlearning. Consider the biblical patriarch Job as he sits on his dunghill, covered with boils, struggling to figure out why God has punished him. What from a medical perspective appears to be simply a problem in dermatology lies at the distant horizon, not the center, of his experience with pain. . . .

The Death of Ivan Ilych offers a vivid illustration of the mobility of pain. The accident that Ivan Ilych first dismissed as insignificant, a trivial event in the course of an ordinary life, becomes over time subject to reinterpretation. Understood with hindsight, his pain sheds its original air of meaninglessness and at last exposes the origin of an unseen chain of events. An insignificant pain finally turns scandalous and terrifying. Like the devil impersonating a country salesman, its insignificance turns out to be merely a clever disguise that death has employed in forcing an entry into Ivan Ilych's otherwise well-insulated life. . . .

The meaning of pain, as Tolstoy develops the story of Ivan Ilych, expands beyond a symbolic union with death. Tolstoy shows us with remarkable clarity how pain continues to change over time. In fact, the specific changes he describes also reveal the larger sense in which pain—far from constituting a single, simple, unified entity—is inherently changeable. *The Death of Ivan Ilych* suggests that pain does not possess an unchanging essence but rather continues to move between the poles of meaninglessness and meaning, even as its meanings continue to change. It is as if pain were never fixed but perpetually in motion across the plane of a human life.

The variable meanings of pain in *The Death of Ivan Ilych* do not stop with the terrifying revelation of its link with death. All at once, after three days spent in screaming and struggle, Ivan Ilych suddenly experiences a deep calm, and his relation to pain changes once again. In effect, he passes through pain to a state of spiritual awakening. After this awakening, he is still aware of his pain—the pain has not diminished or disappeared—but now it somehow no longer matters, no longer torments him. He can address it as one might address an old enemy, long forgiven:

> "And the pain?" he asked himself, "What has become of it. Where are you, pain?" He turned his attention to it.
> "Yes, here it is. Well, what of it? Let the pain be."

The pain of Ivan Ilych now stands stripped of its terrors. His pain is, once again, simply pain. Tolstoy's narrative describes a kind of circular motion. For Ivan Ilych, the pain which began in meaninglessness and later revealed its symbolic link with death finally came to rest once more in meaninglessness. Yet the two types of significance are profoundly different. Ivan Ilych's final disregard of pain marks the attainment of a spiritual, almost otherworldly vision in which human life looks vastly different than it did in his period of career-building and social-climbing. At the very end of his life, Ivan Ilych unexpectedly scales a religious height from which he views his pain—even agonizing, excruciating, terminal pain—as truly insignificant. His final *understanding* of his pain (his acceptance of its place and meaning in his life) is Ivan Ilych's profoundest act. It is, needless to say, an act of interpretation.

The peculiarly changeable nature of pain—its power to take on new meaning or abruptly to lose, to regain, or to transform the meaning it temporarily possesses requires that we understand this most ancient and personal of human experiences as indelibly stamped by a specific place and time. Pain seems the quintessential solitary experience. We are probably never more alone than when severe pain invades us. Others appear to go about their business mostly unchanged, thinking that the world is just the same, but we know differently. The isolation of pain is undeniable. Yet it is thus especially important to recognize that pain is also always deeply social. The pain we feel has in large part been constructed or shaped by the culture from which we now feel excluded or cut off.

Reference

Tolstoy, L. (1967). *Great short stories of Leo Tolstoy* (L. & A. Maude, Trans.). New York: Harper & Row.

Explorations

1. The view that physical pain is constructed within the processes of communication is more easily appreciated by considering the differences among people in the way they experience pain. For example, if you are a female, you may find certain kinds of shoes painful, whereas other females do not. If you are a male, you may find the punishment your body takes in a given sport pleasurable, whereas, many of your peers do not.

   Consider at least one kind of experience that (a) you don't find painful, but many others do; and (b) that you find painful, and many others do not.

   a. _____

   _____

   b. _____

   _____

2. Consider the way your relations with others affected your experiences in exercise 1. How did your relationships enter into your experience?

   a. _____

   _____

   b. _____

   _____

3. List three different groups of people or professions (e.g., manicurist) in which pain may be reconstructed as not painful or even pleasurable.

   a. _____

   b. _____

   c. _____

4. You may have faced conditions in which you felt pain, but found ways to alleviate it being with other people. Consider, for example, getting hurt while playing a team sport or recovering from an operation. Describe an experience in which others helped you reduce your feeling of pain.

   _____

   _____

   _____

5. If the human experience of pain is affected by our communication in relationships, then the same should be true of pleasure. Consider (a) an experience that you find pleasurable that many others do not, and (b) an experience that many others find pleasurable but you do not. You might consider various foods, beverages, forms of music, physical sensations, or your appreciation of nature.

   a. _____

   b. _____

6. Return to these experiences and, in each case, try to describe how you came to like or dislike the experience in question. Focus in particular on the way your relations with others functioned. For example, the first taste of soda for many children is negative. It is fizzy and strange tasting compared to milk. Yet, after finding out their friends like it, children will often come to prefer it over milk.

   a. _____

   b. _____

Key Construction

- Socially constructing pain

READING 3

The Blinding Power of the Real

People cannot get along without making classifications. Yet calling someone a "loser" or a "hero" can have a powerful impact on how the person is treated. One consequence of classifying is that the label blinds us to the "exceptions to the rule." We miss the wins of the loser, and the failures of the hero. We become imprisoned by common constructions of the real. In this famous study, David Rosenhan dramatically illustrates the ways in which our constructions blind us. He shows us how a label of mental illness can become irreversible: Once a schizophrenic, always a schizophrenic. On reading this selection, consider how you or someone you know may feel imprisoned by a common construction (e.g., slow learner) of what others may label as real for you or someone you know.

Reading 3   DAVID ROSENHAN

If sanity and insanity exist, how shall we know them?

The question is neither capricious nor itself insane. However much we may be personally convinced that we can tell the normal from the abnormal, the evidence is simply not compelling. It is commonplace, for example, to read about murder trials wherein eminent psychiatrists for the defense are contradicted by equally eminent psychiatrists for the prosecution on the matter of the defendant's sanity. More generally, there are a great deal of conflicting data on the reliability, utility, and meaning of such terms as "sanity," "insanity," "mental illness," and "schizophrenia." Finally, as early as 1934, [Ruth] Benedict suggested that normality and abnormality are not universal. What is viewed as normal in one culture may be seen as quite aberrant in another. Thus, notions of normality and abnormality may not be quite as accurate as people believe they are.

To raise questions regarding normality and abnormality is in no way to question the fact that some behaviors are deviant or odd. Murder is deviant. So, too, are hallucinations. Nor does raising such questions deny the existence of the personal anguish that is often associated with "mental illness." Anxiety and depression exist. Psychological suffering exists. But normality and abnormality, sanity and insanity, and the diagnoses that flow from them may be less substantive than many believe them to be.

At its heart, the question of whether the sane can be distinguished from the insane (and whether degrees of insanity can be distinguished from each other) is not a simple matter: Do the salient characteristics that lead to diagnoses reside in the patients themselves or in the environments and contexts in which observers find them? From Bleuler, through Kretchmer, through the formulators of the recently revised *Diagnostic and Statistical Manual of the American Psychiatric Association*, the belief has been strong that patients present symptoms, [and] those symptoms can be categorized, and, implicitly, that the sane are distinguishable from the insane. More recently, however, this belief has been questioned. Based in part on theoretical and anthropological considerations, but also on philosophical, legal, and therapeutic ones, the view has grown that psychological categorization of mental illness is useless at best and downright harmful, misleading, and pejorative at worst. Psychiatric diagnoses, in this view, are in the minds of observers and are not valid summaries of characteristics displayed by the observed.

Gains can be made in deciding which of these is more nearly accurate by getting normal people (that is, people who do not have, and have never suffered, symptoms of serious psychiatric disorders) admitted to psychiatric hospitals and then determining whether they were discovered to be sane and, if so, how. If the sanity of such pseudopatients were always detected, there would be prima facie evidence that a sane individual can be distinguished from the insane context in which he is found. Normality (and presumably abnormality) is distinct enough that it can be recognized wherever it occurs, for it is carried within the person. If, on the other hand, the sanity of the pseudopatients were never discovered, serious difficulties would arise for those who support traditional modes of psychiatric diagnosis. Given that the hospital staff was not incompetent, that the pseudopatient had been behaving as sanely as he had been out of the hospital, and that it had never been previously suggested that he belonged in a psychiatric hospital, such an unlikely outcome would support the view that psychiatric diagnosis betrays little about the patient but much about the environment in which an observer finds him.

This article describes such an experiment. Eight sane people gained secret admission to 12 different hospitals. Their diagnostic experiences constitute the data of the first part of this article; the remainder is devoted to a description of their experiences in psychiatric institutions. Too few psychiatrists and psychologists, even those who have worked in such hospitals, know what the experience is like. They rarely talk about it with former patients, perhaps because they distrust information coming from the previously insane. Those who have worked in psychiatric hospitals are likely to have adapted so thoroughly to the settings that they are insensitive to the impact of that experience. And while there have been occasional reports of researchers who submitted themselves to psychiatric hospitalization, these researchers have commonly remained in the hospitals for short periods of time, often with the knowledge of the hospital staff. It is difficult to know the extent to which they were treated like patients or like research colleagues. Nevertheless, their reports about the inside of the psychiatric hospital have been valuable. This article extends those efforts.

Pseudopatients and Their Settings

The eight pseudopatients were a varied group. One was a psychology graduate student in his 20's. The remaining seven were older and established. Among them were three psychologists, a pediatrician, a psychiatrist, a painter, and a housewife. Three pseudopatients were women, five were men. All of them employed pseudonyms, lest their alleged diagnoses embarrass them later. Those who were in mental health professions alleged another occupation in order to avoid the special attentions that might be accorded by staff, as a matter of courtesy or caution, to ailing colleagues. With the exception of myself (I was the first pseudopatient and my presence was known to the hospital administration and chief psychologist and, so far as I can tell, to them alone), the presence of pseudopatients and the nature of the research program was not known to the hospital staffs.

The settings are similarly varied. In order to generalize the findings, admission into a variety of hospitals was sought. The 12 hospitals in the sample were located in five different states on the East and West coasts. Some were old and shabby; some were quite new. Some had good staff–patient ratios; others were quite understaffed. Only one was a strictly private hospital. All of the others were supported by state or federal funds or, in one instance, by university funds.

After calling the hospital for an appointment, the pseudopatient arrived at the admissions office complaining that he had been hearing voices. Asked what the voices said, he replied that they were often unclear, but as far as he could tell they said "empty," "hollow," and "thud." The voices were unfamiliar and were of the same sex as the pseudopatient. The choice of these symptoms was occasioned by their apparent similarity to existential symptoms. Such symptoms are alleged to arise from painful concerns about the perceived meaninglessness of one's life. It is as if the hallucinating person were saying, "My life is empty and hollow." The choice of these symptoms was also determined by the absence of a single report of existential psychoses in the literature.

Beyond alleging the symptoms and falsifying name, vocation, and employment, no further alterations of person, history, or circumstances were made. The significant events of the pseudopatient's life history were presented as they had actually occurred. Relationships with parents and siblings, with spouse and children, with people at work and in school, consistent with the aforementioned exceptions, were described as they were or had been. Frustrations and upsets were described along with joys and satisfactions. These facts are important to remember. If anything, they strongly biased the subsequent results in favor of detecting sanity, since none of their histories or current behaviors were seriously pathological in any way.

Immediately upon admission to the psychiatric ward, the pseudopatient ceased simulating any symptoms of abnormality. In some cases, there was a brief period of mild nervousness and anxiety, since none of the pseudopatients really believed that they would be admitted so easily. Indeed, their shared fear was that they would be immediately exposed as frauds and greatly embarrassed. Moreover, many of them had never visited a psychiatric ward; even those who had, nevertheless had some genuine fears about what might happen to them. Their nervousness, then, was quite appropriate to the novelty of the hospital setting, and it abated rapidly.

Apart from that short-lived nervousness, the pseudopatient behaved on the ward as he "normally" behaved. The pseudopatient spoke to patients and staff as he might ordinarily. Because there is uncommonly little to do on a psychiatric ward, he attempted to engage others in conversation. When asked by staff how he was feeling, he indicated that he was fine, that he no longer experienced symptoms. He responded to instructions from attendants, to calls for medication (which was not swallowed), and to dining-hall instructions. Beyond such activities as were available to him on the admissions ward, he spent his time writing down his observations about the ward, its patients, and the staff.

Specifically these notes were written "secretly," but as it soon became clear that no one much cared, they were subsequently written on notebook paper in such public places as the dayroom. No secret was made of these activities.

The pseudopatient, very much as a true psychiatric patient, entered a hospital with no foreknowledge of when he would be discharged. Each was told that he would have to get out by his own devices, essentially by convincing the staff that he was sane. The psychological stresses associated with hospitalization were considerable, and all but one of the pseudopatients desired to be discharged almost immediately after being admitted. They were, therefore, motivated not only to behave sanely, but to be paragons of cooperation. That their behavior was in no way disruptive is confirmed by nursing reports, which have been obtained on most of the patients. These reports uniformly indicate that the patients were "friendly," "cooperative," and "exhibited no abnormal indications."

The Normal Are Not Detectably Sane

Despite their public "show" of sanity, the pseudopatients were never detected. Admitted, except in one case, with a diagnosis of schizophrenia, each was discharged with a diagnosis of schizophrenia "in remission." The label "in remission" should in no way be dismissed as a formality, for at no time during any hospitalization had any question been raised about any pseudopatient's simulation. Nor are there any indications in the hospital records that the pseudopatient's status was suspect. Rather, the evidence is strong that, once labeled schizophrenic, the pseudopatient was stuck with that label. If the pseudopatient was to be discharged, he must naturally be "in remission"; but he was not sane, nor, in the institution's view, had he ever been sane.

The uniform failure to recognize sanity cannot be attributed to the quality of the hospitals, for, although there were considerable variations among them, several are considered excellent. Nor can it be alleged that there was simply not enough time to observe the pseudopatients. Length of hospitalization ranged from 7 to 52 days, with an average of 19 days. The pseudopatients were not, in fact, carefully observed, but this failure speaks more to traditions within psychiatric hospitals than to lack of opportunity.

Finally, it cannot be said that the failure to recognize the pseudopatients' sanity was due to the fact that they were not behaving sanely. While there was clearly some tension present in all of them, their daily visitors could detect no serious behavioral consequences—nor, indeed, could other patients. It was quite common for the patients to "detect" the pseudopatient's sanity. During the first three hospitalizations, when accurate counts were kept, 35 of a total of 118 patients on the admissions ward voiced their suspicions, some vigorously. "You're not crazy. You're a journalist, or a professor (referring to the continual note-taking). You're checking up on the hospital." While most were reassured by the pseudopatient's insistence that he had been sick before he came in but was fine now, some continued to believe that the pseudopatient was sane throughout his hospitalization. The fact that the patients often recognized normality when staff did not raises important questions.

Explorations

1. Rosenhan's study provides a vivid illustration of a process that all of us confront during our lives. We all are placed into categories by others, and these categories often become static and constraining. Think of a time when you have been placed in such a category by others (e.g., nerd, jock, airhead). In what ways were these categories binding? How did you feel about being classified?

_____

_____

_____

_____

2. Rosenhan's pseudopatients were unable to convince the hospital staff that they were indeed quite sane. However, in daily life we can sometimes change others' ways of describing us. Describe an incident in which you were able to reconstruct or change the reality of how someone had categorized you. What did you say and/or do to achieve this effect? For example, if someone said you were a nerd, you could demonstrate to them that you are socially savvy.

_____

_____

_____

_____

Key Constructions

- How constructions restrict our definitions and actions

READING 4

Breaking the Rules of Everyday Life

If as Wittgenstein suggested we view our ways of communicating as gamelike, we begin to realize the multiple ways the world can be "played." Each ordering of communication also means restrictions. Or, in the metaphor of the game, if we participate in a given language game we must play by the rules. Such demands are fairly obvious when we enter our first course in physics or astronomy. As we learn to speak in these various languages we soon realize that we must leave our everyday talk at the classroom door. If you tried to argue in your astronomy course that God created the heavens, you might possibly draw a critical remark from your professor. God is not usually found in the language game of Introduction to Astronomy. Rules of communication govern most of what we accept as common sense. When a professor is giving a lecture, you will not talk very loudly to your neighbors, turn around in your seat and stare at the students behind you, stamp your feet, or drink a beer. Restricting these commonsense actions is the result of playing by the rules.

Reading 4 is from the classic work of Harold Garfinkel, called *Ethnomethodology*. By the word *ethnomethods* Garfinkel meant the processes of everyday communication that keep our commonsense realities intact.

They are methods (practices) of the people (ethno) for sustaining the everyday world of common sense. For example, if you yawned loudly and stretched in the middle of a lecture, the teacher might stare in disapproval. The stare constitutes an ethnomethod for sustaining the reality of the classroom as a place where students honor the words of their teachers by not exhibiting rule breaking actions such as yawning and stretching during lectures.

To demonstrate the force of ethnomethods in everyday life, Garfinkel asked his students to go out and try to break the rules. Specifically, they were told to engage a friend or acquaintance in conversation, and at some point, begin to question the sense of what the other was saying. Without treating their reaction as unusual, they were asked to act toward the other as if the strange or unusual is now commonplace. A number of the cases are included in the reading.

Reading 4   HAROLD GARFINKEL

Case 1

The subject was telling the experimenter, a member of the subject's car pool, about having had a flat tire while going to work the previous day.

(S) I had a flat tire.
(E) What do you mean, you had a flat tire?

She appeared momentarily stunned. Then she answered in a hostile way: "What do you mean, What do you mean?" A flat tire is a flat tire. That is what I meant. Nothing special. What a crazy question!

Case 2

(S) Hi, Ray. How is your girl friend feeling?
(E) What do you mean, "How is she feeling?" Do you mean physical or mental?

(S) I mean how is she feeling? What's the matter with you? (He looked peeved.)

(E) Nothing. Just explain a little clearer what do you mean?

(S) Skip it. How are your Med School applications coming?

(E) What do you mean, "How are they?"

(S) You know what I mean.

(E) I really don't.

(S) What's the matter with you? Are you sick?

Case 3

On Friday night my husband and I were watching television. My husband remarked that he was tired. I asked, "How are you tired? Physically, mentally, or just bored?"

(S) I don't know, I guess physically, mainly.

(E) You mean that your muscles ache or your bones?

(S) I guess so. Don't be so technical.
   (After more watching)

(S) All these old movies have the same kind of old iron bedstead in them.

(E) What do you mean? Do you mean all old movies, or some of them, or just the ones you have seen?

(S) What's the matter with you? You know what I mean.

(E) I wish you would be more specific.

(S) You know what I mean! Drop dead!

Case 4

During a conversation (with the E's female fiancee) the E questioned the meaning of various words used by the subject:

> For the first minute and a half the subject responded to the questions as if they were legitimate inquiries. Then she responded with "Why are you asking me those questions?" and repeated this two or three times after each question. She became nervous and jittery, her face and hand movements . . . uncontrolled. She appeared bewildered and complained that I was making her nervous and demanded that I "Stop it" . . . The subject picked up a magazine and covered her face. She put down the magazine and pretended to be engrossed. When asked why she was looking at the magazine she closed her mouth and refused any further remarks.

Case 5

My friend said to me, "Hurry or we will be late." I asked him what did he mean by late and from what point of view did it have reference? There was a look of perplexity and cynicism on his face. "Why are you asking me such silly questions?

Surely I don't have to explain such a statement. What is wrong with you today? Why should I have to stop to analyze such a statement? Everyone understands my statements and you should be no exception!"

Case 6

The victim waved his hand cheerily.

(S) How are you?

(E) How am I in regard to what? My health, my finances, my school work, my peace of mind, my. . . . ?

(S) (Red in the face and suddenly out of control.) Look! I was just trying to be polite. Frankly, I don't give a damn how you are.

Case 7

My friend and I were talking about a man whose overbearing attitude annoyed us. My friend expressed his feeling.

(S) I'm sick of him.

(E) Would you explain what is wrong with you that you are sick?

(S) Are you kidding me? You know what I mean.

(E) Please explain your ailment.

(S) (He listened to me with a puzzled look.) What came over you? We never talk this way, do we?

Explorations

1. In the course of a conversation, raise questions about the words your conversational partner is using. Ask him or her what is meant (e.g., "Do you mean this in a physical, mental, or spiritual way?"), respond with puzzlement over what is commonsense and/or otherwise try to treat commonsense ways of talking as if they are strange and unusual. The previous examples illustrate some possibilities. Describe what you said and did in this conversation. What were the results of what was said by the other person? Write down your best recollection of the episode as a dialogue—as was written in the previous case examples in Reading 4.

_____

_____

_____

_____

_____

2. Within the course of a conversation, substitute for one commonsense descriptive term (e.g., *house*, *tree*, *girl*) another term, from another language game (e.g., *single-family dwelling*, *photosynthesis producer*, or *female-gendered person*). Unsettle the common way of naming the world. Describe what happens in this type of conversation.

_____

_____

_____

_____

Key Constructions

■ Ethnomethods
■ Distress that accompanies the disruption of ordinary rules of conversation

READING 5

Discourses of Death

As we have seen, the ways in which we construct the world together have practical consequences. To call an object "a chair" suggests by common convention that one can sit on it. To call the same object "a precious antique" suggests just the opposite. And so it is with the various ways in which we describe each other. In Reading 5, Christopher L. Bodily finds a strong tendency for older qualified nurses to define themselves as "too old" to take on nursing duties. The common phrase "too old for . . ." is not a trivial one. The description suggests that one should no longer carry out various activities or be a certain kind of person. As much gerontology research indicates, it is just such curtailing of activity that hastens death. As we narrow the spectrum of activity through our language choices and actions, and especially an activity about which we care, so do we become increasingly disabled and depressed. As one commentator put it, "We do not cease to be active because we grow older, but we grow older because we cease to be active."

Reading 5 CHRISTOPHER L. BODILY

My own interest in the concept of "age" and the subsequent analysis provided below emerged unexpectedly, from a research project on which I collaborated in 1990. The initial project was part of a growing effort among healthcare researchers to investigate and assess potential solutions to the "nursing shortage." Our specific focus was the shortage of nurses in long-term care facilities, and our aim was to assess the possibility of attracting older, inactive nurses into long-term care settings. Consequently, we conducted a survey of inactive nurses over the age of 50 residing in Illinois. Our rationale for targeting this group rested, in part, on the view that the voices of older, inactive nurses were simply missing from most discussions of the nursing shortage. Given the accumulated experience of older nurses, it seemed more prudent to pursue solutions informed by their voices, rather than amidst their silence.

As I began reading the written responses, I was immediately struck by not only the diversity of what was written, but by the sheer volume of writing. Many respondents answered the open-ended questions succinctly in the space provided, while others let their long, thoughtful reflections flow up and down the margins and over the top of the survey questions. While many comments qualified or elaborated upon previous responses other respondents offered anecdotes, proverbs, poems, newspaper clippings, letters, formative job experiences, stories of frustration, and many other poignant reflections that make up the lore of nursing. It was clear these respondents had a lot to say and the survey provided a discursive space within which they could say it; it functioned as more than a mere tally sheet for demographics and attitudes.

The Emergence of "Ageism"

Mostly as I thought about aging, I tried to rearrange my thoughts.

What interested me most about the ways the respondents were using "age" was that its meaning was being taken for granted; that is, "because of my age" or "I'm too old" were sufficiently obvious to require nothing more than a knowing nod on the part of the reader. Somewhere behind the uses of "age" were routine assumptions that the concept was both sufficiently meaningful and readily interpretable so as not to require further elaboration. One respondent, for example, stated, "I am 76 so you can see I am unable to work." Yet, other than the assumption that I (or any other reader) would readily know what it meant to be 76, it was not clear just what I was supposed to "see" from this statement. Should I have seen actual or perceived functional limitations, chronic illness, or perhaps the fear of being "out of touch" with current nursing practices? Or maybe I should have seen anxiety over the possibility of being discriminated against by employers, a lack of interest in returning to work, or even relief that one's working days are past? While these are a handful of possible meanings that might be lurking behind the phrase "I'm 76," there is nothing given by the respondent conclusively to suggest one over any of the others. About all I did manage to "see" was that this was one of hundreds of examples of the unreflective, unquestioned, and unelaborated use of "age" as an explanatory resource.

To give the reader a better feel for how "age" was used, some specific examples include "My age would not be conducive to working," "Age is a factor at this time," "It would be impossible at my age," "I am past the age," "My age is prohibitive," "The age factor," "I wouldn't consider it at 68 years," or simply "I am 64." Even more curious were comments that ruled out health, illness, physical limitations, and other things commonly associated with "age." For example, "[I am] no longer working because of age although in good physical condition," or "I am too old" even though I do not look my age or feel my age." Similarly, respondents ruled out other possible interpretations by stating them explicitly in conjunction with "age"—"age and health," "age and physical limitations," or "age and illness" to name a few. If health or other physical limitations were indeed the problem, then I could only wonder why respondents slipped "age" into their comments. What does it add? Not one respondent said that their limitations or ill-health were "due" to age. Instead, "age" was offered in addition to such factors.

Respondents not only deployed "age" in the various ways discussed above, but implicit in such deployments is a certain confidence that I (or any other reader) would interpret it appropriately. Consequently, I began to wonder just what it is that might permit "age" to be so confidently deployed? What might compel respondents to give "age" such tremendous explanatory responsibility, but at the same time not compel them to explain what they meant by it? The most obvious prospect, it seemed to me, was that the unelaborated use of "age" presupposes some larger context or construction from which it gains legitimacy as an explanatory resource. To merely say, for example, that "I am too old," and then expect this to be routinely accepted as a sufficient explanation, presupposes something deeper and prior to this particular deployment. Concepts of "age" would then be viewed as dependent on or emerging from a larger, more general construction. It was thinking about just such a construction that eventually pointed me toward *ageism*.

Among its other capacities, the structure of ageism, through our continued maintenance of it, legitimates and encourages the unreflective use of the concept of "age." Most commonly, it allows room for using either specific chronological dates (for example, "65 years" or "past the age of 70") or more general typological ages such as "too old," "over-aged," and "the young." Ageism's power comes from our willingness to take for granted what it means to be "65" or "too old" or simply "young." We bundle up various assortments of limitations, abilities, and characteristics and attribute them to different chronological dates and typological ages. Such constellations of abilities and chronological or typological ages are then readily available as self-contained explanatory resources. As Estes explains:

> The major problems faced by the elderly in the United States are, in large mea-
> sure, ones that are socially constructed as a result of our conceptions of aging
> and the aged. What is done for and about the elderly, as well as what we know
> about them, including knowledge gained from research, are products of our
> conceptions of aging. In an important sense, then, the major problems faced
> by the elderly are the ones we create for them. (1983: 1)

Although Estes is not addressing ageism per se, and I by no means offer this as a criticism, I should note that ageism is not confined to the elderly. That ageism, in the context of political discourse, is a charge often made against "the young" only adds to the confusion. Discrimination against the elderly is only one manifestation of the entire construction which I refer to here as ageism. The explanation, for example, that someone is "too young to understand" is equally a manifestation of ageism. Again, what the structure of ageism permits is the unelaborated use of chronological dates and typological ages as sufficient explanations. The concepts of "age" that emerge from ageism may be directed at young and old alike and may produce both victims and benefactors. Attributing "wisdom" to someone merely because they are chronologically old emerges as easily from the structure of ageism as attributing "irresponsibility" to someone's chronological youth.

While I am satisfied with the opportunity here to bring ageism and its emergent constructions to the table as analytic topics in their own right, I also hoped to avoid "over-determining" them and alienating my own account from future discussions. Rather than reaching some sort of conceptual closure, my intentions were to precipitate a more open or reflexive conversation about ageism and the deployments of "age." While much has been said about the "playfulness" and "reflexivity" of social constructionism, something ought to be said about the serious burden it imposes upon us. The shift from passive "discoverers" of a single reality to that of active architects, builders, and custodians of various "realities," means we have nowhere to turn but to ourselves. Rather than gazing objectively out of windows, we instead find ourselves in an elaborate hall of mirrors—turning one way, then another, but never managing to escape our own reflections.

Whatever the approach, we are never free from the responsibility of carrying on. Even while those so inclined wait patiently for the emergence of scientific truth and certainty, decisions still have to be made and actions taken. The constructionist aesthetic simply suggests that we do not hold our breath and carry on with some understanding of how we are implicated in the various realities that constitute our world.

Reference

Estes, C. (1983). *The aging enterprise.* San Francisco: Jossey-Bass.

Explorations

1. The nurses who defined themselves as "too old" did not create this category in themselves. All constructions of our worlds and our views of ourselves grow from within relationships. Therefore, we may suspect that the constructions of age and age-appropriate behavior may be widely shared within the culture. Is it possible that you, the reader, also have certain views of what is "proper" for people of various ages?

a. Consider a woman who has lived for 70 years. Would you generally define her as young, middle-aged, or old? _____ Would she be elderly or a senior? _____ Why? _____

_____

b. What would you think is proper for such a woman to wear to the beach?

_____

_____

_____

c. What would be inappropriate for her to wear to the beach?

_____

_____

_____

d. Would these same clothes be appropriate for a young woman or girl? If not, why not?

_____

_____

_____

2. Now consider the ways in which your age is constrained through these constructions. List three groups of people (e.g., parents, brothers or sisters, various friendship groups, faculty members) who place you in an age category. What do they expect from you in each case (for example, obedience, help, quiet) and how do you respond to their expectations?

Group of people: _____

Expectations: _____

Group of people: _____

Expectations: _____

Group of people: _____

Expectations: _____

Key Constructions

- Categorizing as constraining
- Ageism

The Challenge of Reconstruction

Reconstructing the real and the good is not always an easy task. For example, we can never step out of all conventions of communication. If we did so, we wouldn't be able to communicate at all. However, one major means of reconstructing is to draw on our ability to use multiple conventions in any given conversation. Because we participate in many relationships over the course of our life, we emerge with the potential to play multiple language games. With numerous conventions available to us, we are always in the position to *reframe*, that is, to locate within our language game repertoire an alternative way of constructing the world. In the popular idiom, if someone tells us a glass is half empty of its contents, we can quickly reframe by saying, "no, it is half full." But let us consider a far more challenging case. As we saw in Reading 4, once an individual is classified as mentally ill, it is very difficult for people to locate an alternative construction. Even when the individual no longer acts in an unusual or disruptive way, people may see him or her as "diseased."

In Reading 6, David Alexander, who was hospitalized during his undergraduate days for mental illness, describes his attempts in reconstructing himself following his release from the hospital. Do you think he succeeds?

Reading 6   DAVID ALEXANDER

One sunny day three months later, I returned to college. The small Catholic school had hundreds of wooded acres to roam. On campus, I was a "Jesus Freak," spending much of my time reading the Bible, praying with the monks, and going to daily mass. I intended to be a priest and began to study philosophy.

The study of philosophy was helpful in looking at my experience in other ways than as a "psychological disorder." A professor friend exposed me to William James, the father of American Psychology, who coined the term "flow of consciousness." William James said that there were plural realities. There was room for my symbolic experience to be a reality. He also spoke of the transmission theory of the mind, where the mind can pick up influences, as in Poetic inspiration or ESP. In his *Varieties of Religious Experiences*, he detailed experiences that reminded me of my own.

There was also literature which validated my experience, such as William Blake's "The Marriage of Heaven and Hell," and Dante's *Divine Comedy*.

But perhaps the strongest source of validation came from my dreams. Due to the noise in the dormitory in my last year, I got a study room in the monastery. I started sleeping there, and when discovered I was allowed to stay. The silence and the fact that I wasn't allowed to have guests made it conducive to meditation and remembering my dreams. One night I dreamt of a series of animal metamorphoses.

From a distance I see the tracks of a sidewinder moving under the desert sand. A snake with dark cross-marks surfaces onto lush green grass. "It's poisonous," I yell, warning my youngest brother. The snake stops by my wall and my eyes focus more clearly. It grows plump and yellow-black. Finally, the snake grows legs underneath, and rises a translucent white horse! It attacks me.

I took these metamorphoses to be like the stages of life: the first was related to infancy and the mother, when one's identity is submerged. The second concerned adolescence, and dealt with death and sexuality. The third stage was the critical one for me. The yellow-black snake I related to my hospital experience. Although it appeared that things were standing still, the true self was coming into focus. It was like the chrysalis where the inner organs of the larvae literally melt down to form a butterfly. The translucent horse represented a more spiritual stage that lifts above the ground. But the horse attacked me at the dream's end. Things were not all resolved.

Based on this dream I developed a mandala, a device where one intuitively divides reality into systems of fours. The four stages of life could be compared to colors, spatial forms, and modes of thinking. I took another walk where I thought I had found signs of the mandala in the foundation of a building under construction. Was I threatening to slip back again? My isolation in the monastery contributed to my starting to think of the world as an "out there," and as "evil."

My brother Frank, the middle brother I had not given much attention to, went to the same college. I still have the image of him studying hard at all hours, with a glass jar over a light bulb for a study lamp. I gave him some attention and help, but I was largely absorbed in my own world.

Nonetheless, I was still able to get involved with others. I camped out with friends, played college ball, and also edited a literary journal. I even wrote a few poems. I also wrote about my hospital experience, something I hoped to publish.

I had a second important dream that involved the presences of God. *I feel a dark wavy presence in the room; then I have the bright yellow thought of God, God! Suddenly, my body rushes out of the bed and I touch God's body. I'm surprised he has one. In another scene I'm approached by some black inner city youths, but I turn them away.*

Later, I determined that the black youths were also the presence of God. I decided that I must go somewhere where I could help the poor.

I graduated from college with honors, an accomplishment. I think this also is an important dimension in healing—to have something positive to separate you from the breakdown experience.

Ironically, by the time I left college, I had lost my faith again. My study of philosophy led me to think that church dogma was too rigid, and further, I felt that Christianity denied one's sexuality.

After I returned home, I had a difficult summer. The world offered few jobs for someone with a philosophy degree. I ended up shelving books in a library and serving as a live-in attendant for a handicapped person. Surviving a couple of lonely years, I decided to get my Master's in counseling. With my parents willing to support me, I headed north with a van I had bought for a $100. In a city, I hoped I would have a better chance to find women friends.

Going for a Master's in counseling was like trying to strengthen my Achilles heel. It was also part of a plan to gain expertise and official recognition for my book project about the symbolic experience. The shaman, I read, not only survived an encounter with the spirit world, but was legitimized by receiving teaching from his elders.

The Master's program was not as intellectually demanding as philosophy. I would raise difficult questions in class—thinking I was being a good student—while the professors were thinking, "There's one in every class." I didn't know that getting a graduate degree was like breaking into a labor union. They didn't want any "crazy people" getting through.

About this time I got involved in my first sexual relationship. Being so inexperienced, I didn't realize we were incompatible. She broke up with me and it caused a crisis. At the same time, in my last semester, I got two C's from this professor, and was expelled from Graduate School.

I searched deep inside of myself. There was a monk friend from the Catholic college, a master artist taught by one of Rodin's students. My friend sculpted and drew religious icons with a science-fiction look. I asked him one day why he believed in God. He asked me to consider the dignity of man. I began to read C.S. Lewis and G.K. Chesterton and certain questions were answered. They said that Christianity wasn't against the body and sex, just that the body was easy to abuse.

So one tear-filled day after a walk in the park, I returned to my belief in God. Eventually I even went back to church, and the community support I found became essential to sustaining my sanity.

I had some fights ahead, especially my expulsion from graduate school. I made transcripts of my work, claimed unfairness, and I threatened to go to the Dean. There was a tense meeting with the department head and the other teacher, but they agreed to let me try to finish, without changing my grades.

I studied for months for the comprehensive exams, feeling that they would try to stop me there. It was the final "test" I had to pass. One case example seemed designed to create anxiety, but I struggled through. One happy day, a professor informed me I had passed and had scored the highest among my classmates on the objective part.

Explorations

1. In the following we use a "popular convention" for describing a person, an object, or an event. In each case, provide two alternative reconstructions.

   Example: Losing a friendship
   (Alternative reconstruction: Opening up some space in my life)

a. A police officer arresting a loitering man on a bench at the bus station

Alternative reconstruction: _____

_____

b. The tragedy of divorce

Alternative reconstruction: _____

_____

2. Return to Reading 6 and locate passages in which the author is attempting to *reconstruct himself* as reasonable and good. Underline passages in which he seems to be making the attempt to reconstruct himself.

3. Reconstruction is facilitated when we can demonstrate a new view of something by providing new evidence. Rather than simply pointing to the person or event and reframing it, we add new information that validates the reconstruction. In Reading 6, Alexander offers new evidence that enables us, and himself, to reconstruct himself as not mentally ill. Highlight passages in which such evidence is offered.

4. Reconstruction is not an activity that occurs alone. As we have proposed, we generate meaning in relationships with each other. In his autobiography, Alexander attempts to recruit others into the process of reconstruction. Locate three different "groups" or "individuals" he draws into the process of reconstruction (e.g., famous authors).

_____

_____

_____

Key Constructions

- Reframe
- Reconstructing one's identity

Key Constructions for Part One

- We create our worlds through communication
- We live and communicate within traditions of communication
- A constructionist invites us to
  - feel liberated, not needing to fight over what is ultimately "right," "real," or "absolute"
  - creatively explore the taken-for-granted
  - be curious about multiple views, positions, and values
  - search for new ways of talking that lead to alternative possibilities
- Form of life
- Language game
- Language as pragmatic
- Picture theory of language
- Playing by the rules
- Socially constructing pain
- How constructions restrict our definitions and actions
- Ethnomethods
- Distress that accompanies the disruption of ordinary rules for constructing reality
- Categorizing as constraining
- Ageism
- Reframe
- Reconstructing one's identity

Suggested Readings

Abhib, M. A., & Hesse, M. B. *The construction of reality*. Cambridge, MA: Harvard University Press.

Austin, J. L. (1962). *How to do things with words*. New York: Oxford University Press.

Bakhtin, M. M. (1981). *The dialogic imagination: Four essays by M. M. Bakhtin* (C. Emerson & M. Holquist, eds.). Austin: University of Texas Press.

Berger, P. L., & Luckmann, T. (1967). *The social construction of reality*. Garden City, NY: Doubleday/Anchor.

Buttney, R. (2004). *Talking problems: Studies of discursive construction*. Albany: State University of New York Press.

Cronen, V., Johnson, K. M., & Lannamann, J. (1982). Paradoxes, double binds, and reflexive loops: An alternative theoretical perspective. *Family Process, 21*, 91–112.

Gergen, K. J. (1994). *Realities and relationships: Soundings in social construction*. Cambridge, MA: Harvard University Press.

Gergen, K. J. (1982). *Toward transformation in social knowledge*. New York: Springer-Verlag.

Gergen, K. J. (1999). *An invitation to social construction*. Thousand Oaks, CA: Sage. London: Sage.

Gergen, K. J., & Gergen, M. (2004). *Social construction: Entering the dialogue*. Chagrin Falls, OH: Taos Institute Publications.

Gergen, M. & Gergen, K. J. (Eds.) (2003). *Social construction: A reader*. London: Sage.

Holstein, J. & Gubrium, J. F. (Eds.) (2008). *Handbook of constructionist research*. New York: Guilford Press.

Leeds-Hurwitz, W. (Ed.). (1995). *Social approaches to communication*. New York: Guildford Press.

Mead, G. H. (1934). *Mind, self and society*. Chicago: University of Chicago Press.

Pearce, B. (1989). *Communication and the human condition*. Carbondale: Southern Illinois University Press.

Pearce, W. B., & Cronen, V. E. (1980). *Communication, action, and meaning: The creation of social realities*. New York: Praeger.

Philipsen, G. (1992). *Speaking culturally: Explorations in social communication*. Albany: State University of New York Press.

Potter, J. (1996). *Representing reality*. London: Sage.

Sarbin, T. R., & Kitsuse, J. I. (Eds.). (1994). *Constructing the social*. London: Sage.

Shotter, J. (1993). *Conversational realities*. London: Sage.

Sigman, S. J. (1987). *A perspective on social communication*. Lexington, MA: Lexington Books.

Stewart, J. (1995). *Language as articulate contact: Toward a post-semiotic philosophy of communication*. Albany: State University of New York Press.

Wittgenstein, L. (1953). *Philosophical investigations*. Oxford, England: Blackwell.

Web Resources

Archives of Harold Garfinkel's papers
http://content.cdlib.org/view?docId=kt087015p0&doc.view=entire_text&brand=oac

Barnett Pearce's organizational and academic websites
www.pearceassociates.com/pearce_associates.htm
www.fielding.edu/hod/faculty/wpearce.htm

David Rosenhan's website
www.law.stanford.edu/directory/profile/52/

Internet Encyclopedia of Philosophy-material about Wittgenstein
www.utm.edu/research/iep/w/wittgens.htm

Jonathan Potter's website
www-staff.lboro.ac.uk/~ssjap/index.htm

Kenneth Gergen's website
www.swarthmore.edu/SocSci/kgergen1/web/page.phtml?st=home&id=home

Bakhtin Center: University of Sheffield
www.shef.ac.uk/bakhtin/

David Morris's website
www.healthsystem.virginia.edu/internet/bioehums/morris.cfm

Jaber Gubrium website (constructionist papers)
sociology.missouri.edu/New%20Website%20WWW/Faculty%20and%20Staff/Jaber_Gubrium.html

Constructionist papers related to social practices
www.taosinstitute.net

Discussion Questions and/or Short Papers

1. The major significance of Part I is to demonstrate the pivotal importance of interpersonal communication in creating what we experience, or take to be real. This is not to imply that there is nothing outside what we construct

together. However, the moment we begin to speak about, to name, or describe, we enter into a tradition of communication.

- Can you illustrate the significance of this view as it applies to your own life?
- What are some obvious constructed realities?
- What realities do not seem to be constructed?
- If you understand these latter realities as constructed, could you imagine or create alternatives to the taken-for-granted?
  - What would be some of the advantages and disadvantages of developing alternatives to the taken-for-granted ways of describing and explaining?

2. Some people claim that people are born with moral instincts—that kindness to others, for example, is a natural good. Others claim that people are naturally out for their own gratification, that we are genetically programmed to be self-seeking. Yet, from the standpoint of Part I, what counts as moral, and whether we are moral or not is dependent on our history of relationships.

- To what extent do you find that morality is a social construction?
  - What are the advantages and possible limitations of this view?

3. This section introduces the notion that "using language is like playing a game together."

- Why is this notion a controversial claim? Give examples as to how looking at language this way may be useful in human relationships, especially interpersonal conflicts.

4. Consider your informal conversations with friends or family.

- In what sense is the conversation governed by unspoken rules?
  - What would be some infringements of these rules?
  - How would others react if you broke the rules?
  - Are there means of "bending" or "transforming" the rules, so that new ways of relating would be possible?
    - How would this happen?

Part Two

The Relational Self

Introduction

Whatever is real, good, or meaningful in life grows from communication. This was the major message of Part I. It is out of relationships that we generate language, and it is within language that the world comes to be this and not that, rational or irrational, good or bad. To put it another way, we come to be who we are through communication. To be someone who thinks, wants, feels, hopes, and fears is to have a history of relationships. Without relationships there would scarcely be anything to call a "self" at all.

When you stop to think about this proposal you soon realize that it runs counter to much traditional thinking about the self. We inherit so many ideas of the "self-made man [or woman]," "the lone hero," and the individual who "did it my way." More broadly, it is said that Western culture is *individualistic*.

Traditionally we believe that the single individual is the basic unit of society. We view groups—such as families, classrooms, and organizations—as composed of individuals. It has not always been so in Western history. In medieval times it was not the individual who counted so much as the family, the clan, or the profession. The very idea that we carry a second, or "family," name is a continuation of this early history.

Nor is the Western individualistic view of the self shared throughout much of the world. As many scholars have described, most cultures in the world are far more communal and collectivist in their conception of the person. It is not individual selves who make up the community, but the community that makes the individual important or not.

In Part II we introduce readings and explorations that develop further the constructionist proposals put forward in the preceding section. In particular, in this section we move beyond both the individualist and the communal traditions. Rather, we emphasize the idea of a self-within-relationship. That is, rather than viewing the self as fundamentally separate and alienated from others, we see how deeply related we are to each other, even in the thoughts and feelings we feel to be most private. Rather than seeing the self as the product of a community, we see the self come into existence within relationships. We move from both the individualist and communal self, to the idea of a *relational self.*

The first three selections demonstrate the ways in which our daily behavior is primarily "for others." These readings suggest that, for the most part, our talk, facial expressions, manners, gestures, dress, and other communicative practices are all fashioned within social traditions. In effect, the self is created for other people according to the socially shared rules of the times.

In Reading 7, the famous sociologist Erving Goffman uses the longstanding metaphor of the human being as an *actor on a stage.* As he sees it, in our daily lives we are like actors trying to create impressions. Our lives are centrally concerned with "impression management." More specifically, we talk and act in ways that will typically define us positively in the eyes of others. Even when we move about in public by ourselves, the way we walk, our posture when we stand or sit, the way we fold our arms, and so on all function to manage others' impressions of ourselves.

Reading 8, by Mary Gergen, amplifies this concern with self-presentation and addresses how even the shape of our bodies becomes a matter of communicating impressions. Gergen presents a fictionalized accounting about the way a group of teenagers see their bodies. As you can imagine, there is great sensitivity to "how one looks for others." In Reading 9, Stephanie Shields takes a further step in understanding how our identities emerge in relationship. Her specific concern is with gender and the emotions. We often take it for granted that both gender and emotion are biologically based anchors of the self. We cannot escape our gender, and our emotional lives are biologically given. These function virtually as birthmarks of identity. Yet, as Shields demonstrates, gender and the emotions are formed within traditions of relationship. Neither is an essential given.

These three readings highlight the profound degree to which self-defining expressions are situated within social relationships. Yet, these readings do not take us far enough. They all suggest a distinction between a "public self"—what we present to others—and a "private self" lying somewhere deep inside. This distinction is particularly strong in the Goffman reading, where we are invited to draw the conclusion that there is a private self inside us manipulating and/or managing our many appearances for others. However, in the remaining readings in Part II we tackle the issue of the private self, the self behind the appearance. To what extent are the ways we think and feel, our desires and our fears, already embedded within our relationships?

To begin this exploration, consider your private understanding of who you are. Typically you think in terms of yourself in the context of a history, how you came to be what you are, why your current activities make sense, and where you see yourself in the future. For example, you might see yourself as someone who has become interested in writing for a newspaper or magazine. For this reason you are taking courses in Communication Studies and now you are hoping that you will be able to find the kind of job that will fulfill your dreams. In effect, you possess a small story about yourself, a way of understanding yourself moving across time. More formally we call these life stories *narratives.* In Reading 10 the well-known psychologist Jerome Bruner discusses narratives of the self. Yet, as you will quickly realize, to understand ourselves in terms of stories is to borrow from the cultural tradition of storytelling. If there were no such tradition, we would be unable to understand ourselves in this way. Our forms of self-understanding are, therefore, dependent on our life storying and restorying within relationships.

Of course, most parents are hopeful that they can influence their children's self-understandings and life story. They hope, for example, that they can raise children who are self-confident or who have a strong sense of moral value. To explore this process of socializing the self, in Reading 11 we include a brief excerpt from a popular children's book by Stan and Jan Berenstain, *He Bear, She Bear.* Here you will have a chance to explore what effects, if any, you think such books can have on children's sense of the self, and most particularly, their gender identity.

Most research on child socialization suggests that influence goes in one direction: The older generation influences the younger. Yet, this emphasis is misleading because it typically leaves out of the equation the child's relationship with the adult. Parents and children are engaged in *relationships*, which means they are engaged in intricate patterns of coordination and mutual adjustment. In Reading 12 Mary Gergen proposes that our history of relationships often remains with us over a lifetime. Metaphorically speaking, we carry bits and pieces of others with us; they are "social ghosts" who privately speak within. They may also speak with each other, agreeing or disagreeing. For example, we might carry the social ghost of our mother who wants us to be cautious in our choices, and a father's voice that says that life is about taking risks. As the poet Walt Whitman wrote, "I contain multitudes."

Finally, in Reading 13 we come full circle to consider again our actions with others. As the collection of readings has suggested, we enter into daily relationships carrying with us a history of relationships. We carry with us narratives of the self, images and voices of significant others in our lives, and a repertoire of possible actions. As we relate with each other we draw from the past in ways that will define ourselves in the present. An excerpt from the work of Rom Harré and Nikki Slocum suggests, however, that the way we define ourselves also has the effect of defining the other. Or as they say, in defining ourselves we *position the other*. If a teacher views himself or herself as "an authority" on a given subject, it will place others in the position of "learner." At the same time, positioning goes both ways. To define oneself as a learner also invites the other to define the self as teacher, or both may reposition themselves as learner-teacher. Ongoing conversation, then, is often a process of mutual positioning. After all, who could any of us be without our relationships to others?

The Self as Dramatic Actor

As Shakespeare once wrote, "All the world's a stage, and all the men and women merely players." This view of the individual as a dramatic actor continues even today to give us insight into ourselves. Is there not a sense in which most of our daily actions are scripted in order to "make sense" to others, just as an actor must do to sustain the play? And don't we feel the pressure to remain in character, to be convincing and to take our cues from others? One of the most important social theorists to explore these ideas was Erving Goffman. Here we excerpt from his pivotal work, *The Presentation of Self in Everyday Life*:

Reading 7 ERVING GOFFMAN

When an individual appears in the presence of others, there will usually be some reason for him to mobilize his activity so that it will convey an impression to others which it is in his interests to convey. Since a girl's dormitory mates will glean evidence of her popularity from the calls she receives on the phone, we can suspect that some girls will arrange for calls to be made, and Willard Wallers' finding can be anticipated:

> It has been reported by many observers that a girl who is called to the telephone in the dormitories will often allow herself to be called several times, in order to give all the other girls ample opportunity to hear her paged.

As an example of what we must try to examine, I would like to cite at length a novelistic incident in which Preedy, a vacationing Englishman, makes his first appearance on the beach of his summer hotel in Spain:

> But in any case he took care to avoid catching anyone's eyes. First of all, he had to make it clear to those potential companions of his holiday that they were of no concern to him whatsoever. He stared through them, round them, over them—eyes lost in space. The beach might have been empty. If by chance a ball was thrown his way, he looked surprised; then let a smile of amusement lighten his face (Kindly Preedy), looked round dazed to see that there were people on the beach, tossed it back with a smile to himself and not a smile at the people, and then resumed carelessly his nonchalant survey of space.
> But it was time to institute a little parade, the parade of the Ideal Preedy. By devious handlings he gave any who wanted to look a chance to see the title of his book a Spanish translation of Homer, classic thus, but not daring, cosmopolitan too and then gathered together his beach-wrap and bag into a neat sand-resistant pit (Methodical and Sensible Preedy), rose slowly to stretch at ease his huge frame (Big-Cat Preedy), and tossed aside his sandals (Carefree Preedy, after all).

The marriage of Preedy and the sea! There were alternative rituals. The first
involved the stroll that turns into a run and a dive straight into the water, there-
after smoothing into a strong splashless crawl towards the horizon. But of
course not really to the horizon. Quite suddenly he would turn on to his back
and thrash great white splashes with his legs, somehow thus showing that he
could have swum further had he wanted to, and then would stand up a quarter
out of water for all to see who it was.

The alternative course was simpler; it avoided the cold water shock and it
avoided the risk of appearing too high-spirited. The point was to appear to be so
used to the sea, the Mediterranean, and this particular beach, that one might as
well be in the sea as out of it. It involved a slow stroll down and into the edge
of the water-not even noticing his toes were wet, land and water all the same to
him!—with his eyes up at the sky gravely surveying portents, invisible to others,
of the weather (Local Fisherman Preedy).[1]

The novelist means us to see that Preedy is improperly concerned with the extensive impressions he feels his sheer bodily action is giving off to those around him. We can malign Preedy further by assuming that he has acted merely in order to give a particular impression, that this is a false impression, and that the others present receive either no impression at all, or, worse still, the impression that Preedy is affectedly trying to cause them to receive this particular impression. But the important point for us here is that the kind of impression Preedy thinks he is making is in fact the kind of impression that others correctly and incorrectly glean from someone in their midst.

I have said that when an individual appears before others his actions will influence the definition of the situation which they come to have. Sometimes the individual will act in a thoroughly calculating manner, expressing himself in a given way solely in order to give the kind of impression to others that is likely to evoke from them a specific response he is concerned to obtain. Sometimes the individual will be calculating in his activity but be relatively unaware that this is the case. Sometimes he will intentionally and consciously express himself in a particular way, but chiefly because the tradition of his group or social status require this kind of expression and not because of any particular response (other than vague acceptance or approval) that is likely to be evoked from those impressed by the expression. Sometimes the traditions of an individual's role will lead him to give a well-designed impression of a particular kind, and yet he may be neither consciously nor unconsciously disposed to create such an impression. The others, in their turn, may be suitably impressed by the individual's efforts to convey something, or may misunderstand the situation and come to conclusions that are warranted neither by the individual's intent nor by the facts. In any case, in so far as the others act *as if* the individual had a particular

[1]William Sansom, *A Contest of Ladies* (London: Hogarth), 1956, pp. 230–32.

impression, we may take a functional or pragmatic view and say that the individual has "effectively" projected a given definition of the situation and "effectively" fostered the understanding that a given state of affairs obtains.

Explorations

1. When we view life as a theater, we are also invited to see ourselves as actors who play many roles for many different audiences. Try out this metaphor by asking yourself what different roles you play for various individuals or groups. For example, you may play the part of a son or a daughter to your parents. What other roles do you play, and for whom? Can you think of six different selves, and indicate each audience?

   a. I play the part of _____ for _____

   b. I play the part of _____ for _____

   c. I play the part of _____ for _____

   d. I play the part of _____ for _____

   e. I play the part of _____ for _____

   f. I play the part of _____ for _____

2. When we view the person as an actor on a stage, we are of course employing a metaphor. When this metaphor of person as actor is applied to you, what objections might you have?

   _____

   _____

Key Constructions

- Self-presentation
- Metaphor
- Impression management

READING 8

Your Body as Communication

We define ourselves for others not only in our talk and our dress, but also in how we talk about the shape of our bodies. In the same way that different groups construct different realities and moralities, so do they generate different conceptions of "the good body." This is most obvious in the case of the communities of ballet dancers and body builders. Here we find dramatic differences in what counts as a "good body." Teenage circles also establish standards for what is acceptable in their community. In Reading 8 Mary Gergen has written a fictionalized account of a group of five teenage girls who meet after school to enjoy each other's company, watch the "soaps" and, in the mix of conversation, end up talking about their bodies.

Reading 8 MARY GERGEN

PATTY: What's going on here? I had a diet Coke in the fridge, and somebody took it. I know it wasn't you, Gail-the-Rail, because you just finished off the ice cream. Hey, who's on a diet here anyway . . . or rather who isn't?

CHARLENE: Don't be so dramatic, Patty, I drank it, and you know there's another case in the fridge downstairs. Anyway, where's the remote so I can get the tv on? And meanwhile why doesn't somebody go down and bring up some more diet Coke.

SALLY: Hey, not me. I don't even like diet drinks, even if I am always on a diet. I just hate my thighs . . . all that ugly cellulite.

GAIL: I wish I had some cellulite. I don't have any curves. I need something more up here and a rounder butt. How am I supposed to be a cheerleader with this body? And look at my arms; they are like rails.

PATTY: No kidding, Gail! That's why I call you, Gail-the-Rail.

CHARLENE: But, Gail's the only one skinny enough to be a model.

KATHY: Maybe, but she's not tall enough. You know this is a crazy group, height-wise. Half of you are short, and the rest of you are tall. Almost no one is my height. You'd think I'd feel normal around you all, but I feel out of it. Either I'm looking up or down all the time.

SALLY: Big deal! I wish I were five inches shorter. The only guys I can date are basketball players. Everyone else thinks I'm a giraffe. I always have to wear flats. I hate how tall I am! And it's not fair! Patty's barely five feet and her lover boy, McGoo, is almost twice as tall as she is. Why can't the short girls leave the tall guys for us?

CHARLENE: I kind of like being short. I can go out with any a guy- short or tall. Trouble is they're just all so stupid! I can't wait 'til I can meet some guys at college, who might at least say something interesting. The guys in our class are so immature.

GAIL: I'd just be happy to go out with a guy who was my height or even shorter—especially if he's a jock. Am I the only one who hates how they look around here, or what?

PATTY: If I were in the shower, and suddenly somebody pulled away the curtain, you know what I'd cover up? My forehead. I hate my forehead. That's the worst part about my body. That's why I always wear bangs. My mom agrees with me, probably because she also has the same ugly forehead.

KATHY: That's crazy. How can anybody not like their forehead? Besides, you have great lips, and a terrific boyfriend. For me it's clear, I'd cover up my hips. Today, Jon called me "Hippo-hips" again. I hate that, and besides, I don't even think I have big hips. Do I? Certainly not like some other people I could mention who aren't currently among us—like Cherry!

SALLY: Yeah, but Cherry has such big breasts, no one even notices if she's got big hips. And you know, what I really can't stand is the way she walks. Like the girl waddles. She is sooo dumb.

CHARLENE: I hear she took ballet classes, that's why they all walk like ducks. I think all Buzzy ever really sees are those 38D's. It makes me want to vomit.

KATHY: I don't know about Buzzy, but I think Jon likes me because he's always making fun of me so that he can get me to look at him.

SALLY: In your dreams, girlfriend. Barb's got him under her thumb, even if he does lust after your bod.

KATHY: Why can't you agree with me just once? You'd better be nice or you'll be walking home.

CHARLENE: Girls, girls, who cares about what the guys think or don't think. There's never been another group like ours to hit this school. Mr. Alwin even told me that we are the cutest and coolest group that he's ever taught. You can tell by the way the other girls look at us that they agree with him. We are sharp!

PATTY: Yeah, lets drink to that! Now somebody go get me that diet Coke. I'm dying.

Explorations

1. Have you ever wanted to change some bodily characteristic, or perhaps you've even done so? If not consider someone else you know who has made some bodily change

   a. Why do you think this change was important? _____

   _____

   _____

_____

_____

_____

b. What did you or this other person hope was communicated by changing one's appearance? _____

_____

_____

_____

_____

2. Often we shape our bodies so they will be more acceptable or desirable to people around us. Yet, there are many different groups and each may have different standards for what is a "good body." Some, meanwhile, may care very little about the body at all.

a. In the previous conversation, what are the various groups that seem to matter to these girls in terms of their bodies? _____

_____

_____

_____

b. Why do you think it matters, or not, to these various groups if these girls change their bodies? _____

_____

_____

_____

3. Many people believe that our desires for bodily change are, in part, the result of advertising. Advertising helps define social ideals, and when we are exposed to certain ads we may see ourselves as less than ideal. Describe an advertisement that influenced your view of your body or someone else's view of your body (e.g., clothing, perfume, food, beverages, prescription drugs, soaps, etc.).

_____

_____

_____

_____

_____

4. Have you ever rejected the ideals presented in an advertisement? Explain how and why you rejected the image.

_____

_____

_____

Key Construction

- Communicating identity with one's body

READING 9

Doing Emotion/Doing Gender

Doesn't our biological makeup determine our actions in large degree? And if so, aren't the most important influences on who I am genetic in nature? Such reasoning is highly common, and supports the traditional idea of individual or independent selves. Yet, in Reading 9 Stephanie A. Shields challenges these common assumptions and proposes that our relationships are primary to who we are. As we communicate with each other, we come to have an identity. The challenge is significant because it reexamines two characteristics of the self that seem so fundamentally biological in origin: gender and emotion. There are strong tendencies in Western culture to view masculine and feminine social and emotional traits as genetic. As Shields proposes, however, both gender and emotion are cultural in origin. To express yourself emotionally (or not) is to perform one's gender for others.

Reading 9 **STEPHANIE A. SHIELDS**

The first time I heard of the notion of "doing gender," I found it confusing. Even though this was some years ago, I vividly remember being stumped: How could gender be a verb? Yet, in a highly influential paper, West and Zimmerman (1987) made exactly that case. They proposed that gender can be understood by examining the interactional work; gender is not something one "has," but is something that one "does." The point is that, even if in our heart of hearts we believe with certainty that we are either female or male, the trappings of womanhood and manhood that assure us (and others) of that identity are always being contested, disputed, negotiated. In a sense, we are always practicing gender, even when totally comfortable within our own skin. With practice we come to own the role in much the same way that a TV actor seems "naturally" the character she or he plays. But unlike the TV actor, we move in and out of situations that make gender "performance" more salient or that require us to improvise ways to meet the challenges of the situation while continuing to believe in the consistency and truth of our own gendered character. We are our own toughest audience.

Textile artist Mary Yaeger has done an interesting series of "woman badges." Using small industrial patches as a base, she applies hand embroidery to create pictures on the patches that are reminiscent of scouting merit badges. There is the eyebrow tweezing badge, the bathroom scale badge, the tampon badge, and, of course, the Girl Scout cookie badge, to name but a few. With the badges, Yaeger reminds us not only of the important rites of passage that mark our development from childhood to adult womanhood, but the sheer quantity and concentration of practice that goes into making the countless action, ideas, and details of woman/feminine/female seem totally natural.

As a social identity, gender is multi-faceted and is expressed through appearance and behavior. The *what* of gender can be learned from physical appearance and from the tangible artifacts of social organization. Barbie models womanhood for girls as surely as toys of pretend destruction signal manly activity to boys. In a holiday catalog, web e-tailer Amazon.com even offers gender-specific guidelines for a range of gifts that are not themselves explicitly gender-coded. (Apparently gender neutral gifts do not sell on their own and customers must be able to comfortably distinguish between "girl gifts" for girls and "boy gifts" for boys.) For boys ages 2 to 4 Amazon suggests *Big Silver Space Shuttle*, an interactive book to "blast off at bedtime"; for girls, the choice is the picture book *And If the Moon Could Talk,* so she can "head straight to dreamland." He *goes* to the moon, she *listens* to it! But gender is more than what we do, it is also *how* we do it. The accoutrements of gender, by themselves, are not sufficient to create a fully successful enactment of "masculine," "feminine," or a self-conscious alternative either. Successful performance of gender as social identity must pass the judgments of others, and more important, it must be experienced as an authentic expression of the self. Neither older children nor adults believe that to "dress like a girl" or "throw like a girl" actually makes one a girl. Appearance must have presence. Gender is expressed through the style and tone of behavior—*how* the dress is worn, how throwing the ball meshes with other actions and the intent behind them.

Emotion plays a role in doing gender. Beliefs about emotion reveal the distinctive "how" of being a gendered person; doing emotion—expressing emotional feelings and emotion values—signals one's genuineness as female or male, feminine or masculine. For example, because emotionally expressive behavior is gender coded, an important component of the child's gender practice (i.e., enacting a gendered identity) involves practicing emotion—its expression, values, interests—as befits gender. Doing gender through doing emotion encompasses not only emotional display, of course, but also emotion values (e.g., real girls value emotional self-disclosure) and beliefs about emotional experience (e.g., anger is appropriate only when one's rights are violated).

I want to emphasize again that neither "doing" emotion nor "doing" gender is a deliberate or even self-conscious act. Certainly one can deliberately make the effort to conform to or reject conventional gender rules and one can play at exaggerating, flouting, or subverting gender convention. The sense in which I am using "doing" gender and "doing" emotion, however, differentiates between superficial management of behavior and expression and behavior that expresses beliefs, values, and goals vital to creating a sense of personal identity. Sometimes my students have difficulty with the notion that genuine emotion or genuine gender could have any discernible "acting" component— after all, they argue, if it's "just acting," it cannot be genuine. It is important, I stress, not to oversimplify and equate the creation of a gendered identity with the deliberate manipulation of one's "social face." Postponing an appointment with the excuse "I have to visit a sick friend," or meeting a rude customer with a friendly smile might be socially necessary, but it is "just acting." I think it is the implied dishonesty and inauthenticity of this type of deliberate emotion acting that makes it difficult to imagine genuine emotion, emotion subjectively experienced as consistent with one's self, as anything other than totally spontaneous.

Reference

West, C., & Zimmerman, D. H. (1987). Doing gender. *Gender and Society, 1*, 125–151.

Explorations

1. To fill out the picture of gender stereotypes a little further, can you identify three common views of how men and women differ in how they express (show) emotion (or the value they place on emotions)?

   _____

   _____

   _____

   _____

2. Such gender stereotypes often carry with them implicit social rules about what people "ought" to do. Return to the differences you outlined in exercise 1 and comment on whether these differences are also supported by informal rules about how men and women should be different. (For example, the

common stereotype is that women cry more often than men; this stereotype is supported by the common male rule that "real men don't cry.")

_____

_____

_____

_____

3. One common means of testing whether biology (or one's genetic composition) is determining a specific behavior is to ask whether you could choose not to engage in that behavior. For example, biology determines our digestive processes, and we cannot suddenly decide "I think I will stop digesting now." However, biology doesn't determine that we take a bus or scan MySpace; we can always choose not to.

   Return to the various emotional expressions that are typically assigned to men or to women. Could you choose *not* to engage in emotional expressions that are appropriate to your gender? Explain. What would be the results if you made such decisions (e.g., as a man, you cry in a movie)? What might people think of you if you did?

_____

_____

_____

_____

Key Constructions

- Gender performance
- Gender identity
- Cultural origin of emotional performance

R E A D I N G   1 0

The Narrative Construction of Self

One of the major limitations of the metaphor of person as dramatic actor is the presumption of an "actor behind the actor—that is, the sense of a "little person inside" who autonomously calculates every move to create effects on others. Such a view is deeply troubling in its vision of social life. It leads us to see ourselves and others as "strategic manipulators." Our trust is reduced and we become skeptical of everything said to us, even by our closest friends. Our trust is replaced by the question, "What are they trying to get from me?" Further, the view of the person as dramatic actor suggests that the strategic manipulator is autonomous. He or she makes the decisions, chooses the strategy, and has self-serving goals.

To appreciate the fully relational nature of the person requires that we press beyond this view of the dramatic actor. First of all, we must come to appreciate how much we are composed of other people. Consider again the language game. As small children we slowly begin to learn the games of language shared within our family. As a result, we later have the ability to use this language in other relations. But realize that the language we use in these relations is borrowed from our earlier experience with our family. In effect, in speaking to others, we reflect our past relationships.

In this sense, the view of the person as an autonomous manipulator seems misleading. In speaking with others, the words scarcely originate with us; we are not autonomous originators of our actions. Rather, we reflect our relations with others. Nor are we necessarily manipulative. Typically words come tumbling out without conscious consideration. We are primed by past relationships for just such action. In riding a bicycle or eating pasta, we don't plan each movement of the legs or the hands; our history renders them automatic. Most of our communication proceeds in the same way.

These points are nicely illustrated in a great volume of work on self-narratives. All of us can tell stories about ourselves, about our childhood, our neighborhood, our relationships, and so on. If pressed, we could probably tell a "life story" about how we came to be where we are; how, for example, we had a good childhood, a stormy adolescence, and we are now seeking an education so that the future will be rewarding.

But also realize that before we can tell our life stories we must first be taught *how* to tell stories. For most of us, stories are part of the language games we learned as children. We learned how stories develop as we listened to parents read or tell stories, or as we watched television. So, as we tell the stories about ourselves, we are also reflecting a history of relationships of which stories were a part. Our self-narratives are never quite "all our own." Without a history of relationships, we would not be able to define ourselves in story form.

In Reading 10, the well-known scholar Jerome Bruner opens discussion on the narrative construction of self.

Reading 10 JEROME BRUNER

"Self" is a surprisingly quirky idea—intuitively obvious to common sense yet notoriously evasive to definition by the fastidious philosopher. The best we seem to be able to do when asked what it is, is to point a finger at our forehead or our chest. Yet "self" is the common coin of our speech: no conversation goes long without its being unapologetically used. And the legal code simply takes it for granted when it speaks of such legal concepts as responsibility and privacy. We would do well, then, to have a brief look at what the self is, the subject that narrative creation of self is supposed to be about. Is there some essential self inside that, somehow, is just there? If so, why would we ever need to tell ourselves about ourselves, and why would there be such injunctions as "Know thyself" or "To thine own self be true"? Surely, if our selves were just there, we'd have no need to tell ourselves about them. Yet we spend a good deal of time doing just that, either alone or with friends, or vicariously at the psychiatrist's, or at confession if we are Catholics. What function does such self-telling serve?

I want to begin by proposing boldly that, in effect, there is no such thing as an intuitively obvious and essential self to know, one that just sits there ready to be portrayed in words. Rather, we constantly construct and reconstruct our selves to meet the needs of the situations we encounter, and we do so with the guidance of our memories of the past and our hopes and fears for the future. Telling oneself about oneself is like making up a story about who and what we are, what's happened, and why we're doing what we're doing.

It is not that we have to make up these stories from scratch each time. Our self-making stories accumulate over time, even pattern themselves on conventional genres. They get out-of-date, and not just because we grow older or wiser but because our self-making stories need to fit new circumstances, new friends, new enterprises. Our very memories fall victim to our self-making stories. It is not that I can no longer tell you (or myself) the "original, true story" about my desolation in the bleak summer after my father died. Rather, I would be telling you (or myself) a new story about a twelve-year-old "once upon a time." And I could tell it several ways, all of them shaped as much by my life since then as by the circumstances of that long-ago summer.

Self-making is a narrative art, and though it is more constrained by memory than fiction is, it is uneasily constrained, a matter to which we shall come presently. Self-making, anomalously, is from both the inside and the outside. The inside of it, we like to say in our Cartesian way, is memory, feelings, ideas, beliefs, subjectivity. Part of this insidedness is almost certainly innate and species-specific, like our irresistible sense of continuity over time and place and our postural sense of ourselves. But much of self-making is from outside in— based on the apparent esteem of others and on the myriad expectations that we early, even mindlessly, pick up from the culture in which we are immersed.

Besides, narrative acts of self-making are usually guided by unspoken, implicit cultural models of what selfhood should be, might be—and, of course, shouldn't be. Not that we are slaves of culture, as even the most dedicated cultural anthropologists now appreciate. Rather, there are many possible, ambiguous models of selfhood even in simple or ritualized culture. Yet all cultures provide presuppositions and perspectives about selfhood, rather like plot summaries or homilies for telling oneself or others about oneself.

But these self-making precepts are not rigid commands. They leave ample room for maneuver. Self-making is, after all, our principal means for establishing our uniqueness, and a moment's thought makes plain that we distinguish ourselves from others by comparing our accounts of ourselves with the accounts that others give us of themselves.

Telling others about oneself is, then, no simple matter. It depends on what *we* think *they* think we ought to be like—or what selves in general ought to be like. Nor do our calculations end when we come to telling ourselves about ourselves. Our self-directed, self-making narratives come to express what we think others expect us to be like. Without much awareness of it, we develop a decorum for telling ourselves about ourselves: how to be frank with ourselves and how not to offend others.

Explorations

1. Consider your own life as made up of various narratives. These are stories that tell you what your background is, where you are going in life, and what your goals are. In these terms, can you describe two narratives that seem central to your way of life?

   Example: I was the firstborn child. My parents and grandparents always stressed how important it was to be the first child in one's family. One result was that my approach to life is to frequently remind myself of the importance of taking care of others. Even today I am reminded by their stories about how many responsibilities a firstborn child has in taking care of those around him or her. I will be a good parent.

   a. _____

   _____

   _____

   _____

   b. _____

   _____

   _____

   _____

2. Our personal narratives are often influenced by various stories to which we have been exposed over the years. These may include family stories, fairy tales, comics, novels, films, video games, blogs, chat rooms, and television.

Can you describe three stories that may have influenced the way you understand yourself and your goals today?

a. _____

_____

_____

b. _____

_____

_____

c. _____

_____

_____

3. Consider how an understanding of narrative in our lives could shed light on a particular phenomenon. How have certain stories about particular events or issues helped in forming your impression about those topics? Consider what stories in your life have played a significant role in how you presently view the following issues:

a. Your taste in popular music:

_____

_____

_____

b. Your moral values:

_____

_____

_____

c. Your thoughts about terrorism:

_____

_____

_____

Key Constructions

- Narrative
- Self-narration
- Self-making

READING 11

Childhood Shaping of the Self

Parents often believe they can shape the values and motives of their children. They try to help the child become a "good person." One vehicle for shaping is storytelling. As proposed in Reading 10, children often learn how to think about themselves and what they may become from the stories to which they are exposed. Reading 11 consists of a page from a well-known children's book by Stan and Jan Berenstain, *He Bear, She Bear*, in which the authors make a concerted attempt to break down traditional gender roles.

Reading 11   STAN AND JAN BERENSTAIN

We bulldoze roads,
we drive cranes,
we drive trucks,
we drive trains.

We can do all these things,
you see, whether we are he or she.

Explorations

1. How effective do you think books such as this are in shaping children's future narratives? Illustrate your answer by drawing from memories of childhood stories you read (or were told).

   _____

   _____

   _____

   _____

2. Books and television are forms of limited communication. The reader or viewer has no immediate or direct voice in engaging in a the conversation with the writer. Do you see limits to this type of mediated communication in terms of its influencing those to whom it is directed? Can you illustrate from your own experience?

   _____

   _____

   _____

   _____

Key Constructions

- Shaping children's narratives
- Gender equality

Hear the story of my life or at least of one life
The kind of life Told by folks like us
The way we tell stories these days. Some stories are good for laughs
Some stories are tear jerkers
Where would I be without good stories? Where would I be without my story?

Social Ghosts: Others Within

One of the most fascinating ways in which we are linked in relationship with each other is through the voices that inhabit us. When we are thinking through the pros and cons of an issue for example, it is largely in terms of these voices. We might privately "hear" the voice of our father warning us against a particular choice or the voice of a friend saying "go for it." Our private reasoning, then, is not so private after all. It is similar to engaging in a public conversation, only we do it without the physical presence of others. In Reading 12, Mary Gergen calls these internal voices social ghosts. She reports on research with her students.

Reading 12   MARY GERGEN

I am frequently engaged in internal dialogue with others who are not within range of my voice. I envision others watching me as I go about my daily affairs. I am in imaginal contact with others as I am reminded of their preferences and antipathies. I see how my children have grown up, and I "hear" my mother's voice cautioning me to enjoy their childhoods because they grow so quickly. Watching the football scores, I "exchange views" with my father about how the Vikings are doing. Sometimes, I try to "advise" the president, as well as his advisors, on matters of public policy. I commend them when they do what I think is right. Putting mayonnaise on white bread, I "hear" my Jewish lover laugh at my "goyish" ways of making a sandwich. If I am troubled about a personal decision, I bring in my therapist for a consultation on the private sofa of my inner chambers. When I prepare to have a difficult interchange with a colleague, I speak to her in advance to soften my words before they have a chance to land. These are just a smattering of details from the welter of imagined interactions with what I call my "social ghosts."

Once I considered how important these imaginal interactions might be in the course of ordinary human life, I became curious about how they might be written about as forms of cultural life. I began to engage more fully in the possibilities of describing who these social ghosts are, where they come from, when they are likely to be most present, and what functions they may serve in people's lives. Until I began this project, I had never discussed my "social ghosts" with others, and I had never heard others speak of their imaginal relations either. Yet I suspected that if I am frequently involved in imaginal interactions with others, especially when I am otherwise alone, then perhaps such phenomena could become realized in discourses with others as well. "Imaginal conversations" might become constructed as part of all human experience and might even take on some greater import within individuals' lives. Through expanding our dialogues with social ghosts, we might be better able to create changes in our ongoing relationships with "real-time" others, changes that would be beneficial to others as well as ourselves. This possibility opens space for applications in the vast world of psychological theorizing, therapy, counseling, and spiritual practices.

> *Frank Farra [is one of my social ghosts]. . . . He taught me to respect myself, my mind and my body. He showed me that when the two are working together there is nothing that I could not accomplish. His inspiration and determination in everything he attempted helped to guide me to finish my college career. I think of him a lot when things aren't going exactly the way I would like them to be. And the thought of him telling me to be the best I can helps me to make the best of any situation [college student].*

Why Ghosts Are Social

When I first began to shape this study, I needed a name for the partner in these imaginal encounters. It didn't seem that there was any label that was suitable at that time. Children were often described as having imaginary friends, but I thought that promoting the idea that we all have imaginary friends would be a highly limiting theoretical move, given the diversity of imagined others I wanted to name. I chose to call them social ghosts for several reasons. First, I wanted to emphasize the social aspect of this phenomenon. I wanted to indicate that these interactional partners were the result of prior social experiences with other people, fictional and flesh and blood, and that relationships with them were also social—that is, the imaginal relationships paralleled those of embodied social life in many ways. The dialogic relationship, although carried on alone, involves familiar scenarios of interchange. To talk, laugh, and wonder, to be surprised, upset, hurt, angry, and amused, and to engage in other physical acts could all be a part of imaginal interactions. The provocation of the word *ghosts* intrigued me. A ghost can be defined as a form of spirit; a ghost can visit, but it is not present in a conventional sense. Also, ghosts can have qualities of creatures who have lived, yet their status is different. Ghosts can also haunt one. They are not always at our beck and call. Sometimes social ghosts are not welcome in one's life. They may remind us of things we would rather forget. At other times they take us back to moments that are intensely significant in our lives, and we feel almost forced to relive those moments through the powerful interventions of our ghosts. Together, the two words *social* and *ghost* remind us of our embedded existence in the social realm; but also our existence beyond the immediate context, in historical moments, as well as in the present. In all our present relationships, we carry the essences of the past.

Background of the Social Ghost Phenomenon

Whereas the social sciences, especially psychology, have been sparse and sporadic in mentions of such fictive figures and interactions, literary sources have been rich with accounts of imagined relationships. Significant roles are frequently played by social ghosts in novels, poems, plays, and other dramatic forms, as well as in the production of action in the plot. Great importance is often placed on characters' fantasies, remembrances, emotional attachments, and imagined constructions of others from the past. Relations with ancestors, ancient heroes and heroines, lovers, parents, companions, and enemies, as well as supernatural figures such as angels, phantoms, and witches, play powerful roles in many fictional works. Ghosts often visit earthly characters to frighten, advise, entertain, and admonish them. We remember Shakespeare's Hamlet as a man tormented by his "social ghosts," as are Lord and Lady Macbeth. Edgar Allen Poe's poems and short stories are dominated by imaginal dialogues, including the famous raven saying "Nevermore." Harvey, the imaginary rabbit, entertained generations of filmgoers, and the Disney empire rests on thousands of imagined stars. However, despite the dependency of diverse literary forms on imaginal dialogues, one may argue that there is a significant bifurcation between the "real world" and the imaginary one. To what extent can one trust literary accounts as keys to unlock the mysteries of everyday life? Should "social ghosts" be treated as literary devices for enhancing drama only, or should they be viewed as having a significant role to play in normal lives as well? Should we think of them as poetic symbols? Or shall we consider them as aspects of normal human thought processes?

Investigating Social Ghosts with Others

When I began this research project, there were no models for me to imitate. Thus, I wondered how I might enter into dialogue with others about these "social ghosts." I wanted to develop ways of exploring this unknown, or perhaps I should say "invented," territory with others. The inquiry became the basis of a research-oriented project, of which this reading is an outcome. It is difficult to frame a question that has never before been asked. Inventing a term, such as *social ghosts,* requires some introduction so that others may be able to give a meaningful response. To gain some appreciation for how others might respond to inquiry about "social ghosts," I created a simple and fairly unobtrusive survey among college students. This initial exploration took the form of a questionnaire entitled "Remembered Persons" (a label designed to be less dramatic or less humorous in tone than *social ghosts* might seem to them). The definition of "Remembered Persons" was placed at the beginning of the first page. The questionnaire then asked respondents if there were people whom they remembered from the past, either real or fictitious, whom they had known personally or read about, who entered into their thoughts about current life activities. If so, they were asked to name each of these persons, with a maximum of three, and to identify their relationship with each of them. They were then asked to describe the ways in which each of these persons affected "your daily life at present." The attempt in the introductory paragraph of the questionnaire was to define the idea of a social ghost as clearly and as neutrally as possible and then to elicit from the respondents a few examples of social ghosts in their own lives. The survey then addressed the question of the function of social ghosts in the respondents' lives by asking for effects on daily life of these imaginal interactions. The questionnaires were administered to 76 college students of varying economic and ethnic backgrounds.

> *[Social ghost:] Speed Racer. I used to think Speed was a great guy when I was 6. I wanted to be a champion in the Mach 5 like him [college student].*

The surveys were content analyzed, with the aforementioned questions of whether people did have imagined interactions and, if so, with what kind of social ghosts and for what purposes. The identities of these social ghosts were assessed, as well as the relationships they had to the respondents and the functions that these imagined interactions with the social ghosts had in terms of affecting these respondents in their daily lives.

Prevalence of Imagined Interactions

The initial question to which the research was directed concerned the prevalence of the experience of imagined interactions with others. Many developmental and clinical psychologists have suggested that only people with very unsatisfactory social lives and those who are mentally or emotionally disabled or immature would report experiences of interaction with absent social figures. Normal people would be unlikely to carry out an extended set of imagined relationships. However, these data support the view that imaginal interactions with social ghosts are commonplace. In fact, except for one respondent, all those surveyed indicated imagined relationships with at least one person. The majority of the respondents wrote about three relationships, which was the space provided for them on the questionnaire, although some people added more experiences. It is difficult from the results of this questionnaire to draw any conclusions about how many social ghosts people might be able to recall. Perhaps there is no finite limit to the possibilities. Clearly, young adults who are intellectually and socially competent and relatively stable emotionally can, with ease, write about their relationships with social ghosts. Support for the notion of the normalcy of these subjects comes from a similar study among adults in which, of the 20 people solicited, only one could not recall ever having had an imagined interaction. (This subject had eight children, however, and she credited the extensive nature of her actual daily relationships with her lack of imagined ones).

> *[Social ghost:] My grandmother, Eunice Mann, a model. Sometimes when I dress up I think I look like her or I carry myself like her. Often I try to act in a way that would please her. I imagine her giving me compliments [college student].*

Identity of the Social Ghosts

Who was selected to be a social ghost? The next significant question concerned the identity of these social ghosts. Psychoanalytic literature would suggest that such significant others should primarily be family members with whom one interacted in early childhood. Symbolic interactionist theory would hold that any important persons who influenced one's early formation of self-concept would be likely to serve as social ghosts. Developmental and social psychologists, especially social learning theorists, might well emphasize the importance of those figures who have high status, power, or diverse resources, such as fictional characters or famous people—entertainers, athletic stars, and other public figures who are idolized and imitated by adolescents.

As the findings demonstrated, the major proportion (37%) of the social ghosts described were friends of the respondents with whom they no longer interacted on a regular basis. Platonic friendships accounted for approximately two thirds of those mentioned as social ghosts, with former boyfriends and girlfriends generating the remainder. Family members were mentioned second most frequently, with 23% of the social ghosts being a family relative. Among the immediate family, fathers were mentioned most frequently (39%), followed by mothers (13%) and siblings (8%). However, many of these relatives were not members of the nuclear family. Grandparents, cousins, aunts, and uncles accounted for almost all of the remaining social ghosts in this group. Former teachers were named in 11% of the cases. Among these, the predominant group, chosen in 50% of the cases, was that of high school teachers. The remaining 29% of the social ghosts were people with whom the respondent had almost never had direct interactions. These included religious figures, fictitious characters, celebrities, and others. Among the famous social ghosts unknown to the respondent, entertainers were chosen over 80% of the time.

Thus, family members were not the primary social ghosts for this sample. Friends and media-mediated personalities were more likely to be named. Interestingly, the preschool period of life was second only to high school as the time in life in which the social ghosts were most likely to be mentioned. Approximately one third of the social ghosts were recalled from early childhood, and about one half were chosen from the high school period. Very few social ghosts were named from elementary school, junior high, or college periods. This lends some support to the notion that the periods of early childhood and late adolescence are important for development, if one also assumes that one of the functions of interaction with social ghosts is to be reconnected with figures who had an important impact on one during critical periods of identity formation. Perhaps there are other reasons for these periods to be crucial for the development of imaginal relationships as well. The age of the sample precludes possibilities for later time periods. Research with an aging sample would be important in determining what periods of life might most stand out as a source of remembrance.

Interestingly, men were chosen as social ghosts to a greater extent than women by both sexes. Of the 200 social ghosts mentioned, 124 (60%) were male figures. These results may reflect the extent to which men are seen as more powerful than women in our society, especially among youth. In addition, men's positions may be more distinct and make a greater impression on young people than do women's positions. One might also speculate that men would be more absent or emotionally distant from them. Thus, one might speculate that conversations take place in fantasy because actual dialogues are not feasible, or because they would be awkward or contentious if actually attempted or because many facets of relatedness are insufficiently developed to allow for intimacies that the subjects wish to achieve.

> [Social ghost:] Clint Eastwood influences me especially when I'm angry or playing a sport. I'll put on my dark sunglasses, and suddenly I'm in control because I think of Clint, as Dirty Harry, as my sidekick.

In summary, respondents were generally very positive in their attitudes about their social ghosts. The majority of them mentioned the respect and regard in which they held the support and advice that their social ghosts had given them. Often they wrote of the way in which the social ghosts had stood as positive models for them. In many instances, respondents referred to the security and hope engendered by the social ghosts; in a minority of cases, instances of increased feelings of loneliness, guilt, and lack of self-confidence were described. Overall, it appears that imaginal relationships with social ghosts lead to more positive self-feelings, although a minority of the interactions seem to be painful and negative.

Explorations

1. We all carry with us "social ghosts"—voices of significant others in our lives. List five persons (living, dead, or fictional) whose voices you feel are important in your own internal life and briefly explain why.

   a. _____

   _____

   b. _____

   _____

   c. _____

   _____

   d. _____

   _____

   e. _____

   _____

2. Choose two social ghosts from the list in exercise 1. Briefly write about what they generally say to you when you are in conversation with them (e.g., "You can do it because . . .").

a. _____

_____

b. _____

_____

3. We have referred to the way in which our social ghosts contribute to internal conversations, for example, about whether a given action is desirable or not. However, these voices also contribute to our emotional life. The images of some people make us happy and others help us feel secure. Other images or voices are critical or accusatory. Consider a social ghost who may often generate positive feelings and describe how they make you feel positive. Then describe how another social ghost contributes to negative feelings.

a. Positive social ghost: _____

_____

_____

b. Negative social ghost: _____

_____

_____

Key Construction

■ Social ghosts

READING 13

Positioning the Self

We enter into relationships carrying with us a history of relationships. It is this history that furnishes us with the resources for relating in the present moment. In effect, the self is born within relationships, and life pursuits are carried out within relationships. One interesting concept that contributes to an appreciation of the relational self is called "positioning." As positioning scholars point out, when we speak with each other or act toward another, we do far more than convey content; we also define who we are. If your teacher or boss says, "please hand in your work this Friday," he or she is doing more than giving you information. These words also identify him or her as "one who is in authority." Or, as it is said, the words *position* him or her as "in charge." At the same time, the same words position you as a student or employee, as one who is expected to comply. In effect, our words position both self and other. As scholars point out, self and other positioning also carries with it a sense of "ought." The teacher or boss in the previous scenario is conveying that he or she *deserves* to be in authority, and that the students or workers *should rightfully* turn in their work by Friday.

Positioning is especially apparent in conflict situations. Each participant may attempt to place the other in an inferior or negative position. Claiming the "moral high ground," for example, is a common way to position oneself in a conflict. In Reading 13, social theorists Rom Harré and Nikki Slocum summarize the positioning process in a communal conflict. In this case, community activists in the Georgetown area of Washington, DC, rallied against the university; in turn the university defended itself against the activists, and personal dialogue became exceedingly difficult. Each attempted to position the other in negative ways, and thereby gain public support. Each side created story lines to bolster their own position.

Reading 13   ROM HARRÉ AND NIKKI SLOCUM

Six main story lines were distinguishable in the discourse through which the conflict between Georgetown University (GU) and the District of Columbia community called Georgetown was pursued. Some of the story lines were met by dissenting opinions that amounted to direct negations, but a negation did not in each case constitute a new story line.

Georgetown Community Story Lines

1. The Students as Savages Story: GU students are ravaging and violating a historic, affluent, beautiful, and prestigious residential community.
2. The Aggressive University Story: GU is encroaching upon the Georgetown neighborhood's territory. GU is arrogant and hypocritical in that it cares only for its students and neglects the interests of the community.
3. The GU as Neglectful Parent Story: GU is a negligent parent and its students are unruly children.

The first and third of these story lines were woven together in some of the discourses of community activists. While the second and third story lines are apparently contradictory, they are sometimes to be found intermingled in the discourse of a single individual.

Georgetown University Story Lines

4. The Malicious Residents Story: Neighborhood activists are hostile extremists who discriminate against students. They are jealous of the students and wish them harm. They are hindering GU development.

5. The Benevolent University Story: GU has been responsible and cooperative. Its students are responsible members of the community and, in general, they are idealists and leaders.
6. The Historical Rights Story: GU and its students were in Georgetown first; the community grew up around the university and not vice versa.

The disagreements that fueled the conflict were maintained, and made orderly and attractive, by virtue of the story lines through which the dispute was expressed.

Story Lines and Associated Positions

In the dominant discourse of the Georgetown community activists, story lines 1 and 3, "Students as Savages" and "GU as Neglectful Parent" were embedded within a broader set of discursive conventions that might be labeled "the American dream." Coming to live in Georgetown is an ultimate realization of the American dream of material success. That dream is not supposed to end with the hero surrounded by drunken, dirty, and noisy savages. In this story line, rights (including the right to position) are acquired to the extent that one pays taxes, owns property, and steps into the dramaturgy of the American dream. Indeed, one so positioned also acquires the duty to "do something about" whatever hinders the dream's proper ending (a full enjoyment of success). The community activists' speech-acts are to be classified, given the activists' chosen positions, as "protests," "displays of righteous indignation," "fulfillments of one's duty to society," "reprimands to the unruly," and the like.

In the dominant discourse of GU, the community activists were positioned as devoid of rights to interfere with the university's development and particularly with the "campus plan." One anonymous GU administrator positioned herself spokesperson for the institution, as having the rights and duties of a "partner" and "neighbor" to the surrounding community and as naturally expecting the reciprocal position to be adopted by the residents of Georgetown. Accordingly, the failure of the community to accept this benevolent positioning must be culpable. Positioned as a "rejected suitor," GU officials presumed their right to issue utterances with the illocutionary force of rebuke, chastisement, and accusation. In rejecting the positionings of GU, the Georgetown community activists appear in this story line as morally defective, as, for example, "stubborn" and "uncooperative."

Just as the generic story line of the American dream underlay the specific story lines of "Students as Savages" and "GU as Neglectful Parent," there was a single, generic story line underlying both the activists' and the GU administration's seemingly antithetical narratives. "Students Are Children and the University Is their Parent" is a narrative structuring both by the community activists' positioning of GU as "neglectful parent" and GU's positioning of itself as "responsible parent." The position in which GU was put involved both rights (in loco parentis) and a duty to manage student behavior. At the same time, GU's generic positioning put the students into the specific position of "persons lacking civil rights," lacking the right, for example, to drink in bars, and as "persons with a duty of obedience" to GU administrators.

Ironically, the antithetical positioning of GU led both contending parties to conclude, yet without seeming to agree, that students should be housed on campus and be controlled by GU to the greatest degree possible. Since a vast majority of complaints regarded students who were not behaving as "proper adults," the problem was in fact perpetuated by GU's assuming the position of "responsible parent" and thus entrenching the positioning of students as "irresponsible children." That positioning *covertly* confirmed the very story line that was *overtly* the locus of the conflict.

Explorations

1. To more fully appreciate the force of self and other positioning, consider the following examples. In each instance the person in question is speaking to you. How would you say he or she is positioning the self, and how are you positioned by what is said?

   a. You are taking your friends out one evening in the family car. As you are leaving your father yells out, "Be sure to be home by midnight!"

      Your father is positioning himself as _____

      You are positioned as _____

   b. You are out with your friends, and one of them says to you, "Why do you have to go home so early?"

      Your friend is positioning himself or herself as _____

      You are being positioned as _____

   c. It is late one evening and you are walking down a dark street. A police car moves by slowly, and a police officer stares at you intently.

      The officer is positioning himself or herself as _____

      You are being positioned as _____

2. Of course, positioning movements function only as invitations. You may be positioned by someone in a certain way, but you are not required to accept the position in which you are placed. You may not agree with what a particular convention says you "ought to be" in the situation.

   a. Can you describe an interchange in which someone positioned you in a way you thought was improper, unjust, or wrong?

      _____

      _____

b. How did you respond?

_____

_____

c. Do you think your response made a difference in the way you were first positioned?

_____

_____

Key Construction

- Positioning

Key Constructions for Part Two

- Self-presentation
- Metaphor
- Impression management
- Communicating identity with one's body
- Gender performance
- Gender identity
- Cultural origin of emotional performance
- Narrative
- Self-narration
- Self-making
- Shaping children's narratives
- Gender equality
- Social ghosts
- Positioning

Suggested Readings

Backhurst, D., & Sypnowich, C. (Eds.) (1995). *The social self.* London: Sage.

Baxter, L., & Montgomery, B. (1988). *Relating: Dialogues and dialectics.* Mahwah, NJ: Erlbaum.

Bochner, A. P., & Ellis, C. (1995). Telling and living: Narrative co-construction and the practices of interpersonal relationships. In W. Leeds-Hurwitz (Ed.), *Social approaches to communication* (pp. 201–213). New York: Guilford Press.

Burkitt, I. (1993). *Social selves.* London: Sage.

Davies, B., & Harré, R. (1990). Positioning: The discursive production of selves. *Journal for the Theory of Social Behavior*, 20, 43–64.

Gergen, K. J. (1994). *Realities and relationships.* Cambridge, MA: Harvard University Press.

Grant, D., Hardy, C., Oswick, C., & Putnam, L. (Eds.) (2004). *The Sage handbook of organizational discourse.* Thousand Oaks, CA: Sage.

Josselson, R., & Lieblich, A. (Eds.) (1993). *The narrative study of lives.* Thousand Oaks, CA: Sage.

Levine, G. (Ed.) (1992). *Constructions of self.* New Brunswick, NJ: Rutgers University Press.

Pearce, B. P. (1989). *Communication and the human condition.* Carbondale: Southern Illinois University Press.

Potter, J. (1996). *Representing reality: Discourse, rhetoric and social construction.* London: Sage.

Psathas, G. (1994). *Conversation analysis: The study of talk-in-interaction.* Thousand Oaks, CA: Sage.

Sampson, E. (1993). *Celebrating the other: A dialogue account of human nature.* Chagrin Falls, OH: Taos Institute Publications.

Sarbin, T. R. (1986). *Narrative psychology: The storied nature of human conduct.* New York: Praeger.

Shotter, J. (1984). *Social accountabililty and selfhood.* Oxford, England: Blackwell.

Steier, F. (1995). Reflexivity, interpersonal communication, and interpersonal communication research. In W. Leeds-Hurwitz (Ed.), *Social approaches to communication* (pp. 63–87). New York: Guildford Press.

Tamm, J. W., & Luyet, R. J. (2004). *Radical collaboration.* New York: HarperCollins.

Web Resources

Berenstain Bears official website
www.berenstainbears.com/

Goffman's bibliography
www.tau.ac.il/~algazi/mat/goffman.htm

Hip-Hop subculture and African American identity bibliography by Thomas Weissinger
www.library.uiuc.edu/afx/Hip_Hop.htm

Jerome Bruner—informational website
http://web.lemoyne.edu/~hevern/narpsych/nr-theorists/bruner_jerome_s.html

Mary Gergen—manuscripts
www.taosinstitute.net/manuscripts/manuscripts.html#marymgergen

Matt O'Sullivan's photographic narrative
http://thenarrative.net/archive/showAll.html

Rom Harré—informational website
http://web.lemoyne.edu/~hevern/narpsych/nr-theorists-hijkl.html#harre

Critique of beauty and body image
www.jeankilbourne.com/resources/beauty.html

Narrative Psychology
http://web.lemoyne.edu/%7Ehevern/narpsych/narpsych.html

Discussion Questions and/or Short Papers

1. A major theme of Part II is to place into question the familiar idea that we exist as independent beings, living in private worlds, and propelled by biology to feel or act in specific ways. This is but one way of constructing the idea of persons, and it is one that rapidly leads to suspicion, self-seeking, and an uncaring orientation to others. In this section, we have encouraged, instead, a view of the person as fully immersed in relationships. We traced the ways in which we act as emerging from our relationships. Most dramatically, we can say that almost everything we do—from getting up in the morning, working, playing, and so on—owes its existence to our presence in relationships. Consider a range of actions that seem to illustrate this point very well.
    *   Are there any actions that you believe to be automatic—that is, so driven by biology that you and those close to you could not decide to act in any other way? (For example, you cannot decide directly to stop the growth of your hair.)
    *   What kinds of actions are you involved in each day that seem most obviously prepared by the relationships in which you have participated?
2. Consider your emotions from the standpoint of relationships.
    *   Although emotions seem natural, and determined by our biological makeup, in what ways are your emotions dependent on relationships?
    *   Are there rules about *when, where,* and *how* you should express various emotions?

- Could you change the way you feel and express yourself?
  a. What would be required to do so?
  b. Could there be advantages in bringing about such change?
3. From a relational perspective an individual is not fully to blame for his or her actions. This is because most of our activities make sense within some kind of relational history. Thus, when we behave badly, we reflect this history of sense making.
   - Discuss the implications of this perspective for
     a. cheating on a committed partner.
     b. evaluating the performance of members of an organization.
     c. assigning prison sentences.
4. Part II makes a strong case for the ways in which our actions are dependent on the relations of the moment—that is, on whom we are with and what we are doing together. However, it is also clear that when we participate in ongoing relations, we also carry with us residues of past relations. Our language is an important example. We use the language we have taken from previous relations, dating to our earliest years of life. Yet, what we say is very much dependent on whom we are talking with and what we are doing with that person in the moment. Consider how your actions, facial expressions, gestures, and the way you move carry forward residues of the past.
   - Can you describe the ways in which these nonverbal actions are drawn from previous relationships, either with actual people you have known, or relations with fictitious or screen personages (e.g., running one's hands through one's hair while nervous or when contemplating—what is the origin of this action?)?

Communication as Collaborative Action

Introduction

In Parts I and II we have seen that it is through communication that the world and the self come to be what they are for us. And it is through communication that the world and self take on value—or not. If our realities, rationalities, moralities, and pleasures are given birth in the processes of communication, then it is imperative to understand such processes. What brings about success in communication? Why does it so often seem to fail? Why are we sometimes engaged—creating, learning, and joyful—and at other times so bored or frustrated? How are our bodies involved in effective communication? What is it to truly listen to another? Questions such as these will be of chief concern in the three sections that comprise Part III of this book.

In Section A, Discourse in Action, we focus on ways in which our discourse together is both ordered and disordered. Although order is essential to sustain meaning, the outcome of our conversations is never determined. Thus, the choices we make in our dialogues are enormously important in creating the future. Section B, Nonverbal Language: Meaning as Action, underscores that communication is not simply a matter of verbal discourse. Here we explore the nonverbal dimension of communication, focusing on facial expression, body language, and clothing. In Section C, Listening as Collaboration, we find it important to distinguish between "hearing" and "listening." To hear another's voice is simply to register that the sound has been received; to listen, in contrast, is to engage in a collaborative process through which meaning is born and sustained. Throughout these readings, we do not attempt to tell you, the reader, the "truth" about communication. After all, our words also stem from our relationships and will construct a particular world. However, even though there is no revealing truth about communication, we do believe that these readings and explorations will offer some interesting and useful ways of understanding our lives together.

Discourse in Action

We first turn our attention to the *verbal* medium of communication. To appreciate the readings we have selected, think for a moment about a recent conversation you have had with a co-worker, friend, family member, or even a passing stranger. From a communication standpoint, there are at least two major features of such conversation. First there is *order*. So much of what we say to each other is conventional. We generally recognize words and phrases, gestures, facial expressions, tones of voice, and so on. We sometimes feel we have heard and seen much of it before. We shouldn't feel uneasy about this conventional ordering; without it we would fail to communicate at all. For example, consider what it would be like to talk to someone who uses no recognizable words and whose gestures and facial expressions seem totally weird to you!

At the same time, almost all conversations are characterized by a certain degree of *disorder*. You use words and phrases in new combinations and tailor your talk for specific audiences. When another person responds to you, you will likely hear sentences you have never heard before in precisely that form. Furthermore, the juxtaposition of what you have said with what the other has responded is likely to be totally novel. Every conversation is a new horizon of possibilities.

The first four readings in this section—all by communication scholars—are designed to explore the dimensions and interplay of order and disorder more closely. Reading 14 by Donal Carbaugh calls attention to the profound degree to which our relationships are ordered. Often we think of ourselves as acting spontaneously, perhaps laughing or shouting in ways that may even surprise us. As Carbaugh demonstrates in his account of audiences at basketball games, even the most seemingly spontaneous actions are bound by convention. In Reading 15 by Richard Buttney, we confront one of the classic distinctions in the study of language, *the adjacency pair,* or more simply, the way in which conversations seem to be composed of conventional pairings (orderings) such as questions and answers. However, as he demonstrates, there are cases in which the conventions are broken. These "glitches" do not go unnoticed; rather they often invite close attention and demand an explanation.

Following this discussion, we examine the down side of order—disorder. Specifically, in Reading 16 Barnett Pearce illuminates the existence of relational patterns that are so deeply engrained in our traditions that we can scarcely imagine breaking them. Worse still, they are patterns that may be destroying our relationships. What do we do, then, with unwanted repetitive patterns of communication? Finally, in Reading 17 William Foster Owen brings these contrasting *tensions between order and disorder* together in his treatment of metaphors. Metaphors are similar to narratives in that they are forms of speech that often center the ways we talk and act. Recall that the narrative is a story form that organizes what we can say about the past. On the other hand, metaphors provide "word pictures" that catch our attention in ways that bring new life to commonplace events. For example, when an authority is called a "tyrant," or a woman friend is called an "angel," we use metaphors. When we talk about the authority as a tyrant, we may resist him or her. When a woman friend is an angel we are likely to treat her warmly. In this sense, metaphors function to stabilize and organize action. This reading is unusually interesting in that Owen demonstrates the conflict that can occur when people have different metaphors for the same situation. As we shall see, competing metaphors about "our relationship" can be destructive.

The remaining readings in Part III look beyond the surface tension of order and disorder into the *deep interdependence that is essential to create our realities, our rationalities, and our sense of the desirable and undesirable.* We first explore more closely the ways in which the flow of interdependence between order and disorder brings about meaning—or destroys it. Reading 18 by Kenneth Gergen challenges our traditional view of meaning as residing in the head of individuals, and he explores the idea that we use words to communicate these private meanings. He finds this view deeply flawed. If communication were about knowing what is inside one another's head, we would always be left in doubt. We can never "see into the mind" of the other, and thus, according to this view, we would never know what words mean. In this selection we find that meaning is created not in the head, but within the process of relationship.

The two readings that follow both emphasize positive dialogue. Given that strong feelings of interdependence in relationships can often bring us into a place of alienating conflict, what then becomes mutually satisfying or productive dialogue in this situation? Robyn Penman, in Reading 19, touches on what she feels are four major components of such dialogue. Then, in Reading 20, Sheila McNamee discusses future talk. Specifically she demonstrates the importance of replacing "problem talk" with dialogue built around "opportunities" and "potentials," in creating more promising futures.

READING 14

Social Scripts: The Organization of Spontaneity

When conversation flows smoothly it is largely because we rely on frequently recurring patterns. We converse without difficulty in the same way we might ride a bicycle. We do so almost thoughtlessly because our actions are well practiced. Scholars often refer to conventional practices of communicative action as *social scripts*. The phrase calls attention to how our conversations often proceed as if we were following the script of a play. For example, if you meet a friend you haven't seen for several years, you will probably ask each other about what has been happening; you will talk about high points and possible troubles. You will also talk about what's going on in your lives at present, and about friends you have in common. Of course, you could talk about the weather, politics, or the price of food, but these topics are not commonly found "in the script."

One of the most interesting things about scripts is that what passes for spontaneous action—unrehearsed and unplanned—is also largely scripted. You may feel that you are acting on the spur of the moment; however, your actions are carrying cultural tradition. Ironically, it may be that our feelings of spontaneity require traditional scripts. If conditions were totally novel to us, we would have to stop and consider each sentence we spoke. We would scarcely feel spontaneous. In Reading 14, Donal Carbaugh shares his observations of fans at a basketball game. Fans typically feel free and spontaneous, but are they?

Reading 14 DONAL CARBAUGH

By exploring social identities through the communication of particular cultural scenes, such as at basketball games, we may gain an insight into the role of communicative practices in everyday social life.

There are five main phases of communication that combine to form a rather integral sequence of conduct. To act within this sequence is, largely, to be a fan at this sporting event. The talk of the sequence, and of each phase within it, may be understood as a playful game in itself. Most of the fans arrive at the basket-ball game between a half-hour and five minutes prior to the start of the game or "game time." During this time they, like the players, are warming-up. This stage of the event is characterized largely by talk about two topics. First, some talk centers on the arena, the crowd, and the event at hand. For instance, about the arena ("Those seats sure look comfortable"); to the crowd ("Hey, there's Bob." "Here comes the guy selling mixer" ["mixer" referring to soft drinks to be "mixed"—illegally—with alcoholic beverages], or "Do you believe how many people are here?"); to unique aspects of the event ("Hey, we're going to be on TV," "We got to get on TV"); to the cheerleaders ("That was a nice routine," or "Boy, she's good-looking," or "Wow, what a hunk"); to the teams ("They've [the other team] got a sevenfooter," or "Camby has been on a hot streak lately"). The second dominant topic is rather generally sociable and refers to current events (the weather, political issues), to common friends, or to previous basketball games. The function of the talk at this stage is to acquaint individuals in the crowd to those seated around them (even if indirectly) and to orient the crowd to the event at hand.

During the above conversations, and at about twenty minutes prior to game time, the arena clock begins a countdown. While the beginning of the count-down has no apparent impact, the clock helps orchestrate an intricately designed sequence of events. With about twelve minutes left until game time, several things begin occurring at once. By this time both teams are on the floor warming up. The band has begun playing several lively songs, loudly. The cheer-leaders are performing dances to the band's music and doing gymnastic mounts. The referees and coaches are often gathered toward center court and talking. Public announcements are being made of upcoming events. There is an incredible amount of visual and aural and verbal stimulation! The conversations become more lively. A crescendo of talk appears, as if someone were gradually turning up the arena's volume. Then, suddenly, with about eight minutes left on the clock, the teams leave the floor.

The Salutation

As the teams leave the floor, the volume in the arena quickly lowers. A military or service group marches onto the floor prominently displaying the American flag (among others). The announcer states, "Now ladies and gentlemen, please rise for the playing and singing of our national anthem." Those within sight of the flag rise to attention, with some "crossing their heart" and (some) singing the national anthem. For most Americans this is not an unusual sight, yet it is interesting to the cultural analyst. Contrast the tone of reverence introduced during this salutation, if not maintained for its entirety, with the frenzy of stim-uli occurring only seconds earlier. By playing a controlled reverence against a frenzied excitement, each symbolic stage serves dramatically to heighten the impact of the other. As the "warm-up" sets the stage for play and wild excitement, the salutation provides Americans with a kind of reverent political gesture, a cooperative activity paying homage to a national heritage. The salutation ritual provides a practice in which all participants rise, attend to, and/or orient to a common symbol, the nation's flag, thereby uniting through this common gesture. Some of the members of the crowd (or readers) may not agree about the full meaning or sense of the salutation (for example, who is being united toward what ends?). Additionally, those from elsewhere can find the salutation stage to be quite puzzling in the context of a sporting event. Nonetheless, the salutation is always an integral part of the American basketball event. In the salutary performance, the fans typically cooperatively stand, in a common and shared way, and thus co-orient to the American flag. In this sense, this phase provides a form whereby a symbol, the flag-nation, is cooperatively celebrated, within the larger competitive ritual of the game itself.

The second (or seconds before) the anthem is over, a frenzied excitement begins.

The Introductions

Soon after the salutation, the teams reenter the arena. As the home team comes into view, the band breaks into song, the crowd claps, and the cheerleaders lead yells. With between forty and fifty seconds left on the clock, the band begins the home team's fight song, which ends as close to "zero time" as possible. With the clock running down, a strongly expressive style pervades the arena (dramatically extended from the tone set at the end on the warm-up). Yelling and "blurting out" characterize the introductions as the crowd discursively divides into two groups of fans, the home-team fans and the "away-team" fans.

The announcer begins by introducing the away team. As the announcer says, "we would like to welcome the visiting (team name) to (the home team's arena)," a moan or at times even a loud "boo" is often heard. If the home team fans orient to the away players at all, their attention seems to follow the rule: one should playfully disconfirm and/or ridicule the other team. For example, when a smaller player was introduced he was met by "Hey runt!" or "Squirt!" Another player whose name rhymed with lemon was called "Lemon" from the introduction to the end of the game. One player with very hairy legs but peculiarly unhairy knees was greeted by "Hey, do you shave your knees?" These exemplify individuals' comments that orient to an unspoken consensus: that fans playfully disconfirm and/or ridicule the other team.

Groups often coordinate communicative acts to orient to the rule that fans disconfirm the opposing team. For example, the band often leads a particular cheer after each opposing player is introduced. The announcer may say "starting at guard, wearing number 44, six-foot-four-inch, John Smith!" He is greeted by the band and some of the fans yelling "So what?" After being introduced, the next player is greeted by "Who cares?" the third by "Big deal!" the fourth by "Go home!" and so on.

Several other coordinated acts orient to this rule. When a university team from Idaho was being introduced, it was met by several dozen potatoes which were rolled across the floor. (Idaho is the state known for its "famous potatoes," as written on its automobile license plates.) When the U.S. Air Force team was introduced, it was met by a barrage of paper airplanes. When another school, which had a canine nickname, was introduced, the fans rolled several dog biscuits across the floor. Another tactic, used while the opposing team was being introduced, involved almost everyone in the main cheering section opening and casually perusing newspapers, negating any concern about or contact with the away team.

Although the above acts may seem nasty or even tactless, they are almost always done in a spirit of fun, in a playful (rather than serious) tone, and are usually understood (even expected) as part of the basketball event. During the away team introductions, the talk is very expressive and competitively based as it emphasizes and embraces lack of support for the other team, and relentless support of one's favored teams.

If the away team consists of disconfirmed players, there is no doubt about *who* is familiar and supported at home. Home team introductions usually follow a sequence of acts, a kind of mini-ritual, which itself functions to celebrate the team. The sequence is initiated by the announcer, who says, "And now, ladies and gentlemen your University of Massachusetts Minutemen!" Upon this announcement, the band bursts into a rhythm, the crowd stands up, claps, whistles, and yells. The cheerleaders form a dancing tunnel through which the celebrated players enter, one by one, into the arena. There is an explosion of sensorial and even sensual energy after each player is announced (although each time it becomes harder to hear the announcement). As the players join each other at center court they slap each others' hands, smile, and take apparent delight in the highly energized scene. After the final player is announced, the band turns the pounding rhythm into an electric song, the cheerleaders dance, the players "psyche up," and the fans continue to applaud, clap, yell, and celebrate. The band plays one last rendition of the fight song, ending right at the moment the game begins.

Through participating in the introductions the fans celebrate the home team while attempting to intimidate and disconfirm the away team. Sometimes it is stated that the fans are the "sixth man" on the team, playing a key role in the game itself. As the differences and competition between the teams, and between the fans of each, is emphasized, the introductory talk is highly coordinated in its performance and competitive style. As the players have, so the fans have come to play.

To this point, the playing of the game itself has no effect on the cultural event. In other words, the sequencing of events to this point is, to a degree, not dependent on the playing of the game. At times, especially if the home team loses, much of the fans cheering and excitement ends here. The final two phases in the basketball event, however, are dependent on the playing of the game itself.

Game Talk

Once the game begins there are several kinds of talk practiced by the fan. Individual comments normally are spoken during the basketball game, as fans express their approval or disapproval of the events in the game. During these times it is appropriate, perhaps even preferred, for individuals to express— sometimes by standing up and yelling through cupped hands—his or her opinions about various plays and players in the game. Continuing the theme of the introduction, these "fan solos" often criticize or disconfirm the opposing players, but also turn similarly to the opposing coach, or the referees. For instance, after an opposing player had made a defensive error a fan yelled, sarcastically, "Nice defense!" Another opposing player had played intense defense on a favorite home player, but the home player eventually scored. A fan responded to this play by yelling "In your face!" Fans also seem to have an affinity for telling the opposing coach what to do. As the coach stands up to advise or admonish his players or the referees, he is told to "Sit down!" or to "Take another tranquilizer!" The opposing players and coach are the recipients of such verbal criticism and disconfirmation.

While the opposing players and coach may also have some supportive fans in the stand, the referees are less fortunate. No one yells in favor of the refs, only *at* them. The referees, as the official authorities in the rules of the game, bear the brunt of many fan solos. When a fan is dissatisfied with the game, he or she does not verbally fault the home team, one cannot fault the visiting team for playing well, so he or she "lashes out" at the referees. During these times the fans might describe their opinion of a call ("Horrible call, ref!" "Terrible call, ref!"); explain to the referee what, in their opinion, the proper call was ("That was a foul, ref!" or "Goal tending ref!"); or they simply tell the referee what they think of him ("You smell!") or what to do ("Take a shower, ref!" "Hey, put your glasses on!" or "You might as well put on a [the opposing team's color] shirt!"). These verbalizations function as an emphatic support of the desired team. An example on this theme makes the point rather clearly. In this case the referee had made an obviously good call against the home team, and a hometown fan seated high in the stadium on the opposite end of the arena from the call yelled, in the commercially televised style of Bob Uecker, "No way, ref!" The crowd chuckled and "took delight" in such an unquestioned and loyal support of the home team.

The communicative phases described above can be summarized through the manner and style of communicative practice involved in each. By manner, I simply point to the kind of relational tone being targeted in the practice of that phase, ranging from cooperative to competitive. For instance, the talk that occurs during the warm-up would appear to be highly cooperative as the participants discuss the arena, the game, or other everyday affairs. Contrast this with the communicative acts of the game talk when fans choose a desired side and thus verbally "play" on the competition in the arena. By style, I point to the intensity of discursive expression in the phase, ranging from rather low, subdued, and conversational to rather high, frenzied, and excited. For example the "warm-up talk" involves conversations in a style that contrasts to the later parts of the introduction phase when the fans fanatically express support of their desired team. Using the two dimensions of manner and style of communication practice, we may parsimoniously summarize the nature and sequence of fan actions in the basketball scene.

Explorations

1. In this case study Carbaugh identifies the scripted character of what might seem to be spontaneous activities of basketball spectators. Can you do the same for other kinds of relationships? Identify the scripted nature of communication in each of the contexts indicated. What are some of the things participants must do or say in order to "make communicative sense" within these contexts?

   a. The beginning of a romantic first date:

   _____

   _____

   _____

   _____

   _____

   b. Talking with classmates after a final examination:

   _____

   _____

   _____

   _____

   _____

   c. Talking with your family at dinner:

   _____

   _____

   _____

   _____

   _____

Key Construction

- Scripted communication

| READING 15 |

Structured Conversation: Adjacency Pairs

In early work on the conversational creation of meaning, scholars were struck by the turn-taking process. Conversations seemed to proceed in paired sequences, such as a greeting, "Hey, how you doin'?" followed by a return greeting, "Just great; how 'bout you?" These turn-taking sequences were termed *adjacency pairs*, and to an important degree the pattern of adjacency pairs structures much of our conversation. Among the most common adjacency pairs are:

Question	Answer
Request	Compliance (or denial)
Accusation	Denial
Invitation	Acceptance (or excuse)
Offer	Acceptance (or rejection)
Assessment	Agreement (or disagreement)

Yet, over time it also became clear that such patterns are not always so predictable. People often disrupt them. As the communication scholar Richard Buttney proposes in Reading 15, such disruptions are very important. When disruptions take place, we begin to ask questions about why. We begin to draw inferences about what the other person is up to. So long as the smooth flow of pairing is sustained (e.g., question leading to an answer), we move through conversation without much thought. When conversational predictions are unfamiliar (e.g., one's invitation is followed by an accusation), then the conversation comes into question.

Reading 15   R I C H A R D   B U T T N E Y

Some conversational exchanges seem so familiar as to be conventional, for example, question-answer, request-comply/deny, greeting-greeting, invitation-accept/reject, offer-accept/reject, assessment-agree/disagree, accusation-denial, and so on. These exchange formats have been identified as adjacency pairs: two contiguous utterances from different speakers, which are heard as connected, such that the first part of the pair makes the occurrence of a second-pair part expected or relevant. While these exchanges like question-answer or greeting-greeting are common enough, the adjacency-pair structure needs to be understood as "rule-governed" or as a "normative organization." Normative in the sense that *deviations* from the projected second-pair are *relevantly absent*, and thereby, something for which one can be held *accountable*. Silence following a first-pair part is not only noticeable, it also provides the grounds for *drawing inferences* about the person who does not respond. For instance, the lack of response to an accusation may involve a range of candidate inferences such as: "admission of guilt," "attempted avoidance," "display of being above having to answer," or simply "failure to hear or understand the speaker." In courtroom settings, defendants who remain silent following accusations commonly are heard as conceding guilt.

Explorations

1. To further appreciate Buttney's point, write down what you might say to yourself in the following situations:

   a. You invited someone to your birthday party and she or he never responds.

   _____

   _____

   _____

b. You told a friend how well she or he had performed on an examination (i.e., the grade was an A). She or he then responds, "I don't know why you would say that."

_____

_____

_____

2. The focus on adjacency pairs emphasizes the way in which conversation is predictably structured. Yet, there may be more flexibility available to us than such research suggests.

   Can you offer an alternative to the conventional response offered to you as the first move in each pair? For example, a greeting is conventionally responded to with a greeting. However, there are other possibilities. A cheery greeting could yield a comment like, "You sure sound energetic today" (an assessment) or "Are you talking to me?" (question).

   a. How could you respond to a question other than by answering it?

   _____

   _____

   _____

   b. How could you respond to an accusation other than by denying or admitting it?

   _____

   _____

   _____

   c. How could your respond to an offer other than by accepting or rejecting it?

   _____

   _____

   _____

Key Construction

- Adjacency pairs

Unwanted Repetitive Patterns

Previous readings suggest that as we communicate with each other we create not only our realities and values, but also our common habits of relating. Yet, among these habits of relating are some that have unhappy consequences. We say things that we know are troublesome, and yet we do it over and over again. These patterns seem so "natural." But of course, they are not so much natural as conventional. And with effort, we can find alternatives to these conventions. Consider these remarks on unwanted repetitive patterns, and begin to consider how you might escape the demands of habitual patterns of conversation.

Reading 16   BARNETT PEARCE

Consider the social event of a heated argument, complete with name-calling and high blood pressure. Two persons with whom I worked became all-too-predictable in constructing this social event. The interesting thing about it was that they both claimed that they did not like to fight with each other and that they did everything they could to avoid fights, but still fights continued.

Several of us took this as an opportunity for research. First, we convinced ourselves that the "fighters" were telling the truth about not wanting to fight. We noticed that they sought out their friends, asking for advice and help. They deliberately employed various strategies that these friends suggested for avoiding fights. They often went out of their way to avoid being with the other person as a way of evading a fight. These strategies, although sincere, were only partially effective: the fights continued.

We next observed the fights more closely. We found that these persons fought only about a certain range of topics, and then only with each other. They did not fight with other persons about these topics or with each other about other topics. Quite sensibly, we concluded that the unavoidable fights occurred because of something having to do with the combination of their relationship with each other and with specific topics.

We did a series of interviews. First we asked what it felt like to be in these fights. They did not like it and felt out of control. Despite their best attempts to avoid a fight they would feel *compelled* to act in ways that *they* knew would lead to a fight. "When he said what he did," each reported. "I had no choice. I *had* to respond as I did." "What did you think he would do next?" "Oh, I knew that we were getting into it again but there was nothing else I could do."

We interviewed a large number of other persons and found that virtually all could tell us about a similar experience where a combination of the relationship with some other person and a topic produced what we came to call an "unwanted, repetitive pattern" or URP. Although the content of the URPs may be highly specific to the individual or the relationship the experience seems quite common: you are in a highly predictable situation where you feel that you *must* say or do something even though you know it will set off an unpleasant, undesirable pattern of interaction.

Explorations

1. Describe briefly one unwanted repetitive pattern (URP) in which you engage.

   Example: My older brother often criticizes me, saying that my choices are idiotic or immature. When he does this I snap back at him, saying some pretty harsh things. Often this leads to a heated and angry argument. So he just walks away angry and we don't speak for several hours.

   Your unwanted repetitive pattern: _____

   _____

   _____

   _____

2. Participation in these unwanted patterns seems so natural that we may believe we cannot do anything else. But from a constructionist standpoint, we know that alternatives are possible. Sometimes we can see how others manage to avoid or step out of these unwanted scenarios. At other times we may have to create new alternatives.

   Now return to the unwanted pattern you outlined in exercise 1. Try to think of a way you could prevent or avoid the pattern. What could you say or do that would interfere with the "natural" but unwanted sequence? How could you change or shift the conversation to make it a better relationship? Explain.

   _____

   _____

   _____

   _____

   _____

Key Construction

■ Unwanted repetitive patterns

Metaphors We Live By

As we have seen, the concept of the narrative furnishes us with an enormously important way of understanding the use of language in relationships. A second important tool for working and playing with language is the *metaphor*. Traditionally, we distinguished between the *literal* and *methaphoric* use of words. In this tradition, we use a word literally when we apply it correctly in context so that if people are arguing we call their actions an argument. In contrast, a description is metaphoric if it substitutes another word for the literal description. For example, to call an argument a "small war" or a "dance" would be metaphoric. Yet, from our discussion of language games, we realize that, strictly speaking, there is no literal use of language. Rather, we take a description to be literal or accurate when it is conventional—that is, when we have used it for so long that we are no longer conscious of it being conventional. Thus, we may say that metaphors are language forms of constructing the world that play with or unsettle conventions.

As you can appreciate, the use of metaphors is enormously important in breaking up our sense of the taken-for-granted. First, when we shift from a conventional to an unconventional form of constructing meaning, we open different possibilities for deliberation and action. For example, if two people are engaged in an angry exchange of opinions, to call it an "argument" in Western culture suggests that there should be a winner and a loser. If we call it a "dance," we call attention to the way people are interdependent. The term also suggests that they could step out of their particular pattern and that they are not obliged to dance this way. Second, when our attention is drawn to the metaphoric basis of the way we talk and act, we come to appreciate that our actions could be "otherwise." Awareness of metaphors frees us to live another way. For example, how many different metaphorical naming possibilities exist in a conversation about an armed conflict that involves weapons and death? Is it a war, dispute, conflict, struggle, insurgency, or something else?

In Reading 17, William Foster Owen explores the metaphors that seem to dominate the words and actions of a young couple as they try to work out the problems of a committed relationship.

Reading 17   WILLIAM FOSTER OWEN

Alice is a twenty-two-year-old, unmarried college senior who had been dating Paul, a twenty-five-year-old, unmarried college graduate for two years. According to Alice, for the past several months Paul had been "pushing for a more solid commitment" which she had been unwilling to make. Still in college, Alice felt that before "settling down" she wanted to work at "getting a job, graduating, working, and being on my own." This situation is a common occurrence. While the roles may change, dating persons often face disparity of commitment, love, and attachment.

Alice structured her relationship with metaphorical discourse indicating two main metaphors: "relationship is captivation" and "relationship is machine." This discourse in turn helped structure the three interrelated themes: "commitment," "manipulation," and "working." In Alice's view, commitment, defined in terms of "a judgment to begin or to continue a relationship," was a result of manipulation, defined as "the active, conscious control of one person by another for self gain" and work is defined as the amount of effort, struggle, sacrifice, or energy required to maintain relationships. Let us first examine the "relationship as captivation" metaphor:

Main Metaphor:	"Captivation"	
Relational Themes:	"Commitment"	"Manipulation"
Manifesting Discourse:	(1) . . . I wonder if I shouldn't just terminate the whole thing and . . .	(1) . . . take him off the *hook*.
	(2) . . . the illusionary *carrot* in front of his face.	(2) I should quit *dangling*.
	(3) No *point* in telling him I won't marry him and then pouring *salt* in the *wound*.	
	(4) Sometimes I feel like *I'm* walking into a *trap*.	

Alice was negotiating a dialectic of individuality and togetherness, torn between attracting and maneuvering Paul into a committed relation and abandoning this coupling for a life alone. The "relationship is captivation" metaphor helped Alice to conceptualize her dilemma. "Captivation" involves the roles of captor and captive and characteristics including entrapment, baiting, stalking, alluring, hunting, avoiding, and even killing. Alice remarked, "I wonder if I shouldn't just *terminate* the whole thing," evidencing her quandary over continuing the relationship or putting it to death in a reified "termination." Interestingly, she ended the utterance above with ". . . and take him *off the hook,*" implying she had manipulated him onto the "hook." Asked what she meant by this utterance, Alice noted how she had "fished Paul out of a large pool" of suitors, occasionally seducing him with the promise of sexual intercourse. This seduction is apparent in her assertion: "I should quit *dangling* the illusory *carrot* in front of his face." The "dangling" represented manipulation, while the "carrot" represented commitment. Conceivably, one must attract a quarry with a rewarding commodity, and the quarry risks injury in the pursuit of such a reward. The "carrot" was the fulfillment or promise of sexual intimacy, time together and, ultimately, the committed continuance of the relationship. Clearly, Alice held Paul committed or captured in the relationship by controlling Paul's costs and rewards, all the while debating her own uncertainty over the commitment. She *withheld* "telling him I won't marry him," both as a reduced cost to Paul and as an expression of her own uncertainty over commitment. For to tell him this, Alice would be "pouring *salt* in the *wound*," just as captors do to their prey. She could promise the *"carrot"* of commitment, but knew that by refusing to marry Paul she would exacerbate, jeopardize, and "injure" the relationship.

Therefore, Alice wanted to keep her prey, Paul, on the *"hook"* by *"dangling"* the *"carrot"* of commitment continuously before him, but she was uncertain over *how* much commitment she wanted. She feared too much commitment (e.g., "Sometimes I feel like *I'm* walking into a *trap*"), but she feared also that by refusing Paul's wish for maximum commitment she might lose him. As Alice noted: "You know, I have Paul—you know the saying: 'A *bird* in the *hand*'—But, sometimes I'm just not sure what to do with him!" However, Alice used one other main metaphor *to* conceptualize her relationship, "relationship is machine":

Main Metaphor: "Machine"

Relational Theme: "Work"

Manifesting Discourse:

(1) It's like when you see a movie where the *soundtrack* is ahead of the *picture.* . . .

(2) I don't feel like my relationship with him is a *"driving force"* in my life. Conversely, I think he views me as a *"driving force"* in his life . . .

(3) Maybe there's not enough *"tension"* to *string* this relationship together for me . . .

(4) For some reason (call it *Chemistry*) he doesn't have the *power* to excite *"passion"* in me.

From the analyses above of the "captivation" metaphor, Alice perceived she had manipulated Paul into a committed relationship—perhaps more committed than she desired. In one sense, she had entrapped Paul; in another sense, she thought they had arrived at a serious romance too easily. The "relationship is machine" metaphor helped Alice to conceptualize this latter sense. Machines overheat and need to be well-timed and oiled so that gears mesh and the devices work. Sometimes human relations, like machines, *"rub,* cause *friction"* or are *"smooth-running,"* indicative of the relational theme involvement.

Alice's discourse indicated both the "machine" metaphor and the relational theme "work." Recall that work was defined "as the amount of effort, struggle, sacrifice, or energy required to maintain relationships." Alice had manipulated her prey into her grasp, but it had been "too easy" and thus was not gratifying for her. Perhaps just as a mechanic feels greater pleasure in continuously repairing, fine-tuning, and even worrying over a machine, Alice felt there was not "enough *tension* to *string*" the relation together, not enough "*power* to excite '*passion*'" in her, and not enough of a "*driving force*" in her life. Furthermore, like the movie projector malfunction that results in an unsynchronous mesh between voice and video, Alice knew her relation with Paul was ill-timed (e.g., ". . . where the *soundtrack* is ahead of the *picture*). Asked to embellish these metaphorical statements, Alice clarified: "It's *Paul* who's ahead of me; he seems to think we can *zip* along into a relationship without a *hitch*. After all, let's face it, I didn't have to put *any effort* into maintaining it. It's too *easy!*" Ironically, then, the manipulation which had worked so well in capturing Paul had been too successful in the sense that little effort or struggle had been needed. Alice felt a commitment had been achieved in machine-like precision, without "*tension*" or the use of "*power.*" But, how do Alice's main metaphors, and the concomitant themes, mesh or contradict Paul's? Paul interpreted his relationship with Alice using one main metaphor, "relationship is worship":

Main Metaphor:	"Worship"	
Relational Themes:	"Commitment"	"Respect"
Manifesting Discourse:	(1) I keep trying to put Alice kinda on a *pedestal*, . . .	(1) . . . I'd do *anything* for her, drop everything to be *at her side.*
	(2) She's always sayin' I treat her like *royalty*, . . .	(2) . . . always *doin'* things for her like uh—when I come over to mow her lawn—like uh—I keep the *castle grounds* in order.
	(3) She says: "You're my *faithful servant.*"	

Unlike Alice, Paul perceived their relation as an "assumed and unquestioned commitment." While Alice negotiated an ambivalent dialectic of individuality and togetherness, Paul already had decided they were committed for life. The "relationship is worship" metaphor expresses this unwavering commitment. "Worship" involves the roles of royalty and servant; characteristics including duty, respect, faith, honor, and vows and promises. Alice noted: "Paul is a guy who treats me like a *queen*," although, she continued, "they [women] love it when you treat them like *dirt.*" Clearly, Paul did not treat Alice "like *dirt*," but instead worshipped her by putting her on a "*pedestal*," treating her like "*royalty*" and attending her as a "*faithful servant.*"

Paul helped to define the complementary roles of *"queen"* and *"servant"* through his respect for Alice. The respect theme has been defined as "the perception of the degree of other-orientation, and the extent of concern expressed by one person about the well-being of the other." Paul put Alice on a *"pedestal"* by doing *"anything* for her" and would "drop everything to be *at her side."* He *would*, for example, keep the *"lawn,"* the *"castle grounds,"* in order. When asked why he did so much for *Alice, Paul* responded: "The way I was raised was that it was the man's *duty* to do whatever pleased his woman. I mean, when you *promise* to be in a relationship you learn to set aside yourself for the other." Thus, Paul's unquestioned commitment was an outgrowth of his respect for Alice.

Explorations

1. Generate three additional metaphors that could be used by couples in talking about a committed relationship. Then explain what the relationship might be like if this metaphor was central to it.

   Example: An adventure:

   If the couple talked about it this way, they might think about the fun they could have, see risks as welcoming, and perhaps appreciate having a chance to learn more about themselves and each other. They might have less fear of what would happen in the future to the relationship, and they could have a more enthusiastic perspective toward their relationship.

   a. _____

   _____

   _____

   _____

   b. _____

   _____

   _____

   _____

   c. _____

   _____

   _____

   _____

2. Generate two metaphors you could apply to yourself, and indicate how this would change the way you see yourself. For example, to understand yourself as a "fox" would suggest a number of interesting things about the way you approached your work and play.

a. _____

_____

_____

b. _____

_____

_____

Key Constructions

- Conventional word usage versus metaphoric word usage
- Relationship metaphors
- Metaphors open possibilities

READING 18

Meaning as Co-Created

Thus far the readings in Section A of Part III have focused on the stabilities commonly found in meaning making. The stabilities are recurring patterns that enable our relationships to proceed harmoniously and effectively. We now turn to dimensions of instability. In terms of human communication, we never stand in the same place in a river. That is, we deal with a constant flow of events that, like currents of the river, are never identical. The first time someone says "I love you" may bring an enormous thrill. The second time it is said will always carry the history from its having been said before. If someone repeated it 40 times in a row, you might even find it boring. And if a stranger approached you on the street and said it, you might even be offended.

The most significant dimension of instability derives from how the meaning of our words are never fully our own. Our meaning will depend on how another responds to our words, and the meaning of their responses will depend on how we then respond. Neither of us can mean anything without the other. In Reading 18 from Kenneth Gergen's work the case is made for the thorough "interdependence" of meaning.

An Individual's Utterance in and of itself Means Nothing

We pass each other on the street. I say, "Hello Anna." You walk past without hearing. Under such conditions, what have I said? To be sure, I have uttered two words. However, for all the difference it makes I might have chosen two nonsense syllables. You pass and I say "Umlot nigen . . ." You understand nothing. When you fail to acknowledge me in any relational way, it matters little what I have said. In an important sense, nothing understandable has been said. I cannot possess meaning for us—alone.

The Potential for Meaning is Realized through Supplementary Action

Lone utterances begin to acquire meaning when another (or others) coordinate themselves to the utterance, that is, when they add some form of supplementary action (whether verbal or nonverbal). Effectively, I have greeted Anna only by virtue of her response. When she responds to what I have said with, "Oh, hi, good morning..." she helps shape our encounter as an act of greeting. Supplements may be very simple, such as a nod of affirmation that another has said something meaningful. It may also take the form of an action, such as, when shifting one's line of gaze upon hearing the word, "look!" Or it may extend my utterance in some way, as in "Yes, but I also think that . . ." In effect, we must rely on others to grant us the invitation of meaning. If others do not embrace our utterances as communication, if they fail to coordinate themselves around the offering, then our communication can be viewed as disengaged from convention and it makes little sense to people.

To combine these first two proposals, we see that meaning does not reside within either individual but only in conjoint action. Both my act and its "supplement" must be coordinated in order for meaning to occur. Like a handshake or a kiss, the individual's actions alone are empty. It takes two to tango, that is communication is inherently collaborative.

Supplementary Action is itself a Candidate for Meaning

Any supplemental communication functions twice, *first in granting significance to what has preceded, and second as an action that also requires "supplementation."* In effect, the meaning it grants remains "suspended" until it too is supplemented. Consider a therapy client who speaks of her deep depression. She finds herself unable to cope with an aggressive husband and an intolerable job situation. The therapist can grant meaning to her talk, as an expression of depression, by responding, "Yes! I can see why you might feel this way; tell me a little more about your relationship with your husband." However, this supplement too stands idle of meaning until the client provides her own supplement. If the client ignored the statement, for example, going on to talk about her success as a mother, the therapist's supportive words would be denied significance. More broadly, we may say that in daily life there are *no acts in themselves*, that is, actions that are not simultaneously supplements to what has preceded. Whatever we do or say takes place within a time and place that gives meaning to what has preceded, while simultaneously forming an invitation to further supplementation by another.

Acts Create the Possibility for Meaning but Simultaneously Constrain its Potential

If a teacher gives a lecture on psychoanalytic theory, this lecture is meaningless without an audience that listens, deliberates, affirms, or questions what he or she has said. In this sense, every speaker owes to his or her audience a debt of gratitude because without their engagement the speaker ostensibly ceases to exist. At the same time, the lecture creates the very possibility for the audience to grant meaning. While the audience creates the teacher as a meaningful agent, the teacher simultaneously grants to the student the capacity to create. They are without meaning or full existence until there is an action that invites them both into being within a given lecture and a particular time and place in the course.

Yet it is also important to realize that in practice, actions also set constraints upon supplementation. If the teacher speaks about Freud, audience members cannot, without sanction, supplement in any way they wish. They may ask a question about Freud's life, but not necessarily about astrophysics. They may comment on the concept of the super-ego but not on the taste of radishes. Such constraints exist because the lecture is already embedded within a conventional *tradition of act and supplement.* It has been granted meaning as a "lecture on Freud," by virtue of previous generations of meaning givers (e.g., teachers and students listening to a Freud lecture).

The history of using a particular "supplement" enables it to invite or suggest certain supplements as opposed to others because only these supplements are considered sensible or meaningful within the tradition. Thus, as we speak with each other, we also begin to set limits on each other's way of being.

Supplements Function both to Create and Constrain Meaning

As we have seen, supplements "act backward" in a way that creates meaning of what has preceded. In this sense, the communicator's meaning is not her or his possession, but is constrained by the act of supplementation.

Supplementation operates after the fact by framing how a speaker may mean one thing as opposed to another. The "supplement" suggests what is meant by the speaker, and may, therefore, narrow the possibilities of what the communication may mean. Thus, for example, if a physician responds to a patient's story by saying, "you seem to be telling me you might be pregnant," the physician establishes a form of constraint. She is saying to the patient, "Your words say, 'I may be pregnant.' " Of course the patient can disagree, but traditions of medicine will make it difficult for the patient to do anything but affirm, "yes, I think you could be right," because the patient traditionally agrees with the doctor's suggestions.

Explorations

1. Consider a case in which a student at a university receives a phone call from her mother. Her mother says she hasn't heard from her in so long, and she was growing worried that something was wrong.

   Her mother's words will gain their meaning from the way they are "supplemented" by the student. In the following spaces, note what the student could say that would construct the mother's words as:

   a. An expression of love:

   _____

   _____

   b. A reasonable expression of worry:

   _____

   _____

   c. A way of undermining her daughter's confidence:

   _____

   _____

   d. An attempt to create guilt:

   _____

   _____

2. Now consider how the mom in the previous example might respond to these various ways in which her words have been supplemented by her daughter. What do you think a common supplement might be to the student's words?

   a. Expression of love:

   _____

   _____

b. Expression of worry:

_____

_____

c. Creation of confidence:

_____

_____

d. Undermining of guilt:

_____

_____

3. If someone says something to us that sounds like an insult or personal attack, we often respond with irritation and possible counterattack. These responses are quite conventional within Western culture. However, these supplements also construct the other's words as an insult or an attack. There is no insult or attack until they are affirmed as such by the supplement.

In the following spaces try to formulate two alternative responses to what seems like an insult or attack from a friend. Create the "attack" as something else, such as a joke or a cry for help. In effect, how could you *supplement* (rework) the words of the seeming attacker so the relationship does not lurch into bitter conflict?

a. _____

_____

_____

_____

b. _____

_____

_____

_____

Key Constructions

- Meaning as co-created action
- Supplement
- Constraining and creating meaning

Toward Satisfying Dialogue

Much communication takes place in conversations between two or more people. When we speak of dialogue we have something more specialized in mind. We say that dialogue is a good thing, that dialogue produces mutual understanding, and that conflicting parties need to be in dialogue. Many researchers now wish to understand dialogue from a positive perspective. They wish to locate an ideal form of communication between people that yields maximum satisfaction to those engaged. Of course, not all scholars share these same ideals, and one might say that they too need more dialogue. Reading 19 is from the communication specialist Robyn Penman, who frames her perception of positive dialogue.

Reading 19   ROBYN PENMAN

Everyone I know who advocates a prescriptive approach to dialoguing would assert that there are no hard and fast rules for ensuring that the practice of dialoguing emerges. Dialoguing cannot be done by following a set of injunctions or by applying technical knowledge. It is something that happens between people, and no one person can be in control. Even with the good intent of all participants, a pattern of dialoguing will not necessarily emerge. Nevertheless, good intent and a certain orientation to the conversation are still essential prerequisites. I want to consider four features of such a practice, from the point of view of what we, as participants, should be doing to engage in this practice.

Engaging in, Acting Authentically

Being truly engaged in communicating is one of the four prerequisites for the possibility of dialogue. This was the key point that Buber (1965) made when he drew a distinction between "being" and "seeming"—a distinction that I find very useful, mainly because so many people in conversations *seem* to be seeming. The being persons offer themselves, as it were, to the others with no concern about how the others are seeing them. There is no concern with impression management here! On the other hand, the seeming persons are mainly concerned with what others think of them, and produce looks to make them appear to be spontaneous, sincere, or whatever else they think is desirable. Seeming persons are not participating in, they are impressing on.

This distinction helps me account for why I find so much of public discourse frustrating and undesirable. As an example, consider the public debates and discussions generated for television current affairs and documentaries. I always get the sense that the interviewer and interviewee are "seeming" and not "being." The whole interaction is oriented to the appearance of the thing; they are performances in which nothing new can possibly emerge. The fabricated nature prohibits dialoguing.

A similar phenomenon can be found in many public consultation processes between governments and citizens. Consider, for example, the community hall filled with irate citizens complaining about some development. Typically, at the front of the hall (and up on a dais) are government representatives running the meeting. Are they really engaging in a process or simply defending their position, with no possibility for change? Are they really being in the conversation, or just seeming to be? More often than not these meetings simply perpetuate a polarized conflict that does nothing to meet community needs.

The point is that an engagement in communicating is an essential prerequisite for the possibility of dialoguing. On the other hand, only seeming to do so precludes that very same possibility. If you are only concerned with how you seem to be, it is not possible to fully participate in communicating.

This notion of "being" has also been referred to as acting authentically or honestly. What is important here is that the participants operate on the presumption of honesty, without needing to discover if the other is authentic or not. You do not need to ask "Is that acting in good faith," and suggest that one of the grounds for dialoguing requires acting faithfully into the situation. It also requires the presumption of good faith on the part of other participants. Without this good faith, this authenticity to the process, dialoguing is not possible.

Future Orientation, Going with the Flow

As part of our acting authentically to the process, then, we need to be open and sensitive to the temporal context of the process in which we are engaging. We need to recognize that our understanding can and *does* change as the process proceeds. For me, the critical element of this recognition is the idea that, in setting the ground for dialogue, we are future orientated.

Dialoguing needs this future orientation toward the momentary order of possibilities—the permissions or affordings—that are offered as a conversation proceeds. Similarly, we need to be oriented to what options are closed as we proceed, and how we can go on regardless. This is a view from within the process, within the practice of communicating. It is an orientation to going on, and generating the means to do so (hopefully well). It is view oriented to future solutions or possibilities, not to past causes of problems. However, I want to emphasize that I do not think it is enough, as some have argued, simply to keep the conversation going. Conversations can go round in circles and can go backwards, often in weird paradoxical loops and often seemingly forever. What is important is that the conversation goes forward into new things, not just continues.

Collaborating

Working to go on and to keep the possibilities open also requires a commitment to collaboration. Individuals acting singularly do not keep the process going; it continues through the mutual, collaborative effort of all. To participate well, this mutuality also needs to be affirmed. However, we need to consider here exactly what can be meant by mutuality. For some, mutuality means equal contribution. This way of understanding mutuality presumes a whole range of contextual factors, including equality of capacities, powers, and so on. But I do *not* think we need or want to make these assumptions here. No relationship could ever exhibit complete equality. Yet, this should not preclude some sort of a mutual process.

Instead, then, I suggest that mutuality can simply mean that all participants are committed and able to make some contribution to the process. In particular, they need to be able to contribute to the joint development of the methods by which new understandings and changes are brought about. It also reflects the arguments of Bennett (1985), in which good communicating increases "the chances of ordinary people to participate in the discovery and transformation of their own condition" (p. 259).

In this view, mutuality is expressed by the nature and quality of the contributions that the participants in the process make. These are contributions that allow all participants to jointly create new understandings and possibilities of importance to them. It is perhaps pertinent to point out that this form of mutuality is only possible when all participants are acting in good faith, or being authentic to the process.

Presence, Immediacy

I cannot imagine being authentic, future-orientated, and collaborating, without being in the physical presence of the other(s). There are good reasons for arguing that it is an essential requirement for dialoguing and these reasons rely on morally knowing, drawing on the work of Gadamer (1992) and Shotter (1993). Moral knowing does not exist independently of the social situation; it is brought about within it.

It is only when we are in the physical presence of another(s) that the moral demand of the engagement continues to pull us forward, as it were. Thus, physical presence generates an immediacy for action. It is in the immediacy of the moment that demands are made to continue. If we recognize those demands and are committed to meeting them, then dialoguing becomes more possible.

I have also been involved in various online conversations about dialogue since 1995, conversing with others vitally interested and involved in dialogue and have not yet experienced or observed any dialogic moments. Although I believe we need to be actually present with another, I will remain open to the possibility of a virtual dialogue. Perhaps with a longer history of conversing this way we may evolve other ways of implicating the moral demand that arises out of embodied presence.

References

Bennett, W.L. (1985). Communication and social responsibility. *Quarterly Journal of Speech, 71,* 259–288.

Buber, M. (1965). *The knowledge of man* (R. G. Smith & M. Friedman, Trans.). New York: Harper & Row.

Gadamer, H. G. (1992). *Truth and method* (2nd ed., J. Weinsheimer & D. G. Marshall, Trans.) New York: Seabury. (Original work published 1960)

Shotter, J. (1993). *Conversational realities.* London: Sage.

Explorations

1. Penman defines four criteria for a mutually satisfying conversation. Following are listed three common forms of conversation. For each of them, indicate the extent to which they meet the "dialogue criteria" proposed by Penman.

   a. Arguing over politics with your coworker at work (e.g., preparing for disasters):

      Authenticity: _____

      Going with the flow: _____

      Mutual collaboration: _____

      Physical presence: _____

   b. Chatting with your friends on the Internet:

      Authenticity: _____

      Going with the flow: _____

      Mutual collaboration: _____

      Physical presence: _____

   c. A conversation at dinner with your family:

      Authenticity: _____

      Going with the flow: _____

      Mutual collaboration: _____

      Physical presence: _____

2. Can you think of other criteria you might add or delete in exercise 1 to achieve a satisfying conversation? (e.g. humor?)

   _____

   _____

   _____

3. Are there some dialogue criteria that you think might be more relevant or applicable to a satisfying conversation in one situation or with one group of people than with another?

_____

_____

_____

Key Constructions

- Dialogue
- Authenticity
- Impression management
- Antecedent understanding versus future orientation
- Mutuality
- Physical presence
- Virtual dialogue

READING 20

The Significance of Future Talk

We often use dialogue to solve a problem, to figure out what went wrong, or to correct a shortcoming. It is just such dialogue that is central to most therapeutic encounters. But the constructionist orientation of this book invites us to be mindful of the particular language we use, for in our choice of words we create realities, values, and relationships. In Reading 20 Sheila McNamee challenges the utility of problem-centered dialogue. Such talk typically centers on the past and what went wrong. In this way it creates the reality of "the wrong" and that there are "causes" that could be corrected. She proposes that dialogue shift to the future, and its potentials. Many therapists are now moving in this direction, emphasizing opportunities and solutions as opposed to problems.

Reading 20 SHEILA McNAMEE

If you examine the field of psychotherapy, you will note that a good deal of therapy talk hovers on the past. Therapists and clients alike explore the history and evolution of the problems that clients bring to therapy. When did the problem begin? How long has it been a difficulty? How have you come to understand (make sense of) the problem? What do you think causes the problem? What do others say about it (and you)? What have you done to try to solve this problem? The questions that therapists ask direct the therapeutic conversation to the past, as do the expectations that many clients bring to therapy. Most cultural presentations of therapy (consider any number of popular films) portray client and therapist locked in a conversation about the past (childhood, adolescence, etc.).

With such an emphasis on these past-oriented questions, there is little room for imagining the future. The potential to sediment the past, to reify the story, and thereby make it static and immutable is tremendous. Probably more important is the logic inherent in the therapeutic focus on the past. By focusing on what has already transpired, we unwittingly give credibility to causal models that are the hallmark of modernist science. We privilege the logic that claims that what went before causes what follows. So, for example, questions such as, "When did you first notice your homosexual tendencies?" or "how would you describe your childhood relationship with your mother/father?" imply that a client's homosexuality is "caused" by some past event or relationship.

Constructionists do not necessarily want to argue for a disconnection between past, present and future. We simply want to raise the issue of narration. The past is always a story. And we all know that there are many ways to tell a story. Not only do we harbor many voices, each with a different set of possible narrations, but others involved in the same "history" will very likely narrate it differently. Thus, the causality of past to present (and implied future) will take different turns, highlight different features, and pathologize or celebrate varied aspects depending on which story is privileged. This orientation allows us to wonder why we never ask when a client first noticed s/he was heterosexual. If we can understand the past cause for the "deviation" (notice a question arises concerning whose standard we are using when homosexuality becomes the "deviation"), we believe we can work toward resolution. Yet, there is never a need to explore a past cause for those practices that we value positively (i.e., heterosexuality).

One reason that future-oriented discourse can enhance relational engagement is because we all understand that we do not yet know the future. We have not embodied it. And thus, to the extent that we engage with others (our clients in this situation) in conversation about the future, we underscore the relational construction of our worlds. We fabricate together what we might live into.

This is not to suggest that talk of the past is wrong or emblematic of non-constructionist therapy. Instead by privileging a particular way to talk and/or particular themes or topics of therapy, constructionist therapy emphasizes the collaborative, situated creation of possibilities and one way to achieve this is with future-oriented discourse. In our talk of imagined futures, we invite coordination of many convergent and divergent understandings of the past and the present. Again, this form of relational engagement moves toward coordinated respect for multiplicity and differences. So, for example, questions like "How would you like to see homosexuality culturally situated in five years? What do you think you could do to help make that happen? What could others do? How could you help them?" place our focus on potential action—the (literal) making of a new reality—rather than a reification of the same old reality.

Explorations

1. Consider a problem that you have encountered in your life. If it is a pressing problem, all the better. First, describe how this problem came about—what caused it.

   _____

   _____

   _____

2. What should you do about the problem?

   _____

   _____

   _____

3. In light of this problem shift to future talk, how would you like to see the future develop? What opportunities are there to make this happen? What resources are there to help you?

   _____

   _____

   _____

4. Compare the results of the two ways (2 and 3) in which to address the question? Was either more helpful (e.g., as a problem or as future talk)? How?

   _____

   _____

   _____

Key Constructions

- Problem-centered dialogue
- Future talk

Key Constructions for Part Three, Section A

- Scripted communication
- Adjacency pairs
- Unwanted repetitive patterns
- Conventional word usage versus metaphoric word usage
- Relationship metaphors
- Metaphors open possibilities
- Meaning as co-created action
- Supplement
- Constraining and creating meaning
- Dialogue
- Authenticity
- Impression management
- Antecedent understanding versus future orientation
- Mutuality
- Physical presence
- Virtual dialogue
- Problem-centered dialogue
- Future talk

Nonverbal Language: Meaning as Action

So far we have focused almost exclusively on verbal communication. Yet, it is also very clear that whereas words are extremely important in communication, they are scarcely the whole story. As we talk our facial expressions are continuously changing, and these expressions can be vital to how we relate. If you are sympathizing for another's grief, you will scarcely be appreciated if your words are accompanied by a big smile. Similarly, our body movements add an important dimension to our verbal expressions. An expression of love accompanied by clenched fists might invite a very different reaction from the verbal expression of affection alone. Often words are not necessary at all for meaningful collaboration. A mutual embrace, dancing the salsa, roughhouse play with children, for example, require no words, but they can be immensely successful forms of coordination.

The readings in this section bring various aspects of nonverbal communication into focus. How do we interpret another in spatial relation to ourselves? How do we make sense of their stance or their eye contact? We begin by inviting you to examine a photograph by A. Rijsman (Reading 21) of a group of adult friends who are walking in Paris. You will be challenged with questions about what they seem to be saying to each other through the use of bodily distance, posture, and gaze.

We next turn to the nonverbal issues raised by this photo: facial expressions, body movements, and clothing and how they generally communicate meaning. We also explore how verbal and nonverbal communications are indivisibly linking people together, as it is when we swear at one another. Our understanding of a verbal/nonverbal action, such as swearing, is often culturally bound. Although there are continuing debates on the degree to which facial expressions are natural or acquired, it is clear that how we communicate facially is specific to our culture. We learn, for example, how to gaze romantically at someone, to look serious, to sneer, to express ecstasy, and to communicate grief. Many unspoken rules for facial expression are well known and frequently practiced in the culture. You can sometimes participate successfully in a group discussion by simply smiling, laughing, frowning, and groaning at the same time—and never utter a word! However, in Reading 22 John Shotter draws attention to the way in which the mutual sharing of even momentary gaze can create a significant sense of connection.

Second, bodily movements, no less than our facial expressions, are enormously important to the collaborative creation of meaning. And, like words and facial expressions, there are conventions or implicit rules that govern their use. Adding gestures to our spoken language can draw others into the realities we construct. However, not just any gesture at any time will do. A raised fist may powerfully punctuate a call to action, but it would destroy a toast at a wedding banquet. Speech trainers can spend hours with political candidates to help them find a perfect fit between words and gestures. We, therefore, offer an exploration into communicating with the body—a poem by Alice Pennisi (Reading 23) in which she discusses a common problem confronted by women: the male who comes too close. How are we to respond when we feel invaded by another person who violates the unwritten rules of spatial distance?

Third, we turn to the use of clothing as communication. We often think of clothing in strictly, practical terms. We ask, how comfortable, how warm, how expensive, how durable, and so on. But throughout history clothing has also been used as communication. Certain garments signified that one was a king, a priest, a judge, or a fool. Today, however, clothing does far more than inform others of one's position in society. We use clothing to tell each other about our musical preferences, our travels, our personalities of being "cool," rebellious," "nice," "macho," and so on. Clothing can be used to seduce, to intimidate, to challenge convention, and to "fit in" with society. In Reading 24, John Fiske takes up the interesting example of jeans. If jeans are so popular, do they cease to communicate anything special? Or is it possible that jeans are essential to one's well-being in relationships?

We finally treat the phenomenon of swearing. Yes, swearing is verbal, but the content of swear words is not nearly as important as its nonverbal complement. If someone screams "Damn it!" you are not likely to ask what is meant by the verbal term "it" in this case. Swearing is an expressive sign, and can often be communicated nonverbally, such as showing clenched teeth or giving the finger. In Reading 25 by Alaina M. Winters and Steve Duck, they ask why people swear, when swearing is not generally condoned by society. They make an interesting case for swearing as a form of social bonding.

READING 21

Reading Public Communication

This is a photograph of friends taken in Tuileries Gardens, Paris, on a sunny summer day. The group is composed of three married couples. One of the women took the photograph. Note that there are many communicative activities captured in this photo: body language, facial expressions, gestures, spatial distancing, and conversational groupings. Although these activities seem spontaneous enough, none are accidental. All the group members communicate in some way.

Explorations

1. Look carefully at the photograph. What do various people seem to be communicating through their facial expressions, bodily movements, clothing, and so on? (Name 5 items you find of interest.)

a. _____

b. _____

c. _____

d. _____

e. _____

2. The group members share varying levels of importance in the conversation. You may be able to tell by their closeness or distance from one another. Who is central and who is marginal to the group? Explain why.

_____

_____

_____

_____

Key Constructions

■ Visual communication—body language, facial expressions, clothing, gestures, spatial distancing, and conversational groupings

READING 22

The Eyes Have It

The eyes are a fascinating source of nonverbal communication. Of course, there are the obvious signals: the wink, rolling of the eyes upward, and the stare. But there are also subtle ways of communicating with the eyes. Here we find the old saying "The eyes are windows to the soul" still carries weight. Consider the way lovers gaze into each other's eyes. As many feel, such gaze is more significant than the words they might exchange. In Reading 22 John Shotter describes a very subtle and yet significant form of visual communication. The mere focus of our eyes as we exchange glances may communicate the sharing of an entire world of beliefs and values.

Reading 22   JOHN SHOTTER

As soon as I begin an interchange of looks with another person, . . . a little ethical and political world is created between us. We each look toward each other expectantly, with anticipations, some shared some not, arising from what we have already lived in our lives so far. . . . We are "present" to each other *as who we are* . . . hence, if it is a stranger with whom we have become involved, we quickly look away again, lest we reveal too much of ourselves unnecessarily. In our living contacts with another, then, our mere surroundings are transformed into a . . . partially shared world that we sense ourselves as being in along with the others. Besides having an ethics and politics to it, besides our having expectations within it as to how the others around us should treat us and are likely to treat us, our partially shared world has, we feel, a unique culture to it. For each of us, it contains a certain set of interconnected things, with certain values to them in relation to which I take on a certain character, and toward which I take a certain stance.

We can get an initial sense of what is at issue here in a little exercise I sometimes have my students do in pairs. If we can induce a friend to bear with us, and allow us not to look at "them," but to use them while we try to see our own face reflected in the surface of their eyeballs (or lenses of their spectacles), they will have a sense of being "looked over," as if merely an object. It is a change that takes place as a looker ceases to regard another person personally and switches to regarding them objectively, seeming only to be "looking over" them or "surveying" them. The gazed at person feels that the looker's face has gone "stony," that the "interplay" of visual activity between them has ceased, and as a result the looker is no longer seeing them as a person. Indeed, as we all know, to stare, i.e., to look steadily and fixedly at another person, is considered rude.

Explorations

1. Describe an instance in which you have shared a momentary but meaningful glance with someone, an instance in which nothing had to be said but that the kind of glance suggested deep agreement of some kind.

   _____

   _____

2. Consider more fully the ways in which we use our eyes to communicate with others. In each of the following cases, how would you react with your eyes?

   a. A strange man is staring at you:

   _____

   b. You are speaking with an attractive person at a party:

   _____

   c. You are in the front row listening to a speaker:

   _____

   d. On a seaside vacation you inadvertently enter a nude beach:

   _____

e. Someone close to you begins to reveal a secret of yours to others:

_____

Key Construction

- Mutual gaze

READING 23

Space Invasion

We have no problem understanding how our language conforms to rules of grammar—at least most of the time. However, we also speak with our bodies through our movements, gestures, facial expressions, and so on. Here, too, there are "rules of grammar," a nonverbal grammar. Least obvious among these rules are those related to spatial distance. Typically we feel we simply move about our social worlds in a spontaneous way. But consider again: If you are walking on an open sidewalk and a man approaches, chances are you will be careful not to brush up against him. You are not even likely to come within 2 feet of him. If you are on the same sidewalk and a stranger is approaching you from behind, you will likely be uncomfortable if he comes up beside you and walks at the same pace.

The classic work on what is called "interpersonal distance" is Edward T. Hall's _The Hidden Dimension_. From his observations of Americans, he concluded that people in general, adjusted their distance depending on how well they were acquainted with another. Specifically, he distinguished among the following distances:

Intimate distance: Those in intimate relations will tend toward distances ranging from zero (actual contact) to 1.5 feet.

Personal distance: With close friends the preferred range is between 1.5 and 4 feet.

Social distance: In more formal relations we tend to be comfortable when we remain between 4 and 12 feet apart.

Public distance: With complete strangers we tend to keep a distance of over 12 feet.

As other investigators have shown, however, there are many exceptions to these rules. Men and women in the United States, for example, have different standards in speaking with each other than with members of the opposite sex. There are what many call _high-contact_ cultures, such as Latin and southern European cultures, in which closer distances are preferred more than in _low-contact_ cultures such as North America and Scandanavia. And of course, much depends on whether the parties are walking in a public place or boarding a crowded train.

Reading 23 consists of a portion of a poem titled "Encounter" written by Alice C. Pennisi about how she is feeling as a school teacher when approached after school by a 12-year-old male student.

Reference

Hall, E. (1969). *The hidden dimension*. Garden City, NY: Doubleday.

Reading 23   A L I C E   C .   P E N N I S I

At the end of the day I'm in my room,
cleaning, straightening.
He comes in,
hesitant,
holding his paper; he is by me.
"I'm not sure I understand this very well."
"Well, let's take a look. I'm sure we can figure things out." Together, we
bend over the paper.
We bend over the paper placed between us on the table. "What part do you
need help on?"
He begins to talk, pointing at an essay.
He's very close.
He is pointing to an area of the paper, but
he is leaning,
leaning his body into mine.
There's something wrong.

No, don't be silly!
But just in case,
I move away,
slightly,
a little to the right, in a subtle way.
I don't want him to think I don't care. I don't want to misread:
This age is so tough, and
he has so few friends.
I don't want him to—

There.
There it is again.
I know that feeling.
It's that shudder that you get, It's between your shoulder blades. It's that
feeling at
parties,
dorms,

bars,
on the street,
even at family reunions.
It's unmistakable,
Though you don't want to believe it.
It's that feeling of invasion.

You try to collapse yourself
make yourself smaller,
without actually moving.
Maybe it will go away, you think.
Maybe I was mistaken.
He's here for help.
You're being too sensitive, he's just
a boy who wants you to help him understand.
—Wait.
I swear I felt a brush on my rear.
I moved away but now he is still definitely way too close.
His body is nearly up against mine.
I can hear his breath,
Feel his tension. And
Oh no, how did I not realize this?
He just touched my rear again.
He is leaning into me. And
He has rested his hand onto me.
Placed it there.
Cupping.
I shudder.
I swat his hand away and back off.
"What did you just do?"
He stands there, blank.
I take another step away.
In fact, I leap back.
"What do you think you're doing?
This is not my usual teacher voice, this is a voice I use in other places.
Still blank, silent.

It doesn't matter who the person is.
It feels the same.

"Kevin," my voice is low, cold and straight.
"You can never do that.
You can never touch someone without their permission."
Still blank.
"Kevin, you can never, never
touch a girl,

without her permission.
There are laws against that *(Where did that come from?)*
Do you understand me?"
"What do you mean?" Now he responds.
"This is mine!" I nearly yell as I cross my arms over myself.

I want to keep them there, but they go slack.
"Nobody has the right to touch me unless I say so.
I did not give you permission.
Don't ever do that again—to me or anyone else."
"There's a law?"
Is that all he cares about? OK,
"Yes, there are laws that say you can't do that.
Never touch anyone like that without their permission.
Do you hear me?"
He nods, looking at me.
I'm suddenly afraid and feel ill.
"Go home, Kevin."

I am in my room, alone, shaking, cold.
I don't know what to do.
I sit down, and begin to cry.

It feels the same.
It does not matter how old the person is, I realize.
It feels the same.
To my body, it *is* the same.
How can that be?
How can a skinny twelve-year-old make me feel so violated?

Explorations

1. Reflect back on your week. Try to recall the bodily distance separating you from others—from friends of both sexes, from people of different statuses and from intimates as opposed to strangers. Then write down some of your reflections about how you felt at the time.

   a. What differences do you notice at the time of your interactions?

   - **Different age** (note whether younger or older):

   _____

   _____

   _____

   _____

- **Different status** (note whether higher or lower):

  _____

  _____

  _____

  _____

- **Intimates** (note whether same or opposite sex):

  _____

  _____

  _____

  _____

- **Strangers** (note whether same or opposite sex):

  _____

  _____

  _____

  _____

b. Why do you think we maintain such spatial differences?

  _____

  _____

  _____

  _____

2. The author of the poem is unsettled by what she feels is an invasion of her space, and ultimately a threat to her sense of who she is. Have you ever had an experience in which someone has "come too close"? Briefly describe the experience and what you did as a result.

  _____

  _____

  _____

  _____

Key Constructions

- Body distance (intimate, personal, social, and public distances)
- Context and spatial distance
- Bodily space
- High- and low-contact cultures

Styling the Self

One of the most important ways we have of presenting ourselves to others is through our visual appearance. Our appearance can be as important in defining ourselves to others as our words. Most of us peer into the mirror at least once a day to check how we look. In spite of our claims to being unconcerned, we do make choices about what we wear, how our hair is combed (or not), and so on. In effect, our appearance creates a public identity, and invites others to treat us in certain ways. In his influential book *Understanding Popular Culture*, John Fiske takes up the importance of jeans in styling and communicating the self.

Reading 24   JOHN FISKE

Of 125 students of mine, 118 were, on the day that I asked, wearing jeans. The deviant 7, also possessed jeans, but did not happen to be wearing them. I wonder if any other cultural product—movie, TV program, record, lipstick—would be so popular? (T-shirts were as widely owned, but much less regularly worn.) Students may not be typical of the population as a whole, though jeans are widely popular among non-students in the same age group, and only slightly less widespread among older age groups.

Let's dismiss their functionality first, for this has little to do with culture, which is concerned with meanings, pleasures, and identities rather than efficiency. Of course jeans are a supremely functional garment, comfortable, tough, sometimes cheap, and requiring "low maintenance"—but so, too, are army fatigues. The functionality of jeans is the precondition of their popularity, but does not explain it. In particular, it does not explain the unique ability of jeans to transect almost every social category we can think of: we cannot define a jeans wearer by any of the major social category systems—gender, class, race, age, nation, religion, education. We might argue that jeans have two main social foci, those of youth and the blue collar or working class, but these foci should be seen as semiotic rather than sociological, that is, as centers of meaning rather than as social categories. So a middle-aged executive wearing jeans as he mows his lawn on a suburban Sunday is, among other things, aligning himself with youthful vigor and activity (in opposition to the distinctly middle-aged office desk) and with the mythic dignity of labor.

My students, largely white, middle-class, young, and well educated, are not a representative sample of the whole population, and so the meanings they made of their jeans cannot be extended to other groups, but the process of making and communicating meanings is representative even though the meanings made by it are not.

I asked my class to write briefly what jeans meant to each of them: these notes were then discussed generally. The discussions produced, unsurprisingly from such a homogeneous group, a fairly coherent network of meanings that grouped themselves around a few foci. These meaning clusters related to each other sometimes coherently, sometimes contradictorily, and they allowed different students to inflect the semiotic network differently, to make their own meanings within the shared grid.

There was one cluster of meanings that were essentially community integrative and that denied social differences. Jeans were seen as informal, classless, unisex, and appropriate to city or country; wearing them was a sign of freedom from the constraints on behavior and identity that social categories impose. *Free* was the single most common adjective used, frequently with the meaning of "free to be myself."

An article once in the *New York Times* quotes a psychologist who suggests that jeans' lack of differentiation results not in a freedom to be oneself, but the freedom to hide oneself. Jeans provide a facade of ordinariness that enables the wearer to avoid any expression of mood or personal emotion—they are, psychologically at least, repressive. This flip-side of "freedom" was not evident among my students, and it appears to be a typical psychoanalyst's explanation in that it emphasizes the individual over the social and the pathological over the normal. Clothes are more normally used to convey social meanings than to express personal emsotion or mood.

The lack of social differentiation in jeans gives one the freedom to ''be oneself'' (and, I suppose, in abnormal cases, to hide oneself), which, of course, points to a telling paradox that the desire to be oneself leads one to wear the same garment as everyone else, which is only a concrete instance of the paradox deeply structured into American (and Western) ideology that the most widely held communal value is that of individualism. The desire to be oneself does not mean the desire to be fundamentally different from everyone else, but rather to situate individual differences within communal allegiance. There were, as we shall see below, signs of social differences between jeans wearers, but while these may contradict, they do not invalidate the set of communally integrative meanings of jeans.

Another cluster of meanings centered on physical labor, ruggedness, activity, physicality. These meanings, again, were attempts to deny class differences: the physical toughness connoted by jeans allowed these middle-class students to align themselves with a highly selective set of meanings of physical labor (its dignity and its productivity, but certainly not its subordination and exploitedness). Jeans were able to bear class specific meanings of the American work ethic.

Their physicality and ruggedness were not just inflected toward work, they also bore meanings of naturalness and sexuality. *Natural* was an adjective used almost as frequently as *free*. The informality of jeans in contrast with the formality of other clothes was a concrete instance, or transformation, of the deeply structured opposition between nature and culture, the natural and the artificial, the country and the city. The body is where we are most natural, so there was an easy cluster of meanings around the physicality of jeans, the vigor of the adolescent body, and "naturalness." This meaning cluster could be inflected toward strength, physical labor, and sports performance (sport allows the middle-class body the recognition of physical prowess that labor allows the working class) for the men, and toward sexuality for the women. Of course, such gender differences are not essential, but they are sites of struggle for control over the meanings of masculinity and femininity. Many women participated in the more "masculine" meanings of jeans' physicality, as did many men in their more "feminine" ones, of sexual display.

These natural/artificial and physical/nonphysical meanings joined with others in a set clustered around the American West. The association of jeans with the cowboy and the mythology of the Western is still strong. The meanings that helped to make the West significant for these students were not only the familiar ones of freedom, naturalness, toughness, and hard work (and hard leisure), but also progress and development and, above all Americanness. As the opening of the western frontier was a unique and definitive moment in American history, so jeans were seen as a unique and definitive American garment, possibly America's only contribution to the international fashion industry. Despite the easy exportability of the Western myth and its ready incorporability into the popular culture of other nations, it always retains its Americanness: it thus admits the forging of links between American values and the popular consciousness of other nationalities. Similarly, jeans have been taken into the popular culture of practically every country in the world, and whatever their local meanings, they always bear traces of their Americanness. So in Moscow, for example, they can be made sense of by the authorities as bearers of Western decadence, and they can be worn by the young as an act of defiance, as a sign of their opposition to social conformity—a set of meanings quite different from those of contemporary American youth, though more consonant with those of the 1960s, when jeans could carry much more oppositional meanings than they do today.

Explorations

1. Select a piece of clothing (e.g., shirt, trousers, shoes, etc) that you are currently wearing. Name at least two ways in which this item may create a positive identity and invite others to relate positively to you.

   _____

   _____

   _____

2. Not all people agree on the meaning of various styles of clothing. What is "cool" for some people may be "silly" for others. Return to the piece of clothing

you just selected. Can you also identify a group of people who would react negatively to such clothing? Why would they do so?

_____

_____

_____

3. Clothing is only one means of styling and communicating about the self. Recently, tattoos and piercings have become increasingly popular as a means of defining oneself to others. Indicate two ways in which the tattoo or piercing helps fashion a positive identity, and two ways in which it might have the opposite effect.

a. Positive implications:

_____

_____

_____

b. Negative implications:

_____

_____

_____

Key Constructions

- Public identity
- Nonverbal presentation of self
- Social differentiation
- Clothing as an identity marker

READING 25

You **@#$**&!@!!: Swearing as Bonding?

Swearing is a paradoxical communicative practice. It is socially unacceptable and at the same time highly common. Because so much swearing goes on in a day, we must be prepared to explore its uses. The authors of Reading 25, Alania M. Winters and Steve Duck, suggest that an important function of swearing is that it helps people bond while it excludes others. Can swearing, then, be used by friends to sustain friendships?

> Why do men swear? When they swear, why
> do they use the words which they do?
> —Patrick, 1901, p. 113

Swearing has a relevance to social experience that makes it interesting to students of aversive social behaviors. In part, our research interest in the phenomenon of swearing is all the greater because this disapproved, aversive activity is extremely prevalent in everyday life. Cameron (1969) reported that every 14th word in a sample of 66,767 words recorded from everyday speech was profanity. Cameron's findings indicated that from 4% to 13% of everyday speech consisted of swear words, depending on the context from which the word sample came (e.g., leisure activity or work). The sheer pervasiveness of expletives in social behavior should warrant examination of the role, functions, and effects of swearing in social interaction, given that it is both aversive and pervasive. Also of interest is that, whereas it is publicly condemned, swearing is nevertheless widely practiced.

An Analysis of Swearing

Profane language is language that is unholy, not sacred, and therefore not permitted to be used except "outside the temple." Hughes (1991) noted that "swearing draws upon such powerful resonators as religion, sex, madness, excretion, and nationality, encompassing an extraordinary variety of attitudes including the violent, the amusing, the shocking, the absurd, the casual and the impossible" (p. 3).

Patrick (1901) began by distinguishing between assertive and ejaculatory kinds of swearing. *Assertive swearing* attracts the listener's attention and is intended to enhance the speaker's credibility as the swearing offers a social emphasis or a firm claim to speak the truth that adds credence to a statement and strength to an assertion. Examples are "Yes, by God!" or "Hell, no!" or the forms of swearing used in legal oaths for the same purposes. *Ejaculatory swearing,* the main focus of both Patrick's analysis and ours, refers to the sort of swearing that is simply exclamatory and may be seen as powerfully insulting, derogatory of others, crude, offensive, and even disruptive of social orders in that it can be used to register disrespect for authority.

Although both forms can still be distinguished, the form most often regarded as aversive in social behavior is the ejaculator, a broad class that covers several different subspecies. Patrick (1901) differentiated seven classes of words and phrases used in profanity: (a) names of deities ("By God"); (b) names connected to "God's wounds"; (c) names of saints ("Jumping Jehosaphat"); (d) names of sacred places, such as Jerusalem or one's mother's grave; (e) words related to a supposed future life "Good heavens," "Damnation," and it's minced forms such as "darn" or "tarnation"); (f) vulgar words forbidden by polite usage (Patrick gave no examples, and we will not do so either) and (g) expletives having unusual force for various reasons, such as "Mercy!" "Gracious," or "For pity's sake" and "other fossil remains of religious terms or ejaculatory prayers" (p. 115). Swearing may also be analyzed broadly at the group or dyadic level, where it serves intergroup purposes (e.g., stigmatizing or derogating out-groups) and can function negatively by expressing prejudices through racial and other slurs. Some of these instances not only express individual opinions and emotions but also serve subtly to reject membership in one group and claim membership of a different group. Indeed, phrases such as "swearing like a trooper," "abusing one another like fish-wives," or "talking like a sailor/tinker" associate the broad act of cursing with particular types of people and social classes.

In an extension of such ideas to the dyadic level, we offer an essentially relational analysis. First, the use of swearing is permitted more freely in interactions where the partners are familiar with each other. Second, swearing can be used to indicate familiarity and informality or acceptance of others. Third, swearing can be used to create relational boundaries, that is, rather like nicknames or personal idioms, which serve to include "members" and exclude others; use of swearing serves to signal something about the relationship between speaker and hearer as well as to convey specific descriptive meanings. For example, swearing is used in relational ways in teasing, joking, relieving social tension, shocking the listener, and rebuking forcefully. It is also a means of social bonding by "playing the dozens" or other forms of mock insult that actually tease partners and help create and define relational bonds. The maintenance of such bonds might be in positive or negative relationships. Language in this latter category, therefore, ranges from the artful exchange of nonserious insults to the deliberate use of denigratory and offensive terms to insult enemies or to commit verbal abuse. For example, "sounding" and "signifying" are long standing and common speech acts of ritualistic exchanges of insults in African American vernacular. Schwebel (1997) even recorded that insult matches routinely occur in a jocular way in college dormitories. The interesting question from a social psychological point of view is why an aversive behavior is used in an affiliative way, and a corollary concern is how this is done. Can aversive behaviors actually serve bonding functions, and if so, how?

Is Swearing Relational?

Whenever people swear they are claiming power and asserting self. Such assertion of power may be a purely individual activity. It is our belief that a behavior that is normally aversive or abusive can be given a different connotation by the relational circumstances of its production and can, in turn, produce different relational meaning. Gossip is both aversive and bonding, so we believe is profanity. Swearing can also exert power in relationships. The most obvious case is when an abusive man swears at his partner in a derogatory way, but less abusive and more informal ways of swearing can also be relational, as when African American informal speech permits the use of the "n-word" as a familiar term between members of the group but reacts to the term as a racial slur when spoken by a White person.

The relational context of use is an important factor in the analysis. Cohesion in social groups or dyads depends to some degree on the shared willingness to break social taboos and to collude in the expression of moral disparagement of outsiders. The development and tolerance of increasingly informal codes of speech in a relationship are social psychological mechanisms for developing greater closeness in that relationship. Willing collusion in a social practice that is otherwise aversive can be used to signal bonding and acceptance. Thus, the use of swear words is relational even though the referential meanings of the terms are aversive, and the practice is generally discouraged in the broader social group. We believe that such a proposal helps us understand why profanity occurs in informal personal relationships when it is an aversive social behavior at large.

References

Cameron, P. (1969). Frequency and kinds of words in various social settings, or what the hell's going on? *Pacific Sociological Review, 3,* 101–104.

Hughes, G. (1991). *Swearing: A social history of foul language, oaths and profanity in English.* Oxford, England: Blackwell.

Patrick, G. T. W. (1901). The psychology of profanity. *Psychological Review, 8,* 113–127.

Schwebel, D. C. (1997). Stategies of verbal dueling: How college students win a verbal battle. *Journal of Language and Social Psychology, 16,* 326–343.

Explorations

1. What are two places or situations in which you are *most* likely to swear?

_____

_____

2. What are two places or situations in which you are *least* likely to swear?

_____

_____

3. Why is swearing invited in one set of instances or places and not the other?

_____

_____

_____

4. In what ways do you think your swearing would affect your relationships in a place in which you are least likely to swear?

_____

_____

_____

5. Do you agree with the reading that swearing increases your feelings of belonging in a particular group? Why or why not?

_____

_____

_____

_____

Key Constructions

- Profane language
- Assertive swearing
- Ejaculatory swearing
- Relational function of swearing

Beyond Words

Key Constructions for Part Three, Section B

- Visual communication—body language, facial expressions, clothing, gestures, spatial distancing, and conversational groupings
- Mutual gaze
- Body distance (intimate, personal, social, and public distances)
- Context and spatial distance
- Bodily space
- High- and low-contact cultures
- Public identity
- Nonverbal presentation of self
- Social differentiation
- Clothing as an identity marker
- Profane language
- Assertive swearing
- Ejaculatory swearing
- Relational function of swearing

Listening as Collaboration

No one denies that "paying attention" is an important part of successful communication. If we don't attend to the other's words and actions, then we can scarcely coordinate effectively. For good communication to occur, stress is often placed on "careful listening." Although scarcely surprising, what does it mean to listen carefully? One traditional view of listening is to "register information." Thus, listening carefully would simply ensure that you take in everything that is said, along with the nonverbal accompaniments. However, the position we have stressed in this book is that communication is a collaborative process. Thus, when one person talks the other is not simply collecting information. Rather, the listener "enters into" what the speaker is saying. Through the listener's gaze, facial expressions, posture, and occasional utterances, he or she joins the collaboration of meaning making.

To illustrate, as professors, all of us have experience in speaking to various groups of students, colleagues, and the public. We all know what it is like to look out at attentive faces, to see heads that nod after a well-argued point has been made, and to hear laugher when we say something that seems amusing. Under these communication conditions we loosen up, words flow freely, and we become increasingly spontaneous and open. In contrast, when we speak with an audience that shows signs of disinterest, boredom, or irritation, our words may become tentative, guarded, or even terse. We may speak in monotone voices and decide not to risk attempts at humor.

In the three readings that follow, the writers attempt to capture important dimensions of collaborative listening. In Reading 26 communication scholars John Stewart and Carole Logan explore three practices that can contribute significantly to what they call "dialogic communication." Their analysis invites us not only to attend to each other in special ways, but also to try out new forms of speaking in coordination with each other.

Barbara M. Korsch and Caroline Harding (Reading 27) focus on the importance of two-way listening. As they demonstrate, in the context of doctor and patient, problems are often created by the lack of attention to what the other is saying. They invite us to consider ways of increasing mutual sensitivity.

Finally, in Reading 28 Donal Carbaugh draws attention to how "good listening" may vary significantly from one culture or subculture to another. If making meaning is a collaborative process, then we must be prepared for important differences in the traditions of coordination. Carbaugh's experiences with the Native American Blackfeet invites openness to other ways of listening.

READING 26

Dialogic Listening

As children we often engaged in what can be called *monologic listening*. That is, a parent or teacher talked to us, and ideally, we were to not only hear what they said but incorporate it into our understanding. Sometimes we might be allowed to ask questions to clarify our understanding; at other times we might be reprimanded for not "just listening to our parents." Yet, as we grow older we participate more with others as full partners in a dialogue and a new form of *dialogic listening* is required.

Dialogic listening requires attention to two forms of activity. First is what is called *back-channeling*, that is, attention to the cues or signals we are giving to the person as he or she is speaking. (Think of the speaker's words as a channel and the cues given off by the listener as the back-channel.) These cues are enormously important in the process of mutually sculpting meaning. For example, if you are trying to say something important in a conversation and the other person seems preoccupied by gazing off into space or by turning his or her body away from yours, then nonverbal language will probably bring your offering to a rapid close. You may even become irritated with the other person and pay little attention to what he or she says next. In effect, the back-channeling has helped sculpt the relationship in an undesirable way.

A second important dimension of dialogic listening concerns *preparation*. Listening is specifically focused in ways that will enable the listener to respond meaningfully to what has been said. Preparatory listening is not an easy matter. If the listener becomes totally immersed in the other's words, such as in the way we listen to a good story, then little preparation may occur. On the other hand, if the listener is preparing a response by deliberating on what he or she will say next, then the other's words will fail to register. Over time, attention to intense listening preparation may begin to subside as we learn to trust that our dialogic responses will be relevant.

We often confront "important conversation," in which there are strong emotional investments. Here skills in dialogic listening must function at their finest. In Reading 26, John Stewart and Carole Logan offer several ways of sharpening skills for dialogic listening.

Reading 26 JOHN STEWART AND CAROLE LOGAN

There is no simple recipe for dialogic listening—no six easy steps or five sure-fire techniques. This is something that anybody who wants to do can *do*, but it requires an overall approach to communicating that's different from the stance most people ordinarily take when they listen or talk. You also need to maintain a fairly challenging tension or balance . . . between holding your own ground and being radically open to the person(s) with whom you're communicating. The best way to get a sense of this approach and this tension is to understand a little bit about the idea of "dialogue."

Focus on "Ours"

Dialogic listening involves a crucial change from a focus on *me* or a focus on the *other* to a focus on *ours*, on what's *between* speaker(s) and listener(s). Contrast this with empathic listening which requires you to try to experience what is behind another's outward communication. When you focus on "ours," you don't look "behind" the verbal and nonverbal cues. You don't try to deduce or guess what internal state the other is experiencing. Instead, you concentrate on the meanings you and the other person are mutually creating between yourselves. Empathic listening can be helpful, but dialogic listening requires a move beyond empathy to a focus on "ours."

It can make a big difference whether you are trying to identify what's going on inside the other person or are focusing on building meaning between. When your focus is on the other's thoughts and feelings behind their words, you spend your time and mental energy searching for possible links between what you're seeing and hearing and what the other "must be" meaning. "Look at those crossed arms. She must be feeling angry and defensive." Or, "He said he'd 'never' pay all the money back". That means it's hopeless to try to get him to change his mind: When you think in this way, you're moving back and forth between what's outside, in the verbal and nonverbal talk, and what's inside the person's head.

From this position, it's easy to believe that what's inside is more reliable, more important, more true, and hence more interesting than the talk on the surface. When you're focusing on "ours," however, you concentrate on what's outside, not what's supposedly inside. We don't mean that you should be insensitive to the other person's feelings. In fact, you will be even more sensitive when you are focused on what's between you here and now. You concentrate on the verbal and nonverbal talk that the two (or more) of you are building together. In a sense, you take the conversation at face value; you never stop attending to IT instead of trying to infer what is behind it. This doesn't mean that you uncritically accept everything that's said as "the whole truth and nothing but the truth." But you do realize that meaning is not just what's inside one person's head. Focusing on "ours" prepares you to respond and inquire in ways that make it clear that getting to the meaning is a mutual process.

Encouraging

Dialogic listening also requires a special form of encouraging. Basically, instead of encouraging the other person(s) to say more, you're encouraging them to respond to something you've just said in response to something they said. So you're encouraging . . . actively and relevantly keeps the collaborative co-construction process going.

Paraphrase Plus. One specific way to do this is with a paraphrase plus. Paraphrase plus consists of: (1) a restatement, (2) of the other's meaning, (3) in your own verbal and nonverbal talk, (4) concluded with an opportunity for the other person to verify your understanding. The paraphrase plus includes all of these elements *plus* a small but important addition.

The plus is your own response to the question, "What's next?" or "Now what?" You start by remembering that the meanings you are developing are created between the two of you, and individual perspectives are only a part of that. If you stopped with just the paraphrase, you would be focusing on the other person exclusively instead of keeping the focus on what is happening between you. So, you follow your verifying or perception-checking paraphrase with whatever your good judgment tells you is your response to what the person said, and you conclude your paraphrase plus by inviting the person to respond to your synthesis of his or her meaning and yours. The spirit of the paraphrase plus is that each individual perspective is a building block for the team effort. For example, notice the three possible responses to Rita's comments.

RITA: I like having an "exclusive" relationship, and I want you to be committed to me. But I still sometimes want to go out with other people.

(Paraphrase)

1. **Muneo:** So even though part of you agrees with me about our plan not to date others, you're still a little uncertain about it. Right?

(Attack)

2. **TIM:** Oh, so you want me to hang around like an idiot while you go out and play social butterfly! Talk about a double standard!

(Paraphrase plus)

3. **Scott:** It sounds like you think there are some pluses and minuses in the kind of relationship we have now. I like it the way it is, but I don't like knowing that you aren't sure. I guess I want you to tell me some more about why you're questioning it.

Muneo responds to Rita's comment with a paraphrase. This tells us that Muneo listened to Rita, but not much more. Tim makes a caricature of Rita's comment; his interpretation reflects his own uncertainty, anger, and fear. His comment is more a condemnation than a paraphrase. Scott offers a paraphrase plus. After explaining his interpretation of what Rita was saying, he says briefly how he *responds* to her point, and then moves the focus back to where both persons are present in the conversation and can work on the problem together. He paraphrases, but he also addresses the "What's next?" question as he interprets and responds to her comments. Then he concludes the paraphrase plus with encouragement rather than simply verifying the accuracy of his paraphrase. When all this happens, both the paraphrase and the plus keep understanding growing between the individuals.

Run with the Metaphor. Another skill you can use in the sculpting process is to run with the metaphor. You can build meaning into the conversation by extending whatever metaphors the other person has used to express his or her ideas, developing your own metaphors, and encouraging the other person to extend yours. Metaphors, of course, are figures of speech that link two dissimilar objects or ideas in order to make a point. "Communication is made up of inhaling and exhaling," "Conversation is a ride on a tandem bicycle," and "Dialogic listening is sculpting mutual meanings," all are metaphors, as are "This place is a zoo," and "She's as nervous as a flea on a griddle." As these examples illustrate, metaphors don't appear only in poetry or other literature; they are a major part of most everyday conversation. In our label for this skill, "run with the metaphor," for example, the term run itself is metaphoric.

This skill consists of listening for both subtle and obvious metaphors and then weaving them into your responses. We have found that when other people hear their metaphor coming back to them, they can get a very quick and clear sense of how they're being heard, and they typically can develop the thought along the lines sketched by the metaphor. For example, in a workshop he was leading, John was listening to an engineer describe part of his job, which involved going before regulatory boards and municipal committees to answer questions and make arguments for various construction projects. Part of what Phil said about his job was that it was a "game." John tried to run with the metaphor by asking, "What's the name of the game?" "Winning," Phil responded. John recognized that his question had been ambiguous, so he continued: "Okay, but what kind of game is it—is it baseball, football, soccer, chess, or what?" "It's football," Phil replied. "What position do you play?" "Fullback." "And who's the offensive line?" "All the people in the office who give me the information I take to the meetings." "Who's the coach?" "We don't have one. That's the major problem." This was a telling response. In fact, from that point on, the workshop was focused on one of the major management problems that engineering firm was having.

Here's another example of how running with the metaphor can work in conversation:

TANYA: You look a lot less happy than when I saw you this morning. What's happening?

ANN: I just got out of my second two-hour class today, and I can't believe how much I have to do. I'm really feeling squashed.

TANYA: Squashed like you can't come up for air, or squashed as in you have to do what everybody else wants and you can't pursue your own ideas?

ANN: More like I can't come up for air. Every professor seems to think that this is the only class I'm taking.

Again, the purpose of running with the metaphor is to . . . build the conversation between the two of you in order to produce as fully as possible a response to the issues you're talking about. In addition, the metaphors themselves reframe or provide a new perspective on the topic of your conversation. A project manager who sees himself or herself as a "fullback" is going to think and behave differently from one who thinks in other metaphorical terms, such as general, Joan of Arc, guide, or mother hen: And the work stress that "squashes" you is different from the pressure that keeps you jumping like a flea on a griddle: Listen for metaphors and take advantage of their power to shape and extend ideas.

Remember our point that all these specific listening skills are like foods on a salad bar: You don't eat everything, and at different times, you select different dishes.

Explorations

1. In focusing on "ours" versus "you" one listens not for the internal state of a motive or intention behind the words, but on the directions they invite in the conversation. Consider someone who criticizes you in a conversation. What advantages might there be in your focusing on "ours"?

2. In Reading 26 Stewart and Logan compose a small exchange in which three different responses are given to Rita's comment on having an exclusive

relationship—*the paraphrase, the attack,* and *the paraphrase plus.* Consider the case of a close friend, with whom you often spend the evening on weekends. In this particular week, she or he tells you: "I was invited out this Saturday night by John and Sarah. . . . I would ask you to join us, but I just don't think I can. I don't know them well enough, and I really need to give them my full attention. If we become friends, then for sure you will be included."

Formulate a response to what has been said that will function in the following ways:

Paraphrase:

_____

_____

Attack:

_____

_____

Paraphrase plus:

_____

_____

3. Consider the following entries into a conversation with a friend. Try to formulate a response that will "run with the metaphor."

a. I have a sinking feeling about my grades this semester.

_____

_____

b. The food here is fit for a pig.

_____

_____

c. This morning you look a little like what the cat dragged in.

_____

_____

Key Constructions

- Monologic listening
- Dialogic listening
- Focusing on "ours"
- Paraphrase
- Paraphrase plus
- Run with the metaphor

Listening: A Two-Way Street

Most of us know someone who never seems to listen, and most of us have been asked at times why we don't listen more closely. However, whether one listens or not depends greatly on the relationship. If someone is asking your advice about a problem, you may listen very carefully. If, however, someone is telling you about a distant relative, your attention may drift. In the first relationship the act of listening is critical, whereas in the second you are merely being amused. In Reading 27 Barbara M. Korsch and Caroline Harding consider the relationship between doctor and patient. Mutual listening in such relationships may be a matter of life and death, and yet failures in listening are very common. Why is this so?

Reading 27   BARBARA M. KORSCH AND CAROLINE HARDING

Most of us could come up with a number of heartfelt complaints about our doctors. No matter where I am—parties, airports, even grocery stores—if word gets out that I study doctor–patient communication problems, I am pursued by the many people who are convinced that they have the most dramatic story to tell. In a matter of moments, a reception I attended recently turned into a doctor-bashing free-for-all:

"You wouldn't believe what the internist said to me yesterday. . . ."
"He doesn't treat me like a human being with feelings."
"She didn't seem to listen to a word I said."
"The gynecologist made me feel so stupid. . . . I wish he would act as if he cared about me."
"Here I waited and waited to see the doctor and, when I finally got in, she didn't answer any of my questions."
"I went to find out what's the matter with me, then I couldn't understand what he was talking about."

Strangers come up to me and complain about their doctors. Just as I was about to board a plane for England not long ago, a young doctor who was traveling with me told the airline reservation agent that I was on my way to give a seminar about doctor–patient communication. The reservation agent immediately stopped work on my ticket and said, *"Have I got a good one for you!"* My heart sank. I was about to hear another tale of woe. She launched into a story about having finally selected a woman gynecologist because her male doctor had never shown any empathy or concern about her condition. Her expectations were unfortunately dashed; not only was her new female doctor abrupt, she didn't seem to listen to her problems, and she even told her that her menopausal symptoms were *"all in your head."* The poor agent had been greatly disappointed to find that her new female doctor was worse than the man had ever been.

Most people don't realize that even doctors are not immune to being treated badly by their own doctors. When I developed glaucoma after having eye surgery my doctor was less than sympathetic. When he saw how upset I was, he quipped, *"What do you expect; nothing's ever simple when doctors get sick. That's why I hate to take care of doctors."*

Before one of my appointments, I had prepared a list of questions for the doctor about my condition. Because my mother had gone blind in the last ten years of her life, I was naturally very concerned. But when I got into his office and pulled out my list, he abruptly cut me off with, *"Oh no. Are we going to have to play twenty questions again?"*

You can imagine how, after that scathing comment, I walked out of his office, my questions unanswered, extremely frustrated and angry. Although this doctor was an expert technician and surgeon, my faith in his general competence had diminished. I felt so brutalized that I never wanted to see him again. My respect for him was gone, and I knew that if he had understood anything about my feelings, he could never have spoken to me the way he did.

Why is it that doctors sometimes seem so unresponsive? Is it impatience or lack of concern? I've heard many patients complain that when they began talking about something that was really bothering them, the doctor cuts them off with,

"Don't worry, it's nothing serious."

The doctor means to be reassuring, but reassurance can sound hollow when you feel that the doctor did not really understand. There are other times when the doctor seems to be busy reading your chart and making notes while you are trying to explain something. How could he possibly be "listening"?

Many of the young doctors I taught have not thought of the role of the physician as one of being a listener; as a result, they have come across as nonresponsive to patients. They are eager to give patients good advice about health behavior:

"You really must get your cholesterol down . . . try to find time to get more exercise . . . cut down on red meat . . . do I need to explain what you're doing to yourself by your continued smoking?"

It takes courage and persistence to get doctors to listen to our health concerns and anxieties. Doctors want to get right to the point—*"How high was the fever? When did you first notice* it?"

They're trained to focus on the medical task at hand, and patients may interpret their seemingly detached behavior to mean, *anything else you want to talk about is none of my business.* So while patients feel that some important issues have not been addressed because the doctor seemed uninterested, in fact doctors need to focus their attention on the medical task. As patients, we do have the right to decide what we want the doctor to hear. What we have to say is important, and we feel that the doctor should pay attention! On the other hand, doctors must be able to get the information they require because they have a limited amount of time in which to take care of us.

While doctors are not responsible for dealing with separate family problems or unrelated emotional problems, they do have to take into account who their patients are, as well as the resources and limitations involved in their life situations. They need to be able to individualize a patient's treatment plan.

In many situations, whether we are taking classes or bringing our cars to auto mechanics, it helps to have the people we interact with understand who we are and why we are there. When you take your car in for service, for example, you feel the need to explain why you need it back as quickly as possible:

"I'll be late for my job."
"I'm scheduled for an important meeting."
"I'm supposed to pick someone up from the airport."

Doctor–patient encounters rarely involve only the immediate task at hand, even in very task-oriented visits. If a child, for instance, is taken to the emergency room with a leg laceration and the doctor simply injects Novocaine and sews up the cut without attempting to find out anything other than what she needs to know medically, she may miss out on valuable information. Perhaps the parents could have provided details about how the accident happened that would have been useful to the physician in counseling them about how to prevent future accidents.

In a different setting, when a doctor asks a patient a few questions about her background, and she launches into a long saga about her troubled childhood, the physician has no other choice but to interrupt, feeling inundated with too much information. The patient then feels put down. Each situation will be different—doctors will have varying amounts of time to spend with patients, and patients will have different issues they feel they need to communicate.

What is appropriate for one encounter is frequently not appropriate for another. It depends on the setting and the purpose of the visit—one patient is extremely ill and needs hospitalization, the next has simply come in for a routine checkup, and another is in for her follow-up after last week's surgery. The doctor certainly knows what he needs to explore, but the patient also knows what he wants to get across. Quite often, a patient will volunteer essential information that the doctor had not expected or asked for, something that turns out to be important to future health care. And if the physician comes across as impersonal and uncaring, that attitude will not be as likely to promote the patient's motivation and cooperation in obtaining the follow-up care needed.

Taking Steps to Improve the Relationship

Although the interactions you have with your doctor can be frustrating, this relationship is one of the most important ones you will ever have. Unfortunately, many people avoid doctors when they know they shouldn't, and others bypass doctors by going to chiropractors and herbalists. These alternative healers are offering something to patients that the medical profession may not have. They make the effort to communicate well with people who visit them as well as provide understanding and compassion. Of course, good communication is not always enough. We all want the best medical care available, but we may not get it when we are not happy with our doctors.

What has happened to the doctor–patient relationship? There are changes in the systems for health-care delivery that are definitely going to make it more difficult for people to have satisfying, long-term relationships with their doctors. Under managed health care, the relationship between patients and doctors is changing; we often are unable to choose our doctors, doctors are inundated with rules, regulations, and pressures, and, above all, our doctors have very little time with us.

In the face of all these stresses, making communication in the doctor–patient relationship as effective as possible is going to be more important than ever. As patients, are we to reach out more to understand our doctors? Shouldn't our doctors make more of an effort to understand and respond to us? With less time available and our health at stake, we need to learn more about our relationships with doctors and what to expect from each other. When all is said and done, it is not the actual health care that people complain about in this country. We have perhaps the best technical expertise available. What people complain about is the lack of communication and the psychological issues.

In many ways, doctors live in a world of their own with a different language, value system, goals, and ways of achieving results. When we go to them for help, we need to talk about our experiences with illness and express our feelings, anxieties, and concerns—and we rarely have enough opportunities to do so. Doctors have too little time and need to get down to business.

We each have our own agendas and, unfortunately, they often conflict. This reading is not about the doctor or the patient. It's about what goes on between them and why we need to be aware of the common breakdowns in communication so that we can overcome them. It is important to remember that our relationships with doctors are not one-sided. When we are unhappy with them, they are usually not happy with us either. We each have difficult roles. For patients, it is frightening to be sick. We may have to place our trust in the hands of someone we don't know very well or may never have even met before. For doctors, they are challenged each and every time they walk into an examination room or stop at a hospital bed. They are in constant demand day and night to respond to their patients' needs. At the same time, they have to adapt to increasing pressures from the changing health-care system. And so do we.

The relationship between doctors and patients is powerful and complex. When you get right down to it, it's really a partnership. We depend on them and they depend on us. There are times in our lives when the relationship is absolutely crucial. It has the potential of making us healthier and helping us to live longer. And to realize that potential, we—and by *"we"* I mean both doctors and patients—are going to have to spend some time working on our partnership.

Explorations

1. If "good listening" depends greatly on the nature of the relationship, then according to Korsch and Harding, what are some of the central features of the doctor–patient relationship that should lead to a successful listening interaction? Identify three features of the relationship that should lead to good mutual listening.

   a. _____

   b. _____

   c. _____

2. Consider the various relationships in which you are engaged. Describe a relationship and a specific time in that relationship in which you were a good listener. What can you specifically identify about the relationship that encouraged such good listening (e.g., a conversation in which someone is apologizing)?

   _____

   _____

   _____

   _____

3. Teachers and students often have conversations that are similar in many ways to the unsuccessful conversations described in the reading.

   a. What factors do you think contribute to less effective teacher–student conversations? (For example, is it a time factor, as mentioned in the reading, or are other things important?)

   _____

   _____

   _____

   _____

   b. What actions might you take as a student to improve your conversations with teachers?

   _____

   _____

_____

_____

c. What actions should teachers take to improve their conversations with students?

_____

_____

_____

_____

Key Constructions

- Mutual listening
- Doctor–patient listening

READING 28

Listening as a Cultural Act: The Blackfeet

Often we speak of listening as a physical act. From this perspective listening involves the reception of sound waves on the eardrum. We listen for the whistle of the train, and when we hear the sound, the act is complete. However, it is also useful to think of listening as a cultural activity. If someone asks you to "listen for the train" as you cross the tracks, he or she is not just interested in the state of your eardrum. He or she may want you to pay attention to the train's approach. In effect the person is asking for a particular kind of cultural performance. If the sound of the train reaches your ears and you say, "The train is coming," you have performed well. If you remained silent, or danced when the sound reached you, you would not be performing properly in Western culture. To listen is to participate in a particular kind of cultural relationship. This point is nicely illustrated in Reading 28, Donal Carbaugh's account of his experiences with the Blackfeet, a Native American group living near the Rocky Mountains.

_____

Reading 28   DONAL CARBAUGH

As he drove down Browning's Main Street Two Bears told us: "There are about 15,000 enrolled Blackfeet tribal members. About 7,000 live on the reservation." "Of these, about four to five percent practiced traditional Blackfeet ways." I had talked with several tribal members who were "living the traditional Blackfeet ways," navigating "the modern day world" through their own traditional practices, Two Bears, Rising Wolf, Slow Talker, and others had explained to me that these provided a rich pool of social resources for contemporary living. Driving down the Main Street of Browning, however, it was difficult for me to envision these cultural ways being practiced here.

On the eastern outskirts of town, Two Bears swerved across the road, drove into a pull-off, and without any warning, continued right out into a field. Almost knocked off my seat, I realized we were following some invisible dirt path which eventually emptied right onto the plains. Rumbling along, I noticed we were situated in a bit of a small bowl, with one very slight ridge around the bowl being created a century earlier by the tracks of the Great Northern Railway.

As I pondered the Railway, Two Bears informed us that we were nestled into a site of traditional activities. "This is a sacred site, the site of the Sun Dance." As we looked around, I noticed the remains of five Sun Lodges. The custom is that each was to be used only once. Asking us not to take any pictures—"the elders request that this site be treated as sacred with no pictures taken"—Two Bears recounted the Blackfeet tale of Scar Face, of a young disfigured boy who was healed by the Sun and thus was able to gather the favor of a pretty young woman. We stood in silence a while.

Two Bears asked:

> Did you ever pray to the sun or leave an offering for the sun? It is the source of light, warmth, and makes things grow. We believe we should be thankful for that. . . . Our religion tells us that all of this (waving his arm broadly) is connected. The rocks, the grass, and the sun. The pipes that we use in our ceremonies are made of stone (he shapes his hands as a bowl). The stone represents the earth (his hands become a globe). The stem is made of wood. It represents all living things. The smoke of the pipe is like a spirit you see briefly, then it disappears, up to the Creator. We believe that all things are connected like this.

Two Bears invites us into a prolonged period of silence, to pray, meditate, or leave an offering—"usually of tobacco"—if we wished. Each of us quietly move away by ourselves to look at the lodges and pray. After a long, silent, reflective period at this sacred site, we slowly gather to leave. As we move to the van, finding it hard to leave the site, Two Bears pauses, looks around at the grass, at the lodges, at the small rolling ridges immediately surrounding us, at the grand mountains in the distance, at the beautiful blue sky. Feeling the warmth of the sun, the coolness of the breeze, and hearing the meadowlarks warble, he is visibly delighted: You can come out here and sit down. Just sit down and listen. In time, you might hear a raven and realize that the raven is saying something to you. Or you might talk to a tree. But you have to listen. Be quiet. Be patient.

If you have a problem, or can't find an answer for something, our belief is that you can come out here, or to the mountains, or just about anywhere, sit down and listen. If you sit and listen patiently, you'll find an answer.

Explorations

1. When we understand listening as a cultural activity, we also realize that there may be many kinds of listening within a culture—that is, different kinds of activities that carry the name of "listening." Consider what it is that each person is saying in the following examples. What is it that they are asking of you, or commenting on? Describe the kind of activity they are referring to.

    a. A teacher says, "Now listen up, class."

    _____

    _____

    _____

    b. A friend says, "I need you to listen to me."

    _____

    _____

    _____

    c. Another friend says, "You are such a good listener."

    _____

    _____

    _____

    d. A police officer says, "You listen to me, buddy."

    _____

    _____

    _____

2. Can you describe a time when you (or a close friend or relative) had an experience in which you "listened" in a way that is similar to the Blackfeet tradition? (Review the last 2 paragraphs.)

    _____

    _____

    _____

    _____

Key Constructions

- Listening as a cultural practice

Key Constructions for Part Three, Section C

- Monologic listening
- Dialogic listening
- Focusing on "ours"
- Paraphrase
- Paraphrase plus
- Run with the metaphor
- Mutual listening
- Doctor–patient listening
- Listening as a cultural practice

PART THREE

Suggested Readings

Birdwhistell, R. L. (1970). *Kinesics and context*. Philadelphia: University of Pennsylvania Press.

Bochner, A. P., & Ellis, C. (1992). Personal narrative as a social approach to interpersonal communication. *Communication Theory, 2*, 165–172.

Carroll, J. (Ed.). (1956). *Language, thought, and reality: Selected writings of Benjamin Lee Whorf*. Cambridge, MA: MIT Press.

Gonzalez, A., Houston, M., & Chen, V. (Eds.). (2004). *Our voices: Essays in culture, ethnicity, and communication* (4th ed.). Los Angeles: Roxbury.

Hall, E. (1977). *Beyond culture*. Garden City, NY: Anchor Press.

Knapp, M. L., & Hall, J. A. (1992). *Nonverbal communication in human interaction* (3rd ed.). Fort Worth, TX: Holt, Rinehart & Winston.

Leeds-Hurwitz, W. (1993). *Semiotics and communication: Signs, codes, cultures*. Mahwah, NJ: Erlbaum.

Pearce, B., & Pearce, K. (2000). Extending the theory of the Coordinated Management of Meaning (CMM) through a community dialogue process. *Communication Theory, 10*, 405–423.

Sharf, B., & Vanderford, M. L. (2003). Illness narratives and the social construction of health. In T. Thompson, A. Dorsey, K. I. Miller, and R. Parrott (Eds.), *Handbook of health communication* (pp. 9–34). Mahwah, NJ: Erlbaum.

Web Resources

John Shotter's website
http://pubpages.unh.edu/~jds/

Donal Carbaugh web vita (includes publications)
www.umass.edu/communication/faculty_staff/carbaugh.shtml

International Online Training Program on intractable conflict (by John Stewart)
www.colorado.edu/conflict/peace/treatment/dialist.htm

McNamee web vita (include Publications)
http://pubpages.unh.edu/~smcnamee/

Dialogue examples of adjacency pairs
www.ugr.es/~inped/module10/m10_5.htm

Metaphors about love
www.macmillandictionary.com/MED-Magazine/November2003/13-Metaphor-Love.htm

A transcribed interview with Edward T. Hall
http://cms.interculturalu.com/node/144/print

Chinese emotions: Photo embedded article
www.ling.gu.se/%7Ebiljana/gestures2.html

Discussion Questions and/or Short Papers

1. A major theme of Part III has to do with the tensions between order and disorder in communicative acts. Both order and disorder are required in communication. Without some form of order (e.g., repetition, expectation, coordination), communication would be impossible. Without disorder, people would be frozen in their traditions with little ability to adapt to changing circumstances. Creativity would be diminished and boredom might prevail. Now consider the classroom: Elements of order are in evidence everywhere.
   - Can you describe instances or periods of *disorder*?
   - In your view, did these contribute to or detract from the educational experience? Explain.

2. Metaphors provide word pictures that organize our understanding and draw our attention to what is being said. For example, in terms of electoral politics, states are described as "red" or "blue" according to whether the majority of voters choose one party over another.
   - What are the gains and losses in using metaphors, such as *red* and *blue* states, to discuss national politics?
   - Can you think of another metaphor that might also describe this difference, perhaps with different implications?
   - Some might say it would be better to avoid metaphors altogether. Is it possible to *not* use metaphors in speech?

3. Analyze a section of the newspaper—sports, style, editorial, news, or business/financial—for the use of metaphors. Or you could also analyze a photoblog for metaphors. Describe some of the popular metaphors used, and interpret the function of these metaphors in creating a word picture of a person or event. Evaluate whether you believe the metaphors you describe function in a beneficial or in a harmful way in informing readers.

4. Cell phones are important accessories for many people today. In a manner similar to John Fiske's analysis of jeans, analyze the way in which cell phones, as physical objects, communicate information about their users. Also discuss any reservations you have about interpreting people by their products (e.g., cell phones, blackberries, iPods. . . .).

5. Experiment with a conversation you have with a close friend or family member. Try to incorporate dialogic listening into your conversation. Note the difference in responses you receive when you listen in this manner, as opposed to how you might usually listen.
   - Describe how your experience was different from the manner in which you usually listen. How did this form of listening contribute to your relationship?
   - Did you discover limitations in the idea of dialogic listening? Provide examples.

Relational Dynamics: From Intimacy to Conflict

Introduction

If you are deep in conversation with someone, you will seldom pause to talk about the conversation itself. If you are in the middle of a kiss, you don't stop to deliberate on the meaning of kissing. It is this "pausing to consider the process" that separates communication study from most normal life. The strong hope is that by inquiring into what it is we do when we communicate with each other, useful insights may be generated. With new ways of understanding, we open new avenues of action. No, you may not wish to pause in the middle of a kiss to consider the dynamics, but periodic deliberation on what we are doing and where it leads us can be enormously fruitful.

It is in this context that we offer the next four sections. Each section treats what are often called "dynamics" of relationship—that is, the play of tensions or differences that pervade our attempts to achieve smooth patterns of relating. We first take up the complexities of friendships (Section A), relationships we deeply value but which are often filled with difficulty. We then move to intimate relations (Section B) and to family life (Section C). Here the complexities are both multiplied and intensified. Finally, we consider conflict (Section D) and ways in which it might be negotiated. We offer no cookbook solutions to the complexities of daily life. However, we, as editors of this book, can say that we have found many of these ideas valuable in our own lives.

The Art of Friendship

We tend to think of friendship as a natural fact of life. We can distinguish between those who are "our friends" and those who are not. And should a friendship end it is often painful. Yet, from a social constructionist perspective, friendship is far from a natural fact. The very idea of friendship is a cultural construction, and over the centuries it has been defined in many different ways. A century ago friendship was often constructed as a deep bond between individuals; one might have one or two friends who would be cherished for a lifetime. Today one might have dozens of friends, and the cost may involve being in continuous motion. The way friendship is constructed also varies from one group or place to another. Many Europeans, for example, view the American form of friendship as too superficial. Additionally, the way people define friendship after a broken romance is quite different from the way soldiers in the field might describe relationships with their "buddies." The definitions of friendship continue to change with the times. Today people can become quite attached to "friends" they have met online where they rarely, if ever, meet face-to-face.

It is largely because of variation and change in the construction of friendship that participating in friendships can be viewed as an art. Friendship could only be an exacting science only if its patterns were as clear and stable across time and space as the laws of chemistry. Yes, there are some patterns across friendships. Every significant form of relationship will present at least three significant challenges of communication:

1. Constructing the Relationship

If the rules of friendship are without consistent clarity and stability, one of the major challenges confronted by participants is to define for themselves the nature of their relationship. Is it an important friendship, a casual friendship, a relationship of convenience? If people are to relate successfully with each other they must negotiate about what kinds of actions are appropriate. Such negotiations are typically indirect. For example, a statement like "I thought you were going to call me last night" tells the other that he or she isn't living up to the kind of relationship they had defined. Because our social lives are in continuous flux, most of our relationships are also subject to continuous negotiation.

2. Constructing the World

A second relational challenge is to negotiate with the "other" about how we make sense of the world. Here we discover perhaps the major fruits of friendship. With a friend you can usually talk about what is good or bad about the world, what is worth doing, or how to approach various problems. It is such talk that reduces ambiguity and gives reason and value to one's actions. Without any friends, life can rapidly become meaningless.

3. Constructing the Self

Communication will construct not only the nature of the relationship and the world but also the identity of the participants themselves. As the participants talk with each other they position each other by defining themselves and their values. A simple request such as "can you help me out" implicitly defines one's friend as trustworthy, possessing resources, and potentially caring. When the friend agrees to help, that confirms the definition.

In the readings that follow we see all of these issues up close. First, in Reading 29 Terri Apter and Ruthellen Josselson comment on a conversation between two 14-year old girls. You will have an excellent opportunity to appreciate the way the two negotiate the social world in which they live, and simultaneously construct their own identities. Further, you can see how these constructions together play into their understanding of their own friendship. In Reading 30, communication scholars, Anita L. Vangelisti, Stacy L. Young, Katy E. Carpenter-Theune, and Alicia L. Alexander, explore how people construct the various ways they can "be hurt" in friendships. This analysis again opens the possibility of removing ourselves from the grip of tradition, so that hurt feelings are not so important to everyday relations.

We then take a closer look at gender differences in forms of friendship. First, in Reading 31 Hilary M. Lips expresses concern over the way in which women communicate together. As she sees it, women's friendships build in a form of communication that may lend itself to the continued oppression and discounting of women in society. This controversial argument is followed by Jennifer Coates's (Reading 32) account of ways in which men establish their identity through conversation. Again, there is room for questioning the broader social implications of our friendship patterns. What does it do for or to men to use bigoted comments as a form of communication?

In Reading 33 we move on to the positive potentials of friendship. The concept of friendship can be applied to many kinds of relationships. As we come to understand a relationship as a friendship it takes on special characteristics. William K. Rawlins proposes that the most effective relationship between teacher and student is one of friendship. This is an interesting proposal, as it seems to challenge the traditional hierarchy of teacher and student. However, when we understand good education as friendship, the relationship between teacher and student has very special characteristics.

We complete this section by considering subtle ways in which we communicate our definitions of self and friendship. As mentioned, we seldom define our relationships directly. Only infrequently might we say, "I thought you were my friend." Most often our communication is indirect. Our actions speak louder than our words. In Reading 34, Cynthia Lightfoot describes the way in which adolescents indirectly use risk taking as a way of defining who they are, and simultaneously, the friendship group to which they belong. Adolescent risk taking is not so much about rational calculation as it is about securing a friendship group.

READING 29

Friendship Talk and Social Survival

Our common conversations with friends may be essential to our survival. Friends can help us create useful understandings of our world and of ourselves. They help us interpret the frequently ambiguous actions of others, and reframe what often seem to be failures or frustrations. Reading 29 focuses on how friends help one another through "private talk." By paying attention to the details of this private conversation, you may see how the participants continuously reshape meanings to protect their identity.

Reading 29   TERRI APTER AND RUTHELLEN JOSSELSON

For girls friendship without talk about feelings and without reciprocal understanding of what each feels, seems little more than a shell. Friends seek each other's help in understanding and managing their feelings: "Jana ignored me today and I just feel so awful," one friend says to another. "Nothing I do seems to go right" or "I can't deal with my new stepfather." They work together, carefully assembling the pieces of a story, in an attempt to understand their world and how they might handle it." They sift through their reactions to their families and to their other friends. As friends explore the world of emotions, one girl is careful to help make the other's emotions bearable and to describe her behavior in an acceptable light: "You did the best you could." "It's not your fault." "He's the one who's strange." One friend gets the message across to the other: "You're okay." And that acceptance is the gift of understanding.

Here Ginny and Francine, both fourteen, work to sort out Ginny's problem with a third friend:

GINNY: When she says things like that—"What've you been up to?"—right in front of everyone, it's like—how can you answer?

FRANCINE: She's slipped the criticism in, hasn't she?

GINNY: Yeah! So everyone thinks "What's up?" and something's wrong, and it makes me feel so strange.

FRANCINE: You looked upset.

GINNY: You could tell? Was it obvious?

FRANCINE: I knew—cause I know you. It wasn't obvious. I mean, they were just thinking about what she said, and you didn't say much.

GINNY: You know, I was just about to cry. It's silly, isn't it. I mean, there was nothing to it. I was just embarrassed.

FRANCINE: My eyes sometimes fill with tears when I'm embarrassed.

GINNY: Yeah—it's not really crying. Your eyes just sting.

FRANCINE: And you hurt inside.

GINNY: It's just so confusing to see everyone looking at you and wondering about you. 'Cause it makes me feel so strange. It was like she wanted to push me away before I got there.

FRANCINE: 'Cause she feels bad about spending so much time with those guys. You know how she used to always wait for you after lunch.

GINNY: So she was covering up—making me out to be the odd one for walking up to her.

FRANCINE: Maybe . . . you could just shrug and walk away.

GINNY: Like she's the one who's strange.
FRANCINE: Well, isn't she?

Here two girlfriends engage in a remarkable emotional-education course. They shift from sympathy to analysis to advice to comfort: Francine acknowledges Ginny's feelings ("You looked upset") and the gravity of the situation. She then sympathizes with her, as though to say "I know how you feel," because she, too, feels pain, and her eyes also water when she is embarrassed. But the conversation does not stop with a simple "I know how you feel." This girl talk is a beautiful example of emotional coaching—a process in which we learn to identify emotions and to understand how emotions arise. As they understand why the third friend behaved as she did, Francine convinces Ginny that the fault or problem is not hers but the other girl's—a comforting, positive spin. Together they read another's feelings from how she acts, then, as they go through possible ways of managing an uncomfortable social situation, consider how other people might be handled. Only another girl who inhabits the same social world can understand the nuances of this interaction.

In talk, girls create and learn the contours of their interpersonal worlds. Friends frequently engage in plotting sessions whereby they ask one another, "What should I do?" They discuss how to get a boy to notice them, how to deal with a difficult mother, how to get out of trouble with a teacher. Should I confront this girl, they may ask, or ignore her? Should I give her a dose of her own medicine? How can I ask this guy out or start a conversation with him? How do I tell my mother? These coaching sessions also offer help with a girl's attempt to handle her feelings—especially that terrible adolescent self-consciousness and the anxiety that accompanies it: "Do you think he noticed?" "What did they think?" "How did I look?"

A friend provides an outsider's view—but is an outsider who understands. Francine, as a good friend, understands that Ginny was upset, but she can also assure her, as an "outsider," that no one else noticed. They discuss others reactions to them ("Why did she react like that? I didn't mean to upset her"). They form an alliance against those who do not understand. The need for being understood is primitive and deep, arising in infancy from our need for others to respond to us in ways that, first, simply keep us alive (as we communicate hunger, pain, and fear) and then, later, shape our basic humanity. Throughout our lives, talk with friends continues to offer emotional feedback and helps us make sense of our experience.

Explorations

1. What are some of the ways that Francine helps Ginny cope with her friend's apparent rejection? To answer this question, underline the comments made by Francine in the reading that you think help Ginny.

2. Listen closely to an audiotaped segment of a conversation in which you and a friend reconstruct or reframe a negative event (e.g., losing a game, a prize, a job, a girlfriend/boyfriend). (If you don't have an easily available conversation, invent such a scenario or record it from a television show.) Write 8 to 10 lines from your audiotaped dialogue between you and your friend that address your feelings about the negative event.

_____

_____

_____

_____

_____

_____

_____

_____

3. Can you identify any examples from your dialogue above that illustrate "emotional coaching"? Describe them.

_____

_____

_____

Key Construction

- Emotional coaching

READING 30

How Can You Hurt Me: Let Me Count the Ways

We have tried throughout this volume to emphasize a view of communication as coordinated actions that construct what we take to be real and good. When we coordinate with others in the game of basketball, "three pointers" and "slam dunks" become real; when we coordinate with others in doing chemistry, "chemical elements" become real. The implication is that in close relationships we are continuously creating the realities we live by, whether it is the reality of "our love" or of "my disappointment." In close relations we enter a tradition in which "being hurt" or emotionally injured is a commonly constructed reality. In Reading 30, the researchers demonstrate the many ways in which being hurt can be constructed. They gathered questionnaires from almost 300 undergraduates at a large southwestern university. Almost two-thirds were female. They were asked to describe an interaction in which someone hurt their feelings. The researchers then coded the responses to locate common categories, and to determine which were the most common. Some of the major findings of the research are included in the selection. The table presents the categories and some illustrative phrases.

Reading 30 ANITA L. VANGELISTI, STACY L. YOUNG, KATY E. CARPENTER-THEUNE, AND ALICIA L. ALEXANDER

At one time or another in almost every relationship, people's feelings get hurt. Harsh words are spoken, sensitive issues raised, secrets betrayed, and special dates forgotten. In some cases, people see the cause of their hurt as fleeting or inconsequential—they explain away their feelings and continue their relationship with the person who hurt them as if nothing happened. In other cases, people regard the hurtful event and its impetus as very serious—individuals may terminate a relationship because they see the cause of their hurt feelings as an irrevocable breach.

Cause of Hurt	My Reaction
Personal attack: disparagement of some unchangeable characteristic or quality of the individual	"He made me sound like a crazy woman." "I never thought something like height would play into whether someone would like me."
Undermining of self-concept: Provocation of feelings of inferiority or self-doubt	"It made me feel incompetent." "It made me question my entire self-worth."
Shattering of hopes; discouragement or working obstruction of the individual's hopes, efforts, or dreams	"It's been something that I've been on for a while and I thought I was doing good." "I felt as though everything I did "was in vain."

Truth-telling: accurate reference to a sensitive issue or undeniable fact	"It was something about myself that I've always hated."
	"It was the truth . . . I can't change the past."
Humiliation: public embarrassment or degradation of the individual	"It was insulting in front of a large group of people."
	"He embarrassed me and humiliated me."
Inappropriate communication: unfit or uncalled for verbal or nonverbal behavior	"It was the tone of voice."
	"They were harsh, negative, angry words."

Explorations

1. When you claim to be hurt, how is this expressed to the person who has hurt you? Indicate three of these expressions or reactions in the left-hand column (for example, you may become sullen and quiet):

_____   _____

_____   _____

_____   _____

_____   _____

2. For each of these reactions (left hand column above), what is the likely response of the person who has hurt you? Indicate this in the right-hand column in exercise 1. (For example, if I respond to hurt with being quiet and sullen, the other may question me about why I am so quiet.)

3. Now consider the function of the response to the hurt. Might the other person apologize, feel punished, or something else? In other words, the performance of being hurt has a social function, but not all ways of performing are successful in sustaining a good relationship.

   What, do you feel is an effective way of responding to being hurt, and what is ineffective or detrimental to a relationship?

   _____

   _____

   _____

4. There is no action that requires us to respond with the performance of being hurt. Even if a close friend insults us in front of a group, we are not required to react with hurt. Performing being hurt is a tradition, and we are not required to participate. Revisit the findings reported in Reading 30. Can you imagine alternative ways to respond to any of these cases other than performing "being hurt?" Would they lead to more or less success in sustaining a good relationship?

_____

_____

_____

Key Construction

- Constructions of "being hurt"

READING 31

"The Girls": Friendships Among Women

Women's friendship ties are extremely important in their lives. At the same time, ways of communicating among friends vary across different cultural and social groups. Racial, social class, and national differences are also important. Reading 31 gives an overview of the research on women's friendships in many social contexts.

Reading 31   HILARY M. LIPS

The British feminist Mary Wollstonecraft, writing in 1792 on women's rights, declared that friendship was "the most holy bond of society" and "the most sublime of all affections." A person without friends is considered unfortunate in the extreme, or even flawed in some serious way. In North America, friendships tend to be spontaneous and informal; however, this is not true in every culture. Among the Bangwa people of Gameroon, parents often arrange a best friendship for their children in the same way they arrange a marriage.

Friendships Between Women

Despite the generally agreed-upon importance of friendship, women's friendships have often been trivialized and mocked, and women have been portrayed as incapable of true friendship (Rose, 1995). This portrayal apparently has its roots in general prejudice against women, as both the historical and psychological research on women's friendships indicates that, far from being trivial and fickle, such friendships tend to be deep, intimate, and enduring. For centuries, women have formed passionate, close friendships, as women's private letters and diaries attest. These relationships have emphasized self-disclosure, emotional closeness, and empathy, and have often been a core part of women's emotional lives.

A central theme in women's friendships is talking. Even in early childhood, girls talk and share stories with one another, whereas boys are more likely to spend their time together in active play. Girls tend to develop fewer, more intimate, friendships whereas boys are more likely to have large groups of friends with whom they do, rather than talk. A study of African American girls from preschool to high school showed they spent much more time in talking than in play activity. Adult working-class and middle-class women report that shared activities with friends are mainly valued as opportunities to get together to talk, and that they bond with other women through talk, support, and sharing feelings.

The talking that women do with friends is aimed at building intimacy. Indeed, the most valued function of friendship for women of all ages appears to be intimacy-assistance: discussing private, personal feelings and receiving help. The orientation toward intimacy may be particularly intense during adolescence, but the encouragement, support, and affirmation that women receive from female friends is linked for women of all ages and from diverse groups to positive feelings of well-being, high self-esteem, and life satisfaction.

Women's friendships tend to change over the course of their lives and according to their involvement in heterosexual relationships. Dating or marriage often interferes with women's friendships, and among married couples the man's friends tend to take center stage as the couple's friends (Rose, 1995). Parenting young children may be disruptive of friendships because of the amount of time and energy required; however, women do manage to sustain friendships through these times, often sharing their difficulties and coping strategies. Perhaps not surprisingly, women's friendship networks tend to expand after divorce, following an initial reduction. In one study of European, American and Mexican American divorced women, both groups reported that they had more friends after the divorce because their ex-husbands could no longer prevent them from socializing as they chose. Women also tend to expand their network of female friends in later life, probably because many are widows, and they depend on other women for support, companionship, and help.

Diversity in Women's Friendships

Factors such as culture, social class, race, sexual orientation, and physical ability may be linked to variations in women's friendships. More research is needed to understand how friendships are shaped by the values, resources, opportunities, and restrictions that exist for different groups of women. For example, the Aboriginal women of central Australia have a long tradition of women's camps, or *jilimi*, which serve as refuges for women, places where women's religious rituals are centered and to which women come frequency for conversation and emotional and social support. The permanent members of such camps are widows and married women who do not live with their husbands. The *jilimi* are also more temporary refuges for single girls who are not ready to go to their promised husbands, women traveling without their spouses, women who have temporarily left their spouses because of a dispute, those who are ill or in need of help or support, and those who are in mourning. Sometimes married women come to the camps by day to socialize with other women, returning to their husbands at night. The *jilimi* are taboo to men, and provide women with a safe space, a power base, a place where they and their activities are central. These formally designated women's spaces provide opportunities for women to form strong bonds with one another, and such bonds can extend across generations.

By contrast, other cultures in which women often find themselves in spaces that are segregated from men may not provide the same nurturance for female friendships. In the strongly [historically] gender-divided world of the Saudi Arabian royal families, for example, girls and young women form friendships that may be based on a shared desire to rebel against men's institutionalized power or on shared commiseration over their anticipated fate of arranged marriages. They may derive comfort but little sense of power from these friendships, which can be broken up at any time by a patriarch's decision to marry off a daughter or divorce a wife and send her away, never to be seen again by the other women in the family or community.

In Europe and North America, social class can affect the form that friendships take. Working-class women may disclose more to their friends than upper-class women do, perhaps because working-class women are less likely to socialize as couples. One British researcher found that White middle-class friendships often spanned a variety of activities and included entertaining friends at home, but the friendships among the White working-class sample tended to be specific to particular activities and settings. The latter group seldom entertained friends at home, which was reserved for the family.

This difference may reflect not only class values, but also the fact that middle-class women have larger, more comfortable homes for inviting people in. Other research, however, suggests that women with limited economic resources are more likely than their more affluent counterparts to integrate friendships into kin relations, counting friends as family rather than segregating them to particular activities. Limited resources may, of course, create an emphasis on more localized friendships, ones that do not require expensive transportation and long-distance phone calls.

Racial differences in female friendships are also apparent. One small group of White and Black women who were meeting regularly to talk about and try to bridge issues of race reported that they had surprised one another with their discovery, at one meeting, that all of the Black women and none of the White women had been to one another's homes. This discovery seems to fit with Suzanna Rose's (1995) comment that "a pattern of regarding friends as part of an extended family network appears to distinguish African Americans from white Americans, at least among the poor, working, and middle class" (p. 86). African Americans are more likely than their White counterparts to have an extended network of friends that are counted as family and from whom help and support can be sought.

Black women in professional occupations that are dominated by White men may seek one another's friendship not just for the reasons of help, social support and companionship already discussed, but also as allies in assessing and coping with issues such as racism at work. Black women in professional occupations are often experiencing "bicultural" stress, feeling torn between the demands of the White male culture of their job and the Black community. Friendships with other Black women who are feeling similarly torn can help them manage their feelings of conflict and bridge the two cultures.

Sexual orientation may influence women's friendships, but research in this area is just beginning. Both lesbians and heterosexual women place high priority on such factors as similar interests, understanding, and support when evaluating friendship with women; however, lesbians emphasize equality and trust within friendship more than heterosexual women do. Among lesbians, friendships with women are highly valued; also, friendship with a lover may be viewed as more important than sexuality and may be maintained after a romantic partnership has ended. Also, lesbians often develop close friendship groups, endeavoring to situate their lifestyle and partnership choices in a larger network of social relationships.

Some Paradoxes of Women's Friendships

In her memoir, bell hooks (1996) describes the intimacy that developed among the women in her African American family around the weekly practice of ironing their hair:

> There is a deeper intimacy in the kitchen on Saturday when hair is pressed, when fish is fried, when sodas are passed around, when soul music drifts over the talk. We are women together. This is our ritual and our time. It is a time without men. It is a time when we work to meet each other's needs, to make each other beautiful in whatever way we can. It is a time of laughter and mellow talk. (p. 92)

Years later, as a senior in high school, she decides she never wants to get her hair pressed again; rather, she wants to wear an Afro. At that point, she sees the hair-straightening ritual as a rejection of Black women's beauty, an attempt to look White. In their Saturday morning sessions, she feels, the women supported one another in rejecting their own beauty and conforming to someone else's standards. "The intimacy masks betrayal. Together we change ourselves. The closeness is an embrace before parting, a gesture of farewell to love and one another" (p. 93).

In this example, women friends supported one another, but that support was a mixed blessing, because it made them more comfortable with a culture that denigrated them. Do women's friendships in general act to support the status quo? To preserve rather than undermine gender ideologies and gendered social arrangements? Some authors have argued that the answer is yes: At least some of the time, women's support for one another is solidly situated in support for the prevailing gendered power arrangement. Women's friendships tend to keep unsatisfactory or oppressive marriages intact by giving wives an outlet and a source of sympathetic support, by fulfilling needs for intimacy that are unmet within the marriage, and by defusing anger. One study of the bridal shower, a female friendship ritual that often precedes weddings in North America, notes that these events reinforce a number of traditional patriarchal notions about femininity and about female–male relationships: that marriage is more important to women than to men, that the domestic role is the province of women, and that marriage is the most important relationship in a woman's life.

Women's friendships may also unwittingly support women's weaknesses rather than their strengths, and may reinforce stereotypical notions that femininity is synonymous with nurturance and emotionality. Women's friendships allow for a great deal of self-disclosure; however, that self-disclosure is usually focused on weakness and pain, not on strengths and victories. As Suzanna Rose (1995) notes, "in friendships women emphasize their vulnerabilities rather than their skill, their helplessness rather than their power" (p. 98). She also points out that women tend to expect their friendships to be entirely supportive—an expectation that is based on stereotypes. Women may deny parts of themselves and limit their friendships by refusing to acknowledge the existence of more "negative" emotions in their friendships: emotions such as envy or competitiveness.

Yet women's friendships can also provide a climate in which women can explore new self-definitions and ways to challenge social structures and stereotypes that are detrimental to them. Friends can support one another in resisting the restrictions and limiting expectations that women encounter. Louise Bernikow (1980) notes that, across many cultures, "Women friends help each other to remain perpendicular in the face of cultures that attempt to knock them over with the hurricane forces of ideology about what a woman should be or . . . [deny] the validity of their experience, [denigrate] their frame of reference, [reinforce] female masochism, self-doubt, passivity, and suicide" (p. 144).

Women from different racial, ethnic, or class groups may have different communication styles, hold different values, and be comfortable in different environments. A first step in building friendship across such differences might be to avoid the assumption that behaviors, choices, or spoken words mean the same thing to members of both groups. For example, going to an expensive restaurant for lunch may mean only pleasure and a chance to talk for an upper-class woman; for her working-class friend, however, it may mean feeling awkward about how to behave and paralyzed with anxiety about how much her lunch is going to cost. Canceling a lunch date with a friend in order to go home to be with a sick aunt may feel like a necessary choice to an African American woman who has been raised with a strong concept of extended family. To her European American friend, whose notion of close family is more restricted, it may seem as if the other woman was merely making an excuse to avoid the lunch.

Marsha Houston and Julia Wood (1996) offer four general suggestions for communicating and forging relationships across group boundaries. First, understand that you may not understand that your own vantage point and cultural background shape the way you interpret communications. Second, do not impose your own cultural standards on others; shift your response from "That's wrong" to "That's interesting." Third, respect the ways others interpret their experience, and offer, at least, a respectful hearing. Finally, acknowledge but do not totalize differences: Do not pretend not to notice that your new acquaintance is of another race, but also do not relate to her only in terms of race or expect her to "represent" her racial group on every issue.

References

Bernikow, L. (1980). *Among women.* New York: Crown.

hooks, b. (1996). *Bone black: Memories of girlhood.* New York: Henry Holt.

Houston, M., & Wood, J. T., (1996). Difficult dialogues, expanded horizons. Communicating across race and class. In J. T. Wood (Ed.), *Gendered relationships.* (pp. 39–56). Mountain View, CA: Mayfield.

Rose, S. (1995). Women's friendships. In J. C. Chrisler & A. Huston Hemsreet (Eds.). *Variations on a theme: Diversity and the psychology of women.* (pp. 79–105). Albany: State University of New York Press.

Explorations

1. Which group's communication style with friends in this reading seems closest to your own style of communicating with your friends?

   _____

   _____

   _____

2. Are there communication patterns among friends described in this reading that you wish you could adopt (e.g., having friends who are so close they feel like family)? What would they be?

   _____

   _____

   _____

3. How can you help create this kind of communicative pattern when developing new friendships?

_____

_____

_____

Key Constructions

- Friendships between women
- Culture and friendships
- Cross-cultural friendship and communication

READING 32

Friendship: Man to Man

We often think that the purpose of listening to a conversation is to understand what is being said. What is the topic? What is being communicated about the topic? What emotions are being expressed? However, social constructionist ideas invite you to listen in a second way as well. Here you move beyond the specific content to ask about the social function of the talk. Who is affected by what is said, and in what way? What expectations are created; what isn't being said and why not? All these questions can become significant through the lens of social construction. In Reading 32, Jennifer Coates considers the way in which talk among male friends defines who they are, and subtly informs one another how they should be treated.

Reading 32 JENNIFER COATES

We all in part construct who we are through *saying who we are not*. But for men, the denial of homosexuality is particularly salient. Deborah Cameron spells out the norm as follows: "men in all-male groups must unambiguously display their heterosexual orientation." The following example is a story told by Jim, a [17 year old] male student, about an evening out with his friend, Bill:

> The night before I left to come here
> I was driving down the road
> and I've just seen this long hair little f . . . mini-skirt.
> I've beeped the horn,
> this f . . . bloke turned round,

I've gone "aaaggghhh!," <SCREAMS>
<LAUGHTER>
Bill yells, "what what?,"
"it was a bloke,"
I say, "turn round, turn round,"
and he turns round
and you could just see these shoes hiding under this car
and he must've thought we were just gonna literally beat the
crap out of him. . . .
I've driven past,
opened the window,
"come out, come out, wherever you are.
here queerie, queerie, queerie."

This story operates on two levels: first, it tells of a series of events when the narrator and his friend pass someone who looks like a woman but who turns out on closer inspection to be a man dressed in a mini-skirt. More importantly, this story does important work in terms of establishing the narrator's identity: he positions himself as uncompromisingly heterosexual both through his initial interest in the person with long hair wearing a mini-skirt, and also through his horrified reaction when he realizes this person is actually a man. His fantasy that the cross-dresser feared they would "beat the crap" out of him hints at the violent feelings unleashed by this encounter. The story ends with the narrator presenting himself as venting his fury at this subversion of conventional gender boundaries by shouting taunts and insults at the man.

This story demonstrates how powerful narrative can be as a tool of self-presentation and self-construction. The narrator is at an age when his sexual identity is still fragile and the function of this story is to establish his credentials as a "normal," heterosexual man.

Reference

Cameron, D. C. (1997). Performing gender identity: Young men's talk and the construction of heterosexual identity. In S. Johnson & V. H. Meinhof (Eds.), *Language and masculinity* (p. 232). Oxford, England: Blackwell.

Explorations

1. What is your reaction to the author's interpretations of this conversation? Do you agree or not? Explain.

2. Saying negative things about another group is often part of a conversation among males and females. Are there other reasons (besides self-construction) that a man might tell such a negative story? What are the reasons for why people from certain groups might lash out at others from a different group?

   _____

   _____

3. In this conversation there are several grammatical errors and strange placements of words offered by Jim. Do you think this is because Jim is "linguistically challenged"? Or are there social reasons served by using slang, incorrect grammar, and the like? Please comment.

   _____

   _____

   _____

Key Constructions

- Self-construction through conversation
- Gender identity

READING 33

Teaching as Friendship

We typically think of friendships in terms of same sex-peers. However, the concept of friendship may be applied to virtually any relationship. When it is applied we encourage a particular set of highly valued activities. In Reading 33, William K. Rawlins proposes that college education functions most effectively when the relationship between teacher and student approximates a form of friendship. Friendship for Rawlins has three components. First, teacher and student should function more as equals, rather than as superiors and subordinates in a status hierarchy. Second, they should care about each other's welfare, rather than maintaining a formal distance. Finally, there should be mutuality, that is, recognition that each has something valuable to contribute to the relationship.

At the same time, Rawlins proposes, all friendships carry with them certain tensions. These tensions are not to be viewed as negative, for they typically involve a conflict between two valued goals. For example, most friendships carry with them a tension between independence and dependence. As individuals we may wish that our friendship did not constrain us or reduce our freedom, and yet, we want a relationship in which we can count on the other for certain things. As Rawlins sees it, these tensions exist in a "dialectic" relationship. When goals conflict we may work with friends in managing these tensions toward a resolution. However, each resolution may also set the stage for further tension. We grow and mature through this cyclical process. Here Rawlins describes two tensions that function in classroom friendships and how he has wrestled with them as an instructor.

Reading 33   W I L L I A M   K .   R A W L I N S

Dialectical Tensions of the Educational Friendship

In studying (and living) friendship, I have learned that, throughout life, friends must continually manage dialectical tensions in their communication with each other. In discussing these issues with students in various courses, it has become increasingly apparent to me that they could be considered critical tensions and resources in teaching, if we view and live teaching as a mode of friendship. In fact, writing this essay has itself been an educational activity for me, undertaken in a spirit of friendship with others. I contacted current and former students of mine and asked for their perceptions concerning the general notion of teaching as friendship. I also sought to understand their experienced truths of what I may or may not have accomplished as a teacher with them. I asked them if anything about how I have gone about being an educator in their lives approximates the ideals or feelings of friendship? If so, how so? If not, why not? The resulting dialogue has been an exciting, instructive, and deeply humanizing experience for me, and two of these co-learners' voices are woven into this essay.

The Dialectic of the Freedom to Be Independent and the Freedom to Be Dependent

Friendships involve ongoing tensions between the freedom to be independent of and the freedom to depend on each other. Tensions between independence and dependence permeate the educational friendship as well. Once a person has enrolled in a course or obligated him- or herself to teach it, being in the class is not voluntary. Friendship, however, is always a matter of choice; persons cannot be compelled to be friends with each other. The spirit of friendship celebrates the freedom of each person to choose independent or dependent action, neither requiring nor preventing one or the other choice.

I am pleased to have worked with several students who could not but become who they are, and they changed me in their quests. Meanwhile, "allowing" a student to be his or her own person requires significant readiness on the part of a teacher. Can teachers handle freethinking creativity, and challenging students? If not, why not? What does it take to facilitate this kind of readiness in teachers or, more accurately, between teachers and their students? How do we, as teachers, give students guidance and direction without unduly restricting their choices? How vulnerable and flexible can a teacher become without risking the student's confidence in his or her grasp of the issues at stake?

The pinch here is that students should not be forced into independence if they are not ready, nor compelled or tacitly socialized into being overly dependent. I consider it unfriendly either to, as faculty at one institution where I used to teach put it, "give them enough rope to hang themselves," or subtly and comprehensively manipulate students into depending on faculty for all of their projects to the extent that their very identities are risked in bogus collaboration. Faculty who are too busy or above working with "mere" students, or who build their productivity around required student labor, violate the conjunctive freedoms of friendship as well.

Jim DiSanza poignantly describes the tugs and pulls of these crosscutting requirements in our relationship:

> Whatever the cause, I still remember my first baby steps at independence occurred, when I said no to something you suggested for the first time. You were counseling me about the final stages of my data collection for my dissertation one week prior to the Thanksgiving holiday. You had suggested collecting a final day of observational data the Friday after Thanksgiving. You correctly reasoned that I would be able to watch the tellers, newly socialized to their bank experiences, handling a difficult, stressful banking day during the start of the Christmas rush. I winced at the suggestion. Nancy and I were scheduled to visit family in Cleveland, and I was looking forward to the trip. I had made many family sacrifices for the degree; I wasn't going to add this to the list. Despite the obvious logic of your argument, I said no. I disagreed with the plan. It didn't feel all that great because I had no logical reason for denying your proposal, only my emotional commitments. But it was a stand for my own independence. . . .
>
> On the other hand, I could not have thought, done, or written the things I have if I had not established my independence. I needed you, then I needed to be away from you. (What a male trajectory this whole thing has taken.) This powerful swing from strong dependence to strong independence may be a result of the fact that ours was never a pure friendship; it was also a teacher–student relationship. Our relationship may resemble the parent–child relationship more closely than the ideal of friendship. In the end, I have to thank you both for allowing me to depend on you, and for granting my independence.

The Dialectic of Judgment and Acceptance

How do we, as teachers, reconcile our attempts to communicate acceptance of students as people and developing scholars with our responsibilities to evaluate their work? In addressing this tension, I often try to clarify for students and carefully communicate the distinction between judging them as people and judging their work. I tell them that I try to be a positive and well-intentioned person, and that I tend to like students and want to have fun together in our classes. Even so, I warn them not to slip into a false sense of security with me as an evaluator. They shouldn't think that because I act goofy and mention Tori Amos, Sublime, or Wu-Tang in class, I won't expect the very best from them and bring rigorous standards to bear in evaluating their work. Even so, the accomplishment of my legitimacy as a person who likes, accepts, and enjoys students as people, but sometimes finds their essays wanting, is an ongoing communicative challenge in trying to serve the requirements of educational friendship.

I also tell them the truism that teachers who care the most about them as students will spend the most time evaluating and commenting on their work. Unfortunately, and perhaps correctly, students do not always believe this, maybe because of the way some teachers make them feel through their comments about students' work, by the overall climate created in their classroom, and by their stance toward students. Some teachers convey a commitment to abstract standards, not to the students or to living learning. I believe that many persons' talk about standards in this context is primarily a flight from the responsibility of engaging substantive questions about the value of what and how they are teaching their students and about how the students' labors fit with the lives they are trying to live (and seeking to learn about). Caring can be conveyed by taking students work seriously and expecting the most from them. However, it is not enough in the educational friendship to impose an abstract template of expectations or enforce standards. The caring of friendship must also be communicated and felt by students. Even so, the standards of the educational friendship are robust, not soft or sentimental, with regard to expectations for quality, astuteness, and humane performance in learning together.

Eric Fife's observations make me feel as though I have, at times, achieved some success in reconciling these contradictory responsibilities:

> On the one hand, Batson (and you) encouraged thinkers to be liberated, to think "outside the box," to challenge perceptions and assault the paper constructs of established scholars. Thus, the questions and contentions allowed a tremendous freedom of writing and thought, and my final paper was able to be both scholarly and whimsical. And yet, on the other hand, you let us know that you were a tough critic—and had high expectations for our work, and certain standards would need to be met. So there existed a certain freedom of thought and expression, but at high standards we were not free to violate [your] high standards.

Explorations

1. Rawlins argues for a relationship of friendship between the college teacher and student. Draw from your own experience in comparing a class in which a teacher and student had a friendship versus one in which there was none. How do you compare the "educational" effectiveness of these two different kinds of classroom experiences?

_____

_____

_____

_____

2. As Rawlins suggests, all friendships carry with them certain tensions and the development of the friendship can be viewed as an unfolding dialectic tensions. Rawlins outlines two common tensions that exist when teaching takes the form of friendship (i.e., independence—dependence; judgment—acceptance). Select one of these, and describe a case in which you have experienced such a tension in a friendship either inside or outside of class. What was the result?

_____

_____

_____

_____

Key Constructions

- Teaching as friendship
- Dialectic tensions
- Independence and dependence tension
- Judgment and acceptance tension

READING 34

Risk-Taking as Communication

Parents often wonder why their adolescent children take what seem like crazy risks. Often they can become angry with their children for such "idiotic" behavior. Yet, as Cynthia Lightfoot proposes in Reading 34, taking risks may be a form of communication, and more specifically, a way of creating strong social bonds with their friends. She describes a study in which teenagers talk about their risk taking and why it is important to take risks together.

Reading 34 CYNTHIA LIGHTFOOT

Adolescents are in the process of forging identities in fellowship with their peers, and risks and adventures have a privileged role to play in this process. As "deep play" they disclose aspects of self and its relations. This is apparent in the following study, in which the participants were asked to speculate about the interpersonal consequences of sharing risks with close friends or acquaintances, and about how the consequences might vary according to the degree of risk involved. The scenario concerned a teenager who was offered a marijuana cigarette at a music concert:

> This is a story about a guy named Eric who won four tickets from a local radio station to see a big-name rock band perform at the Smith Center. He asked three friends to go with him, and they were really excited because the concert had been sold out for weeks. They met at Eric's because his parents said he could use the car. After the car was parked in the stadium lot, one of the friends pulled a joint out of his sock. His older brother had given it to him to smoke before the concert. The friend lit the joint, and passed it to the other friends who each smoked some of it. Then it was passed to Eric. None of the friends had ever smoked pot before, and Eric felt a little unsure. Would Eric be more likely, less likely or, equally likely to smoke the pot with his best friends compared to friends who weren't as close? Why? If Eric smokes the pot with his best friends, will that affect how the friends think and feel about each other or not necessarily? Why? If Eric doesn't smoke the pot with his best friends, will that affect how the friends think and feel about each other, or not necessarily? Why?

Nearly all of the teenagers (85%) in the study argued that the story character would be more inclined to smoke with acquaintances compared to close friends. Reasons focused on the power of shared risks to transform different types of relationships: "It's a chance to impress them"; "To become part of their group"; "It's easy for friends who aren't close to form a bad opinion of you"; "Close friends look into the person, not the person's actions." Nonetheless, declining to participate in a risky activity, even in the company of close friends, places one on the outside of a shared experience, and if indulged in too often, may threaten one's membership in the group. Several individuals (20%) noted that Eric could have provided reasonable justifications for his refusal (he had to drive), which would vitiate the negative consequences. A few even suggested that the responsibility of driving should rotate so that all can participate. Here are a few examples:

> If his friends are doing it, and [he knows that] his brother does it, then he'll probably do it. He doesn't want to rain on their parade. You don't just think about yourself when you're with your friends. You're not self-centered. You think about if

they have fun. And it will definitely bring them closer. Like a brotherhood-passing the test, the initiation, sharing a new experience and doing something totally new that you'll remember for quite a while. You remember who you're with. You can make an analogy with sex. The first person you have sex with you're going to be closer with because it's new and different.

He doesn't want these people who he doesn't know well to think that they don't like him. But if he's with his really good friends and decides not to, they're not going to hold it against him. With real good friends it wouldn't matter; with acquaintances it would. But he won't have as much fun because hell be second guessing himself in his mind: Maybe I should have smoked it.

He's already established with best friends. He's secure there so he can relax more and focus more on what he wants. [If he doesn't smoke it] they could still have a lot of fun. The people who got stoned—their experience would be different than his, so they may have bonded more with each other than with him, but that could be overcome. The people who got stoned would be closer. It's just like any other new experience. It would pull them together because it's a new thing-bonding.

It happened often that personal experiences were brought to bear on discussions of the hypothetical scenarios. Many of the individuals who were interviewed showed uncanny insight into the social processes and motivations of themselves and their friends:

People always look at getting high together as a sort of bonding experience, but I never see it that way. A good example is that I have heard these semi-friends talking, and I don't think they were that good of friends with themselves, but yet one of them was saying to the other, "Well, gee, I don't know what to write [in the yearbook]. What did we do together this year?" And the other one said, "Well, we got drunk a lot." It's like if you got drunk or stoned together you are supposed to automatically become great friends and it just doesn't work that way. I think that's stupid, but I think that a lot of people believe it.

Risks are extra-ordinary by these reports. They are a fount of memories and secrets, of shared knowledge and experience, and invested with the meanings of group identity. Shared risks are seen as instrumental in the development of interpersonal relationships and group cohesion, and are often described as symbolic or demonstrative of such relationships. Moreover, the meanings inscribed in risk activities are seen to vary according to the social psychological histories of those involved: For those in the process of forging a collective identity, shared risks are understood to provide an interpersonal, experiential conduit for entering or forming a group; for those whose relational histories are more articulated and secure, risks take on meaning as icons of identity. In either case, the adolescent's relational history is of high relevance to what it means to take a risk, and risk involvement, in turn, is an expression of who one is and would like to become. It is prospectively oriented, largely experimental, and, in these respects, a hopeful sort of activity.

The adolescents interviewed were virtually unanimous in believing that today's risks are tomorrow's memories: "The friends you have right now are the best you'll ever have, so you do things with them so that you can remember."

Explorations

1. Describe a time when you engaged in risky behavior with friends.

   _____

   _____

   _____

   a. Compare your explanation of why you did what you did with the reasons given in the reading.

   _____

   _____

   _____

2. How do you think your own risk-taking behavior is communicated to others?

   _____

   _____

   _____

   a. Did it bring you closer to anyone or any group? If so, how so?

   _____

   _____

   b. Did it have a negative or positive effect on any of your relationships? If so, how so?

   _____

   _____

Key Constructions

- Communicating risk taking
- Risk taking
- Relationship building

Key Constructions for Part Four, Section A

- Emotional coaching
- Constructions of "being hurt"
- Telling secrets
- Friendships between women
- Culture and friendships
- Cross-cultural friendship and communication
- Self construction through conversation
- Gender identity
- Teaching as friendship
- Dialectics tensions
- Independence and dependence tension
- Judgment and acceptance tension
- Communicating risk taking
- Risk taking
- Relationship building

SECTION

The Intricacies of Intimacy

If friendship is an achievement in communication, then intimacy is an advanced course. What we typically mean by calling a relationship "close" or "intimate" is that we are deeply invested in it. We depend on such relationships in significant ways: When the relationship is successful we may be elated or when it is troubled we are troubled. Often we say that we are "emotionally involved." This may mean that emotional expressions are a crucial ingredient of the relationship and expressions of love are the most obvious examples. Emotional expressions may also be used to keep the relationship on a promising course.

Expressions of joy inform the other that "this relationship is good." In contrast, irritation and anger may be used to correct the other and to urge that an unwanted action is not repeated. Emotional expressions may also be used to mark the importance of a relationship. There are rituals of "termination" available when a romance begins to fall apart and rituals of grief at the death of someone close. In effect, our emotional states are important elements of the communication process.

The intricacies of intimacy are introduced by William W. Wilmot in Reading 35. Wilmot makes very clear that we cannot know in advance what kind of actions will contribute to a close relationship. This is because there are ways in which "closeness" may be defined, and they are undergoing continuous change. For example, whether sexual intercourse defines a couple as being close depends greatly on both culture and situation. For some it is the prime ingredient of a deep relationship and for others it is merely "hooking up." Even within a close relationship the meaning of intimacy may change over time. Among aging couples the act of intercourse may be less important to their sense of intimacy than frequent, gentle touching. In his selection Wilmot introduces the important concept of *context sensitivity*. If intimacy is to be achieved, participants must pay close attention to the "competing definitions" found in a specific context.

This emphasis on contextualized sensitivity is nicely amplified in Reading 36. The authors Peter M. Kellet and Diana G. Dalton demonstrate the enormous problems faced by a romantically engaged couple when they are insensitive to how the other constructs the relationship. This case is especially interesting in that it illuminates that most of us have inconsistent or mutually conflicting constructions of what we want from a close relationship. For example, most people want openness and honesty in such relationships, but they don't want the other to say things that will hurt them. In the same way, we want relations to hold us together, but simultaneously we want to be offered freedom. We want there to be reliability and structure, but we also want novelty and spontaneity. To repeat, intimate relations are an advanced course in communication.

Negotiating about these various issues is complicated because culture is always on the move. New concepts, values, and activities are continually emerging and penetrating our social realities. For example, it has become fashionable in many circles for couples to plan weddings at an exotic location: on the beach, on a mountain, or on an island. These may be attractive ideas, but how are they to be integrated into the more traditional view of marriage as a linking of families and communities? In Reading 37 by Stuart Schrader and Catherine Dobris we present a short excerpt from the wedding vows of a young couple who tried to find a way of reconstructing traditional and liberal values into their marriage.

Linda Acitelli, author of Reading 38 on relational awareness, continues the theme of intimate relationships in marriage by looking at the ways couples define the "use" of their relationship. The importance of theory as a framework for examining communication patterns is central to her work.

Both to give you pleasure and provoke you, we have also included in this section a short poem. In Reading 39, the poet and therapist Peggy Penn fantasizes romance with a bear. Alas, the bear also lacks the proper skills necessary to build and maintain an intimate relationship.

READING 35

What Is a Close Relationship?

What is it to be close to another person? Close relationships are usually very important to us. We sacrifice a great deal for those with whom we are close. However, we have no clear way of identifying a close relationship. As William Wilmot proposes, one of the major reasons for our ambiguity in being close to another is that there are many different forms and definitions of "closeness." In particular, for many people consistently active verbal communication is central to intimacy. Yet, as Wilmot demonstrates, there are many subtle and indirect ways of expressing closeness. Developing a close relationship may depend in great part on sensitivity to these nonverbal signals.

Reading 35 WILLIAM W. WILMOT

If our relationships are created via our communication, then the road to relationship enhancement also resides in communication behavior. Relationships don't just change all by themselves; they change due to the actions and interpretations of the participants.

Even though communication is the central ingredient in the relational stew, it is not so simple to just say "do this and that" and you'll have a good relationship. The meaning of communicative moves always is dependent on each relationship context. For example, if you come from a culture where direct talk is not done, to improve the relationship by "talking about our problems" would be counterproductive—others will react to you breaking the norm. In most families, for example, direct talk about concerns is not the accepted way of dealing with difficulties. And, on the opposite end, some relational cultures require talk. Contemporary romantic relationships, for example, are now under the "you oughta communicate" belief—that direct communication nurtures and enhances the relationship. In this type of relational context, to not communicate is against the rules.

Context-sensitive communication is adaptive to the particular relationship, factoring in the cultural and personal preferences of the participants.

A context-sensitive approach validates silence, symbolic and methaphoric moves, and relationship talk as avenues for enhancement.

The largest component of a context-sensitive approach is to recognize that not all relationships have to be close or intimate to be fulfilling. If you do a survey of your own relationships, ranging from work, to classes, to friends, romantic partners and family, most of those relationships will not be intimate in nature. Most people actually have very few close, intimate relationships, and to impose an "intimacy" model onto other perfectly healthy and functional relationships distorts them and brings unnecessary dissatisfaction.

A second component of a context-sensitive approach is to grant that, even when you want a sense of "intimacy" or closeness, it can be accomplished in diverse ways. Lots of jokes currently abound regarding guys doing "male bonding": when two male friends are planning a back country ski trip together, they might say, "We are going to do some male bonding—skiing in Yellowstone for 2 weeks." Clearly, males (and others) do bond through activities, and it is a perfectly legitimate way to build a relationship of quality and substance. We overgeneralize if we see intimacy only as talk per se. Intimacy is probably more accurately defined as appreciation, warmth, and affection rather than as a synonym for self-disclosure.

A context-sensitive approach openly asks what the cultural norms are, and thereby opens our eyes to diverse ways of communication. For many cultures (and subcultures) indirect and symbolic forms of communication are the most important to master in most contexts. It is to those indirect, subtle, symbolic, and powerful forms of enhancement and enrichment that we now turn to. Indirect forms of enhancing relationships occur in all cultures, and in some cultures it is the only avenue for improvement. In societies where the protection of the other's "face" is a central value, communication needs to be indirect. Indirect communication occurs when you communicate to the hearer more than you actually say by referring to some mutually shared background information or relying on the listener's powers of rationality and inference. Often East Asian foreign students in the United States are puzzled why they are constantly being asked what they want when they are visiting American homes. In their countries, the host or hostess is supposed to know what is needed and serve accordingly.

Norms for indirectness can, of course, become rather extensive. An American from the United States (or an American from Canada) might ask you, "Please shut the door," or if trying to be indirect, say, "The door is open." In Japan, the indirectness would come out as, "It is somewhat cold today," more indirect because the door is not even referred to. If you properly understood this indirect speech, you would get up and shut the door. Another form of indirectness occurs when, in East Asian cultures, it is very important . . . to engage in small talk before initiating business and to communicate personalized information, especially information that would help place each person in the proper context. It is presumed that each person is engaged in an ongoing process; that the relationship is continually in flux.

It may well be that indirectness is the most common mode of relationship enhancement, even in western cultures. Many a young person has been dismayed when he or she goes home and asks for a "talk" with the family only to find that the family members are not willing or able to talk directly about an issue. One's parents may have grown up in a time (or place) where the popular emphasis on open communication and direct expression of conflict was not present. Many marriages, rather than being based on open expression and verbal intimacy, depend on the competent performance of role expectations—she cooks and he earns a wage. Rather than conducting marriage based on negotiation, many couples have a high respect for tact and discretion.

Gender Effects

In many cultures derived from European roots, such as in North America, males often are less expressive than females. Yet these inexpressive males do develop relationships! For many males, relationship talk is not valued as an end in itself. For example, when things are going well, there is no need for such talk (Acitelli, 1988). Males seem to value their close relationships differently and react to intimacy and control differently than do females. Because words can provoke conflict and expose vulnerability, communication is somewhat frightening for men. Male silence is discomforting to women as they require words for intimacy and feel distant from their partners in the absence of verbal sharing. If a male operates according to these generalized notions, it would be easy to dismiss an inexpressive male as "not caring." If we make "intimacy" synonymous with verbal disclosure, we bypass seeing the richness and complexity of symbolic, indirect moves made by males (and females too). As Wood and Inman (1993, p. 280) suggest, we have developed a "noninclusive view of closeness in which feminine preferences for verbal disclosures are privileged, while masculine tendencies toward instrumental activities are devalued." We have to be careful of putting such value overlays on relationships, and if we only look at verbal disclosures we will miss many of the important events that carry relational meaning.

Indirect gendered communication has also been important because it is *symbolic*; it has a rich meaning that transcends the simple acts being performed. "Being there" carries a lot of weight, especially when everyone understands its importance. In ministerial circles, it is often called the "ministry of presence"—just sit with the person at the hospital, and they know you care for them. Showing up on time, doing small favors, going out of your way to help someone, are all ways to relationally say "I value you." One example of how a concept can be unpacked for its symbolic significance is *play*. Play also serves an indirect function of relationship building. Elaine and Mike can play and giggle for hours, and their marriage is strong and growing. The sense of mutual understanding, building a shared reality, and release of tension all make play very effective. Play at work can serve indirectly to support relational closeness.

One final comment about indirect, symbolic communication. It has, of course, a power of its own, and in addition it often is at work when it is taboo to talk about certain topics. Baxter and Wilmot (1985) asked people in opposite-sex romantic relationships about what topics are "taboo"—that can't be discussed. They found that state of the relationship, relationship norms, prior opposite-sex relationships, conflict-inducing topics, or negative self-disclosure were topics best avoided.

How then does one "signal" to a partner their importance to you? Through indirect, symbolic acts that you hope will make the point to the other without having to talk about it. Indirect and implicit forms of communication need far more study; we have tended to downplay them in our focus on talking, dialogue, and "working through" issues. Clearly, relationships are built and enhanced through indirect acts.

References

Acitelli, L. (1988). When spouses talk to each other about their relationship. *Journal of Social and Personal Relationships, 5,* 185–199.

Baxter, L., & Wilmot, W. W. (1985). Taboo topics in close relationships. *Journal of Social and Personal Relationships, 2*(3), 253–269.

Wood, J. T., & Inman, C. C. (1993). In a different mode: Masculine styles of communicating closeness. *Journal of Applied Communication Research, 21,* 279–295.

Explorations

Wilmot stresses that there are many ways in which closeness can be achieved in a relationship. Verbal exchanges, such as "self-disclosure" and "talking about a problem in a relationship" may be important to many people. Wilmot suggests their importance may be exaggerated as requirements for closeness or intimacy. Just being present with someone or helping them in time of trouble can also kindle a sense of closeness.

The following quotes are all supplied by undergraduate men and women. While reading the quotes consider these questions:

- Can you choose the ways in which their definitions might suggest indirect (nonverbal) as well as direct verbal means for being "close" in friendships and romantic partnerships?
- How closely do their descriptions follow the gender lines as described by Wilmot?

WOMEN'S COMMENTS: How do you describe what it means to be close to a same-sex friend?

"To be female means it's very easy to have a close relationship with your girl-friends. We talk about things that take place in our everyday lives, e.g., how school was, what happened in class, if you saw a boy. You may be stressing and need to talk to someone, basically the need to vent, someone to look to for advice, and how to go about handling a situation. Some things are kept to yourself or discussed with friends who I feel are more reliable."

"I am very close to all my girlfriends. We tell each other our secrets, personal problems, etc. There is nothing I wouldn't tell any of them. I hug and kiss them (on the cheek) every time I see each of them."

MEN'S COMMENTS: How do you describe what it means to be close to a same-sex friend?

"I can say me and my close friend we share chemistry. We like to do the same things, such as drinking, hanging out with groups and both of us like to play sports, especially basketball. We don't talk much, but mostly we talk about cars, computers, video games, and stuff. We don't tell each other our secrets [because] we want to keep that within our self."

"I think the first bond I have with friends is the ability to laugh and have a good time with them. Another level of 'intimacy' is discovering that someone is on the same wavelength as you and that's when all subjects of discussion are fair game. My really good friends have cried with me, talked about feelings, romance, sex, rough times, the entire spectrum really."

WOMEN'S COMMENTS: How do you describe what it means to be close with a romantic partner?

"I consider being romantic close, very open, caring and loving. I think that being close with your partner does not just have to be sexual but as well as being able to tell that person anything and trusting them with it. I also think that you should be able to tell your partner your feelings on many things."

"To be close with a romantic partner is not too much different than being close to a friend. The only difference is the intimate factor, the sex. I tell my romantic partner all the things I tell my girlfriends. He is just as much my boyfriend as well as my best friend."

MEN'S COMMENTS: How do you describe what it means to be close with a romantic partner?

"It means you have a good relationship together. It means you are friends and not just romantic partners. You go out to nice restaurants and enjoy yourselves. [You] hang out with other close friends. You talk about everyday life. Talk about each person's family. I think you would tell each other certain secrets."

"To be close with a romantic partner means that you trust each other, are intimate, and share the same feelings for each other. You go to dinner, watch movies, and have sex. You talk about how great each other is. You tell your girl things you can't tell your boys and you tell your boys things you can't tell your girl."

1. How closely do these descriptions of close relationships follow the Western gender expectations described by Wilmot?

_____

_____

_____

2. How do these descriptions differ from Wilmot's position?

_____

_____

_____

3. How did the women's definitions include indirect as well as direct communication for being close in friendships?

_____

_____

_____

4. What differences did you notice between the way women and men described their romantic relationship?

_____

_____

_____

Key Constructions

- Cultural norms
- Context-sensitive approach to intimacy
- Indirect, implicit, and symbolic forms of communication
- Gender differences in expressing intimacy

READING 36

Games People Play

Couples want to know about each other, and they don't want to know about each other. When the information is difficult to integrate into a new loving relationship, it is hard to know what is best to communicate and what is best left unsaid. In Reading 36, this high-wire act becomes difficult to walk and two lovers nearly break up. The story ends happily, however, as they find ways to reconstruct the damage. Through certain helpful communication strategies, a rupture that seemed permanent was mended.

Reading 36   PETER M. KELLET AND DIANA G. DALTON

My boyfriend Jon and I have a very close relationship. We have only had one major conflict during the time we have been dating, but it almost ended our relationship.

I met Jon in July when I began working at Rock-ola Cafe, where he works as a cook. We played cards together after work a few times, and I felt myself becoming attracted to him toward the end of the year. I noticed that he was very nice, very funny, and loved animals just as I do.

Our manager had a party at his home for the Super Bowl in January, and I went, anticipating that Jon would be there. We finally got together that night. Since that night, we have spent almost every day together. I think that our relationship has developed from spending so much time together. We see each other every day, and spend the night together almost every night. During this time, we have learned about each other mostly by interacting together. We have also had many profound conversations about our own past experiences, things that are important to us now, and what we expect from our futures. However, there are topics that I think we declined to discuss for a reason—because we didn't think they were relevant issues to our relationship. For example, we never talked much about past love relationships. More important, we never discussed past sexual experiences. It is my feeling that discussions like this can hurt both parties much more than they could ever help. This is a very important detail to remember in considering the conflict.

The actual conflict took place one night when we decided to play an old game, "truth or dare," with my roommate Val. In retrospect, I can see that the decision to play this game was unwise. Before the game began, Jon and I promised that we wouldn't get mad at each other about any of our responses when we had to tell the truth. I told Jon to be sure not to ask me anything he didn't really want to know. He agreed that this was very important. However, the three of us drank beer and took shots as we played the game, and the words began to flow more and more freely. We all started out with some silly dares, but realized after a while that once you get to be a certain age, the dares just aren't as exciting. So we continued just to play truth. After we had asked each other a lot of very basic and silly questions, Jon turned to me and said, "how many people have you slept with?" To this I replied, "Remember that we agreed not to ask each other anything we don't really want to know."

For a while, Jon left this subject alone. It really bothered me that he even asked me that, but I tried to overlook it. After it seemed that, once again, we were running out of interesting questions, Jon asked me the same question. Again, I tried to stop him from asking this. However, he would not leave it alone. Finally, with the aid of several beers, I blurted out a very honest answer to his question. He got very upset when he found out the truth. He started running around the house, yelling about how he couldn't believe I had just told him that. He was shocked that I had actually told him the number of people I had slept with in the past. I was angry that he had pressured me so much, and even more angry that I had revealed something that I never intended to reveal to him or anyone else. It was really none of his business, and it wasn't what he wanted to hear. I told him to "get the hell out of my house." Jon left my house with all of his clothes, his Nintendo, and his dog. He walked six miles home. At that point, I felt that our relationship was over. The trust and respect that we had for each other was gone.

When I went to bed that night, I told myself that I didn't want to be with Jon anymore. I was sure that he felt the same. I did not see any way that we could repair the damaged feelings that we both had after this happened. When I woke up the next day, I got together the rest of Jon's belongings that he had left behind. I discussed the situation with my roommate and two of my closest friends. Everyone was surprised by what had happened. They all agreed with me that there was no way to fix this problem.

Later in the day, Jon called me and asked me if he could come over and talk. His tone over the phone revealed little. I could not tell if he was disgusted with me, upset with himself, or a little of both. I planned everything I would say. I felt that Jon was wrong for pushing me to tell him the truth about something and blowing up when I told him the truth. I could not allow myself to feel guilty for things that had been done in the past.

When Jon arrived at my house, he had roses and a card for me. He apologized for asking me the question when I had repeatedly warned him not to do so, and for the things he said to me afterward. He confessed that the truth had disappointed him because, as he said, "No guy wants to hear that he wasn't the first." He said that the actual number wasn't important, it was the fact that I was so willing to tell him. I reminded him that I was not at all willing until provoked by his nagging. I also told him that I felt bad for revealing something that might make him feel somewhat inadequate. We stayed calm and worked our way through the problem. We finally both agreed that this problem wasn't big enough to ruin our relationship. We agreed to accept each other's disappointment and put the past behind us. Now we laugh at what happened. I just honestly feel that we have both forgiven each other over it.

Interpreting the Quality of Dialogue and Negotiation

In some ways, Pam's narrative creates a sense that the conflict is both inevitable and necessary in her relationship with Jon. It is inevitable in that she describes the experience with Jon as the only major conflict the couple ever had. Because conflict is such an integral part of relational development, we may infer they were, in a sense, due for a conflict. By avoiding taboo subjects, such as past relationships and sexual history, the couple had not negotiated the dialectic of openness and closedness to reach a mutually acceptable balance. The conflict was also inevitable in that they agreed to play a game involving a great deal of personal risk and self-disclosure. The conflict was necessary so the couple could begin to negotiate the contradiction of openness and closedness together and move the relationship to a different place. In retrospect, the couple's ability to renegotiate the relational defi-nition together, bringing them closer together, was beneficial.

On the other hand, the conflict can be interpreted as damaging to the rela-tionship in two ways. First, what was said in anger can never be taken back. Second, Jon now knows something about Pam she states she never wanted to reveal about herself, which is a very real personal risk for her. However, as she explains, they now laugh about what happened. You can assume they have truly dealt with the experience and have been able to move on together.

There are several myths about relationships and communication at work in Pam's narrative. One is that relationships are built through interaction in the present, that the past is not important. Inappropriate topics from the past should [also] be avoided. Pam explains that they never discussed the taboo topic of past sexual history because she does not believe it would have done any good. She is implying the communication is not just strategic, but should be used for only positive discussions, and not for issues irrelevant to the relationship. This assumption ties into her approach to conflict as a game of "all or nothing." She states she thought their relationship was over after Jon stormed out because trust and respect had been broken. She could not see how the relationship would recover from such an event. She also sees communication as a very seri-ous process where you do not ask questions when you are not prepared to hear the answer. Her understanding of Jon and the situation led her to decide the answer to his question would not be well received. Her all-or-nothing approach to both conflict and communication, however, limited her options. She could have lied, not answered the question, or distorted the truth. However, from her perspective, the only possible response was what she calls "a very honest answer." In turn, Jon chose to interpret her answer as an act of aggression.

What Pam and Jon may learn from this conflict narrative is that there are multiple interpretations available. If you accept that you are responsible for your own experiences, you can begin to make wise choices as to what interpretations you want to use. In essence, Jon chose to feel threatened, just as Pam chose to feel required to answer, although they may not have seen it that way at all. For example, another interpretation of Pam's disclosure is that she is proud of how many people she slept with, but because of cultural constraints, it is not accept-able for her to openly announce how sexually desirable she can be. As a result, she is "pressured" into disclosing the truth. You could construct her as a woman of the world, a woman who is highly desired and in a position of power. Jon could have decided what was important was that regardless of who she could have, Pam had decided to be with him. The partners in this conflict can learn a great deal by studying this narrative and expanding their possible alternatives by explicating multiple interpretations.

Pam and Jon effectively negotiated this relational conflict by renegotiating their relationship's rules and boundaries. They decided together that this episode was not important enough to end their relationship. They listened to each other's point of view and decided to put the past behind them. This happened after Jon ran around Pam's house yelling and stormed out. It is not until they have both had a chance to come to terms with their anger that they were able to negotiate a new relational reality. Their conflict style at first is very all-or-nothing and heated. However, they confront the conflict directly. They do not avoid and repress it. They talked through the conflict together once their initial anger had subsided. They are direct and the conflict ends up being handled constructively. Ultimately, they appear to take each other's perspectives, engage one another, and reach a mutually satisfying decision about their relationship.

Explorations

1. Do you believe there are limits in what two people should share within their close relationships? Explain.

    _____

    _____

    _____

2. What have been some of the advantages and disadvantages of limiting the range of what you shared in close relationships?

    _____

    _____

    _____

3. What ways do Pam and Jon discover together that help them revive a relationship that seemed to have been "assassinated" by anger?

    _____

    _____

    _____

Key Constructions

- Communication conflict
- Dialectic of openness versus closedness
- Personal risk
- Self-disclosure

- Negotiating relational conflict
- Multiple interpretations

READING 37

Marriage Ceremonies: New Voices, New Values

The traditional marriage vows are just that: traditional. They are based on early forms of constructing gender, gender roles, and the relationship of marriage. Yet, cultures are in continuous motion, with earlier traditions comingling in various novel ways, and new forms of life continuously emerging. Thus, many people contemplating marriage today are not content with the traditional vows. They seek ways of reflecting and integrating newer discourses and ways of life. The following excerpt from the marriage vows of a Jewish couple illustrates the attempt to reconstruct the relationship of marriage.

Reading 37   STUART SCHRADER AND CATHERINE DOBRIS

We commit ourselves to one another according to the living traditions of the Jewish process and to our individual and collective philosophies of relational union. We resolve to further build on our loving relationship, and to nurture and support each other through unity and diversity, joy and despair. May our commitment enable us to grow as individuals and as a family, enjoying laughter, health, friendship and serenity. May we construct a bridge between our home and Jewish culture, heritage and changing traditions. May we continue our creation of a home guided by reverence for study, a perpetual exploration of spirituality, a continual struggle against social injustice, and the celebration of Jewish festivals. This commitment to unity is founded on principles of compassion, empathy, equality, openness, honesty and understanding. These attributes, along with love, spirituality, education, consonance with nature, and consciousness of global connectedness, underpin and guide our union.

Explorations

You will recognize in Reading 37 relational commitment grounded in particular ideals found within Jewish culture and traditions. However, return to the reading and underline or highlight phrases that suggest that the couple is attempting to integrate into their marriage the following:

- A political commitment
- A feminist commitment

- An ecological commitment
- A cultural commitment

Key Constructions

- Ritual
- Commitment and communication

READING 38

Relationship Awareness

The Western tradition is highly individualist, in the sense that we tend to think of society as composed of independent individuals, and to prize the person who is autonomous or self-directing. In Part II we challenged this view, and instead emphasized the importance of relationship in generating the very construction of the self as independent and autonomous. This issue arises again in considering the challenge of intimacy. We tend to think of intimacy in its ideal state as a bonding of individuals. We come *together*, or become one. Yet, such a bonding challenges our traditional sense of self as independent, a free spirit. This conflict gives rise to intense ambivalence about intimacy and commitment. Reading 38 reports on research with married couples, and demonstrates that talking about the "we" of the relationship can be highly valuable to their marriage.

Reading 38   LINDA ACITELLI

Relationship awareness involves attending to relationships. One can attend to relationships by thinking or by talking about them. Thus, the concept of relationship awareness bridges cognition and communication. The idea in this paper will cross another bridge, the bridge between theory building as an intellectual, scholarly, systematic process and theory building as a result of chance encounters, everyday events, and circumstance. This paper will describe the formal observations and ordinary circumstances leading to the process of theory development. As Isaac Asimov is reported to have said, "The most exciting phrase to hear in science, the one that heralds new discoveries, is not 'Eureka' (I found it!), but "Hmmm . . . that's funny."

Often, theories are born out of puzzlement. The theorist sees puzzles in everyday things that most of us take for granted. Theory building is as much about how the theorist thinks as it is about what the theorist thinks. Therefore, the process involved in developing a theory (the how) [could explore] "if you and I are talking, which kind of talk will make us feel closer: me talking about myself and you talking about your self, or us talking about how we relate to one another?"

Relationship awareness has been introduced to provide a framework for studying the effects of thinking and talking about relationships. Relationship awareness is defined as a person's focusing attention on interaction patterns—comparisons or contrasts between partners in the relationship. Included are thoughts about the couple or relationship as an entity. This awareness is not meant to imply how accurate an individual's portrayal of a relationship is, but rather the frequency of an orientation toward thinking in relational terms.

In an earlier study, 42 married couples (84 individuals) were asked to talk about their lives, as opposed to their relationships, and open-ended responses were reliably coded for relationship awareness based on the definition previously provided. Results showed that, for wives, both marital and life satisfaction were related to the proportion of time spent talking about the marital relationship. Conversely, the husbands' marital and life satisfaction were not related to relationship talk. This study suggests that focusing attention on the marital relationship is important to wives' satisfaction. Similar analyses on data from 238 couples in [the] Detroit area have replicated and extended this work. Men's and women's relationship talk (based on the same open-ended questions) is negatively correlated with both partners' depression and positively correlated with a sense of equity in the relationship. However, for women, relationship talk was also associated with six additional outcome variables: greater satisfaction with the relationship, feeling competent as a relationship partner/wife, feeling cared for in the relationship, having less tension about the partner and their sexual relationship, and having less anxiety in general. Although there are some links between relationship awareness and men's outcomes, these data seem to indicate that there are more areas in women's relationships and lives where focusing on relationships has implications.

Explorations

1. How do you explain the gender difference in the importance of relational awareness for marital satisfaction? Why does talk about one's relationship seem more important to women than men in relation to how happy one is in a relationship?

_____

_____

2. This report suggests that when couples talk about their relationship they are likely to benefit. However, much may depend on the content of their conversation, the kinds of things they talk about, and their opinions about the relationship. Discuss two kinds of relationship talk that might add happiness and two that might be threatening to a relationship.

Contributes to the Relationship: _____

_____

Undermines the Relationship: _____

_____

Key Construction

- Relationship awareness

READING 39

Dancing in the Dark

Sexual excitement, mystery, fear and fantasy combine in strange circumstances. Here communication occurs between (wo)man and beast. The poetic collision is envisioned by Peggy Penn, as she recounts a night alone in her house, with a bear on her porch.

Reading 39   PEGGY PENN

Tin cans rolling across the patio
wake me. Creeping downstairs I make a plan—
fling open the door to scare the raccoons
when a piece of the darkness separates
itself into a blurry massive shape:
on my lawn there is a bear! *a bear!*
Saliva all over the patio
where he's drooled and strewn four days of garbage.
Striped by moonlight, I watch his snout thrust deep
inside half-grapefruit rinds. He sneezes,

crams his dripping tongue inside a herring jar,
lumbers toward the compost heap and tossing
the matchstick fence over his shoulder
sits on top of the heap: bear so hungry . . .
moonlight caught on crystal tips of fur.
I reach for the phone, *they will shoot him. . . .*
Rearing, he stands upright, swaggers
to the ash tree, beefy haunches plie
up and down, loosening his back in a long rub.

I abandon the phone and my hand
floats spellbound like an oar on the air.
Between the pointed teeth in wet black gums
saliva rolls down his chest, and I feel
beads of my own sweat moving uncertainly,
finally looping under my right breast.

Reeling back to the patio he begins
a dance among the cans, a clattering,
paddling, sashay step! He turns, head up,
and through a confetti of moonlight I hear,
Dancing in the Dark. Beneath a mirrored ball
I dance back, swaying to his brush-step swing,
following his feet, just two on a floe,
a hoodlum freedom in my head, rocking
and stomping, bear on the patio, me
in the kitchen, his secret partner, turning
when he turns, lifting my bosom *to* him . . .
kicking my silent cans. But suddenly
he stops, drops down, lurches near my window

as though looking for something lost: a glove, a dance card?
Outside now, I stand in the smell, the lure
of rotten cantaloupe and mango skins
mixed with his steamy sulfurous sweat.
Forbidden Fruit hangs in the air; love
must be somewhere. I go back up the stairs
and put a blue hibiscus in my hair.

Key Constructions for Part Four, Section B

- Cultural norms
- Context-sensitive approach to intimacy
- Indirect, implicit, and symbolic forms of communication
- Gender effects in expressing intimacy
- Communication conflict
- Dialectic of openness versus closedness
- Personal risk
- Self-disclosure
- Negotiating relational conflict
- Multiple interpretations
- Ritual
- Commitment and communication
- Relationship awareness

The Fragility of Family

We often view families as "just natural." Many people even speak of their "natural family." However, family is a social construction just as friendship and intimacy are. What it means to have a family, or to be "in the family," is subject to continuous negotiation. Adolescents may sometimes feel themselves "not in the family"; adopted children may feel this way; sons and daughters can be written out of their parents' will. Many children are raised by their grandparents; sometimes groups of parents and children may come together and form what they consider a family. In some cultures families may consist of generations of related people that may number in the 100s. Occasionally friends may come together and call themselves a family.

Yet, not only is the concept of family subject to negotiation, so is the array of rights and duties that follow from being a member. In many families, only the husband is expected to provide income; in others both husband and wife are expected to produce income; often single parents alone, usually mothers, provide for their children; in some families, adolescent children are counted on for family support. In some families, everyone is expected to give their family higher priority than their friends; in other families there are few demands made on family members.

If families were like isolated islands, these issues of definition might be unproblematic. Without any interference, the participants might reach firm agreement about the family and its requirements. However, families are not isolated; their members also participate in other relationships. These relationships not only have their own demands, as do friendships and romance, but they may also influence one's definition of the family. A mother's boss may tell her that she must make business trips each month, and say to her that "the family will simply understand." The father's poker-playing friends tell him, "you deserve a night out now and then." These parents are left to negotiate these issues with the rest of the family.

The readings in this section illustrate and elaborate on the challenges of negotiating family life. Reading 40 begins with a wedding. Communication scholar Laurel Richardson relates how she is excluded at the marriage of her stepdaughter. Cultural differences add to the drama of a blended family. In many families the most enigmatic member is the father. In Reading 41 by Maggie Kirkman, the focus is on the discovery by a woman after a father's death that he was not her biological father, and the turmoil this produced for her own identity. Her inability to have some opportunity to communicate with her father adds to her anguish.

Gender differences in expressiveness are also related to differences in the way men and women define the relationship of marriage. Failure to negotiate across this divide can also create tension, and ultimately lend itself to divorce. Catherine Kohler Riessman speaks at length (in Reading 42) with men and women who have been divorced. Pivotal in many divorces is the definition of intimacy and how it is expressed. She suggests it is not that men do not wish emotional intimacy, but that their preferred forms of expression differ from women's. Women may see talk about relations and feelings as central to intimacy, whereas men more often may center on supportive behavior and sexual availability.

When a family member is threatened, family members typically put aside their differences and make strong efforts to help the individual in need. Indeed, a common construction of families is that they exist to nurture and support their members. In this vein, in Reading 43 the communication scholar Carolyn Ellis shares with readers her experiences with her dying husband. This touching account not only demonstrates her nurturing support, but shows us that even in troubling circumstances the challenge of meaning making remain. New definitions of both self and relationship may be required, definitions that may be painful to accept. Finally, in Reading 44, family therapist Froma Walsh distinguishes families that are highly resilient in the face of distress from those less successful. She describes several key attributes she has discovered in her therapeutic practice.

Wife and Stepmother Communication: Distress in Blended Families

Because of the increasing prevalence of divorce, many families today are "blended." The mother and father may bring into the marriage children from past marriages. The blended family creates particularly difficult problems in communication. Our common conception of family is one that includes allegiance. Commitment to one's family comes before other relationships, and certainly to other families. Yet, when children enter a second family they typically have commitments to the first. Who is to be given priority? Is it possible to develop a new conception of family or of multiple allegiances?

These tensions are illustrated in Reading 40 by the communication scholar Laurel Richardson. She writes a letter to a good friend about the difficulties she confronted as a stepmother attending the wedding of "her daughter." Ritual functions such as weddings are particularly difficult times for blended families because they publicly demonstrate allegiances. If the bride gives her mother priority, the stepmother will appear "second-rate." To give her stepmother priority would represent a slap in the face to her mother. In this case, the challenge of the stepmother is not to feel excluded and disrespected. The communication distress is magnified in this case because the wedding takes place in a foreign land among strangers, and the bride and stepmother do not see eye to eye. The communication between them is full of distrust.

Reading 40   LAUREL RICHARDSON

So why *did* I go to Beirut? You know why. I assessed Ernest's needs as greater than my fears, and I love him. Before we left I was telling everyone that my daughter, Helen, was getting married in Beirut. I liked how exotic it sounded, how important I felt, and how rehearsing nonchalance lulled my fears. I think I had almost convinced myself that it was true—that my daughter was getting married.

Within minutes of us getting into her fiance Jean-Paul's Mercedes 500 SEL at the Beirut airport, Helen said she wanted her "real" mother and dad to ride in the car with her to the wedding, walk her down the aisle, and for them to sit together during the ceremony. After a pause, she said those were the customs in Lebanon. In the rear view window, I saw Jean-Paul raise his eyebrows, swallow, and shake his head "no." Oh, I thought, this is familiar—Helen as conduit for her mother; Helen finding ways to protect her mother, lessen the turmoil.

Turning to look at me in the back seat, Helen said, "It's not that I don't want you here, Laurel."

I nearly choked on her words. Why would she even think to say she didn't want me here unless she didn't want me here?

"Laurel's been my wife for twenty years and she's not come half-way around the world at great personal, physical, and financial expense to be treated badly," Ernest said. The tension in the car was palpable. I almost cried. I had come to the wedding, not for Helen's sake after all, but for Ernest's sake. You know how tense and awful everything gets when the girls are around their "real" mother; how Ernest never knows what will set things off; how he's viewed as [an] accessory, like a wallet, useful when full. Already, it was starting and my presence was the catalyst.

But the marginalization of Ernest was already in the scheme of things, I think, whether I was there or not. We were assigned a seventh-floor room; Ernest's children, grandchildren, and ex-wife 15th-floor rooms. Helen left us a bottle of drinking water and baklava, telling us to enjoy ourselves and she'd see us the next day. This was early afternoon.

Everyone else was at a party at the groom's house in a village forty minutes inland, a way up into the mountains.

We nearly missed the wedding. No driver came to take us to the village until late in the afternoon, barely in time to taste the sweets and witness the "bejeweling ceremony." Jean-Paul's parents, Marianite-Catholics, live in a stone fortress enfolding four sumptuous living rooms, five baths, a look out tower, and a private well and generator, which they were using because the power had not yet been restored from the last Israeli bombing. Surrounding the house are acres of innocent looking flower beds; beyond them an electrified fence. Under the full width and breadth of the house is another house, their bomb-shelter, intended to protect them from Israelis, Syrians, and Moslem Lebanese. The people who were to be our protectors were themselves at risk.

Speaking French, Jean-Paul's father explained the Lebanese wedding customs to Ernest: the bride rides to the church with her father only; he gives her to the groom at the door of the church; the wedding couple walk down the aisle together. Would that be all right with Ernest? Of course, it was. And, of course, I felt vindicated.

Villagers lined the streets to see the bridal car, completely covered with flowers, and to get a glimpse of the bride, as if she were a royal, not merely marrying into wealth. Helen was beautiful, Jean-Paul handsome, and the cathedral wedding mass lovely and long. Six priests, three languages, flowers everywhere. The oldest priest told Jean-Paul to remain faithful to his wife and told Helen she couldn't get divorced. At the reception Perrier water flowing like wine, food for the multitudes: a whole lamb, pig, goat, salmon, unnamed fish, a three-foot sword brandished by Jean-Paul to cut the ten-layer wedding cake, a pair of doves set free, and fifteen minutes of fireworks over the Mediterranean. After dancing with Helen, Jean-Paul's father asked me to dance and the band to play jazz in Ernest's honor.

I am exhausted thinking about the contrasts—sea and mountains, rich and poor, Jewish and gentile, Christian and Moslem, mothers and step-mothers, lies and truths.

All of my academic theorizing about breaking down oppositions, decon-structing binaries doesn't help me now in any practical sense. Or has it? Has it already?

You can tell I'm home again—at home, again—using my life as entry to the realm of the un-theorized.

Meanwhile, Helen will make her life in Lebanon, while I am only comfort-able in the Lebanon of my past—my fourth-grade studies of Phoenicia.

Thanks for listening.

Love,
Laurel

Explorations

1. According to the stepmother's letter, what did the bride do to make her feel unwelcome at the wedding celebration?

   _____

   _____

2. What do you think motivated the bride to behave in this manner toward her stepmother?

   _____

   _____

3. From your own experiences in families, blended or not, what might be some ways to improve communications among these family members so that ten-sions might be eased?

   _____

   _____

Key Constructions

- Blended families
- Wedding rituals
- Intercultural family communication

READING 41

Family Stories: Who Am I?

Much has been said in preceding pages about the importance of narratives in making sense of our relationships and ourselves. Family stories are particularly important. For one, they are significant in giving a definition to the family. Stories of our vacation together, or when we had to move, give the family a sense of reality. However, they also define the members of the family. In significant degree, you know who you are in the family by the stories that are told. Stories about how you were a difficult child who really flowered as a teenager, or a wonderful child who became a difficult teenager, are important in how you view yourself and how you act toward others. Reading 41 by Maggie Kirkman deals with the outcome of destroying a story, which in this case is about the identity of one's father. Not only does it illustrate the emotional significance of family narratives, but how dependent we are on narratives in defining self and others in the family.

Reading 41   MAGGIE KIRKMAN

When I was 35 years old, nine years ago, my dad died of cancer. A few days later my mom told my sister and I that we had been conceived using donor insemination. She said, your father may not have been your real father. Initially my reaction was to feel greatly relieved. This new information explained so many unanswered questions I had; resolved a fog of confusion I had. As time went on, some of the realities of this situation sank in. I became very depressed for a while. I wasn't the person I thought I was. And my parents, the people I should be able to trust the most in life, had lied to me for 35 years about something so vital: about who I was. Rather than grieving my dad's death, I was incredibly angry at him. My mom said that when we (my sister and I) were teenagers, she had wanted to tell us about the DI, but my dad made her promise not to tell us. I am glad to know the truth, the truth is always better, but her timing was horrible. I was also upset that now I wasn't able to talk to my dad about it. As a human being, I should have a right to the truth about my own identity and history. I would like to be able to sit down and chat with [my donor], but I have accepted that most donors, especially from that time period, don't want any type of relationship. . . . I should be able to know who all of my blood relatives are, including the donor's family members and all of my half-siblings through his sperm donations, so that I wouldn't marry my half-brother, and so that my children won't marry their first cousins. It was so important to my parents for me to fit into the family because they were hiding my genetic background from the whole world: from family, from friends, from neighbors, from the school, and from my doctor. They

spent my whole time with them trying to squash me to fit into the characteristics of the family, to mold me in their image. Unfortunately, I just didn't fit into their mold. It was so painful to find out my dad had lied to me our whole life together about our true relationship, and that he felt it was none of my business. I had to redevelop my sense of identity, because I wasn't the person I thought I was.
(Kelly, DI offspring, USA)

Family stories of birth and conception, stories of how our family came to be, are fundamental to the idea of narrative identity. It is through stories that family members understand themselves and their place in the family. Parents are the narrators from whose stories their children begin to construct their own narrative identities. When the facts of life conform to the traditional narrative of sexual reproduction and biological connection, even those parents who shirk the reproductive details can rely on the schoolyard or other instruments of cultural transmission to fill in the gaps. If the facts of life deviate from the norm, however, parents must confront the need to construct an original story. They are likely to feel impelled to imbue their stories with normalcy. In a culture that elevates genes above all else, children whose family stories include an anonymous donor of gametes or embryos may feel ill-equipped to negotiate an acceptable sense of self.

Explorations

1. Can you describe a shared family narrative that is significant in defining or giving value to your family?

_____

_____

_____

_____

2. Can you describe another story shared in the family that defines the kind of child you were?

_____

_____

_____

_____

3. What if you later learned that this story was not about you, but a neighbor or sibling, or was simply not true at all? Can you describe your feelings, and their cause?

_____

_____

4. Can you speculate on why blood relations are given so much importance in contemporary society? Other than for medical reasons, why should it be so important for most people to know who their biological parents are?

_____

_____

_____

_____

Key Constructions

■ Family narrative
■ Self-definition

READING 42

Failed Relationships: Men and Women on Divorce

How do divorced people explain the breakup of their marriage? Communication failures are often at the heart of the dissolution—whether it is refusing to engage in small talk, express feelings, or agree to love making. However, these relationship failures are described differently by women and men. As the author Catherine Reissman concludes in Reading 42, marriage is based on two ideologies with specific visions forming the basis each gender uses to explain what went wrong. This reading explores these differing constructions of marriage.

Reading 42 CATHERINE KOHLER RIESSMAN

To explain why they divorced, individuals often use the phrase "lack of communication," and in doing so they are making sense of private experience by drawing on an ethic and vocabulary of love that is particular to contemporary American culture. Women, more than men, identify this interpersonal aspect as missing in marriage.

Deep Talk and Small Talk

Talk with a spouse is how women think emotional intimacy ought to be realized. At the same time that they want to talk about both "deep" topics and everyday events, they also want communication that goes beyond words and that is reciprocal. They constantly complain that [their] husbands were silent about their feelings, both positive and negative, as this proofreader describes:

> I had, for so many years, beaten my head against the wall and cried and screamed and said, "Talk to me. Tell me how you feel." And he'd go upstairs and read a book and leave me sitting down here with a bottle and nine million cigarettes, snuffling.

Not only do women want to talk about emotions, they also want "small talk"—about mundane things that happen during the day at the job or at home. They especially want verbal interaction about work—their own as well as their husbands'—but, as they construct it, their husbands are at fault because they will not talk about these topics, at least with them.

A particularly vivid example of the importance of talk for women and the conflict it creates in marriage is given by Betty:

> Well, one time he was sitting here reading his newspaper (points to chair in living room). I just wanted to talk, walk over and say, "Hi, I remember you," you know, anything. I set his newspaper on fire to get attention. I did that once and boy he got mad. See, playing is so important to me, you don't know how important, especially after being married to someone who was not playful. Yeah, there was a lot of times when I felt like I was being crazy and I was being crazy all by myself.

The Expectation of Reciprocity

Women expect reciprocity in verbal exchanges but, as they look back on their marriages, too often they see "one-way love." [One women states:]

> I felt like I was talking to a bank president, you know, who was telling me about a loan I was defaulting on. I was just so discouraged. There was no compassion. There was no hug. And it reminded me of other times I had cried and how he always turned to stone.

Women of all social classes often make reference to friendship in explaining what emotional intimacy ought to be like.

A woman on welfare looks back on her marriage and invokes the image, saying, "My husband was never a friend to me, we were like bedmates." Friendship, women of all backgrounds suggest, entails talking and listening, giving and getting, equality not hierarchy.

Primacy and Companionship for Women

A common explanation for divorce in the accounts of both women and men is that they had "nothing in common" with their spouses. This reflects the belief about modern marriage that the conjugal relationship is the primary relationship, one that takes priority over all others. Joint activities and shared leisure are expected because they vivify the bond between the spouses. More than half of those in the sample make sense of their divorce in the context of problems with companionship and its corollary complaint—that the commitment to the marital tie was not primary enough. Women interpret the relationship between primacy and companionship differently than men do, and women in different social circumstances see the issues in contrasting ways, as well.

Women do not expect husbands to relinquish ties to kin and friends nearly to the extent that men expect this from women. Women usually do not fulfill this expectation. Repeatedly, women note that their husbands were resentful when they wanted to spend time with close friends. Often, but not always, conflicts arose when women were needed by friends or family members in crisis, as this salesclerk describes:

> My mom was going to have a mastectomy. And I told him I was going home. And he never wanted anything to do with my family. I was his and no one else's. As soon as he found out I wanted to go home, [he said], "No, you are not going," to which I replied, "I am going, she is my mother, if you don't like it, too bad." And I went.

"I was his and no one else's"—this lament is echoed implicitly or explicitly by many women. As women construct it, they do not expect this exclusivity from husbands. They do not define the marital relationship as emotionally exclusive, relegating kin and friends to a marginal position.

Rather than keeping husbands to themselves, women seek to integrate the family into a larger social world of kin and friends, and sometimes they even use these ties to buffer and preserve the troubled marriage.

Women do not expect primacy nearly to the extent men do, but they still expect companionship in marriage—to "do things together." Women's ideas of what these joint activities ought to be differ markedly from men's. An office manager describes one of the hopes she had when she married that was never realized:

> We got married in April and the first Christmas, I mean, see, I always have these dreams and everything has to go with the way the dream is. . . . I wanted to go to midnight Mass with my husband, only he didn't want to go. . . . It used to bother me going to Christmas alone, church alone.

"Going to Christmas alone"—this woman's slip of the tongue reveals the loneliness of a companionless marriage.

As women construct it (especially women whose husbands had working-class occupations), "male" leisure pursuits get in the way of doing things together. A clerical worker interprets her resentment this way:

> See, the type of recreations he had were, like I say, more male-oriented. Like, "Let's go to the bar, or Hialeah, or the dog races," things like that which I didn't care to attend. And he didn't want me to come anyway. It's like there were two worlds and there was no way of putting them together.

Women's accounts suggest that they have strong feelings about where and how joint leisure ought to occur in marriage that, in turn, reflect gender divisions. Women, particularly those in working-class occupations, speak over and over again of wanting to "go out," intimating that the home is no place to spend time that is not focused on household chores and child care.

Women's Views About Sex in Marriage

Sexual gratification for both wives and husbands is a core aspect of modern marriage, something taken for granted.

Given the high value placed on sex in American culture, it is not surprising that sexual issues figure in nearly 60 percent of the divorce accounts. Women and men interpret sexual events in distinctive ways, however.

Sexual infidelity was mentioned in 34 percent of the accounts. Women take this action very seriously and interpret it as evidence of betrayal or as the catalyst for divorce. For Gloria discovering the affairs was significant to her because they were proof that her husband could not be trusted. In this construction (which other women share), it is not only the sexual behavior itself but what it signifies about the spouse's character that is disturbing to the wife. This deeper discovery—that the husband is not the person the wife thought he was—is especially troubling because it compromises her ability to love in return.

Gloria makes this point clear:

> Although I still had the love, the freedom to love him just got absolutely slammed shut even though we had a relationship after that [discovery of the first affair]. Not with my heart in it.

For another group of women, affairs mean something different. Although these women still view affairs as very serious and as key turning points in the decision to divorce, they believe that the marriage was "over" in an emotional sense by the time that the affair occurred. In this construction, the affair is the catalyst for separation but the web of explanation for the problem goes deeper.

Not only do women see their husbands' infidelities as the catalyst; they define their own in this way as well. A recurrent plot exists in some women's accounts: their marriage existed "in name only," they then "met someone" and fell in love, and this provided the "push" needed to end the marriage. A teacher speaks directly about the emotional logic, which was also implicit in several other women's explanations, behind this scenario:

> It really took meeting somebody else before I could leave. I might have left anyway, but I think it would have taken a lot longer. . . . I think it might have taken meeting somebody else because I'm so afraid of being alone.

By making sense of infidelity in these ways, women are drawing on a gendered belief that sex and emotional closeness go hand in hand—that sex and love cannot be separated. In this belief system, women's sexual infidelity is justified in the absence of deep emotional ties to a spouse. Similarly, husbands' affairs are legitimate cause for ending a marriage because they mean that the husbands are giving away their love—to the women they are sleeping with, rather than to their wives.

In women's talk about sexual gratification there is additional evidence that women tend to link sex and intimacy. A number of women raise the issue of marital sex while talking about emotional closeness in their marriage. As closeness began to wane, so did sex. A factory worker talks explicitly about the connection between physical and emotional intimacy:

> To me, sex isn't just sex. It doesn't bother me not to have sex. To not have a relationship would bother me more than not having sex. In a close relationship, in a close feeling with someone, of sharing and confiding, and being together and cuddling, to me sex is a natural thing. Without that I don't want it. Consequently, there were many times we had problems [and] he wanted to have sex and I wasn't interested.

Men's Constructions of Emotional Intimacy

Like women, some men blame divorce on "lack of communication." Only one-third of the men (as opposed to two-thirds of the women) say they did not get the emotional intimacy they expected from marriage.

In their accounts of their marriages, men blame themselves for not living up to women's standards of intimacy. . . . They were the silent partners in marriage, not giving wives enough "love and understanding." When they talk about specifics, however, it is clear that their style involves less talk and more action. [One man states:]

> I think that was the problem in the marriage . . . my wife felt I didn't talk enough. I keep things very much to myself, and I'll act and she'll feel, like, "Where in the hell is this coming from because there's never been any prelude to this, we never talked about this and all of a sudden, he's done something." In my own mind, I've worked it out. But I'm not the type of person to sit down and discuss things with people at any length.

In men's definitions of emotional closeness, talk is not the center piece. Rather, men expect wives to be there for them in much fuller ways. . . . Men want a variety of physical and other concrete demonstrations of intimacy. A factory worker vividly depicts what was missing in his marriage:

> When you come home from work at night . . . just to have somebody greet you at the door with open arms, you know, kiss and ask how you are, or how your day went. I never received that.

It is important that his wife be at the door, with "open arms" and a kiss—physical manifestations of caring. Note that his expectations for intimacy here are unidirectional. Like a number of other men, he complains that he did not "receive" love. In his view, marriage is a kind of haven, a place to retreat to, where he can be tended by a wife, away from the pressures of alienated work. In exchange for her emotional support of him, he expects to support her financially. This is reciprocity as many men understand it.

Primacy and Companionship for Men

Men assume that they will have easy access to their wives when they marry. They expect that the marital tie will be the primary tie for them and for their wives, that the couple will be self-contained. Consequently, men count on spending considerable time with their wives—alone together, as a couple.

Men's central complaint (nearly half mention it) is that wives are not "there" for them because they are not emotionally exclusive. In their minds, their wives' other relationships limit the time the couple can spend alone together and undermine the primacy of the marriage. Continuing bonds and obligations to kin are often seen as the problem.

Men in middle-class occupations are more likely than those with working-class jobs to complain about wives' kin ties. Joe, though he has mentioned growing up in a large, close extended family, wanted a different sort of life with his wife. He described in a vivid way the variety of relationships that occupied his wife and, even more, took over their home:

> Jackie was like a little old lady in the woods who lives with sixty-four cats. Anytime something wandered to the back door that was injured, which is fine, I mean, if an animal is injured, I took it in too and I played doctor. But I didn't want to keep them, and she ended up gradually building up to a whole house full of animals.

Cats, brothers, sisters, mothers and the obligations wives feel to them—men echo this lament over and over. As men see it, wives' over-involvement in the lives of others interferes with marital "privacy," especially when wives respond to others' trouble by giving them a temporary home.

A handful of men resent the time and attention that children require from their wives. This is especially true if the children are from the wife's previous marriage because they acutely compromise the primacy of the couple relationship.

Men want the home to be their haven from work. Children and relatives (particularly if they move in) severely diminish peace and quiet at home and interfere with easy access to emotional support. Husbands have a hard time enjoying their wives and getting what they need from them with so many others around. Under these conditions, men feel that they have to compete—that there is not enough attention to go around. They believe that the home should be their space, for they have worked hard to get it, and that they should not have to share it. (For some, having a wife and children is similarly their accomplishment, evidence of their lineage.) A lawyer spoke of his resentment of the collectivity of his wife's women friends, who, as members of a consciousness-raising group, invaded his home on a regular basis.

A related ideal of modern marriage that both men and women prize is doing things together with a spouse, enjoying companionship when not working. Husbands expect easy access to their wives for leisure activities but, as they experience it, their wives are either too busy or do not want to do what they want to do. Tension over different leisure interests is especially characteristic of marriages that working-class men describe. Free time is especially important for these men, who have little control over their work, yet working-class marriages (more than middle-class ones) tend to be sex-segregated, and consequently, men's leisure interests are often different from women's.

As one man lamented:

> I don't think she ever rode my motorcycle. Which is no big deal, but I thought she should try it. It's not that big a thing, but enough things like this add up.

Although men with professional occupations complain less about lack of shared leisure with wives, when they do it is almost as if the existence of contrasting interests constitutes "proof" that the marriage is not viable. These men reason that if a marriage does not provide companionship, it offers nothing at all.

Institutionalized Roles

Men and women make sense of their divorces by drawing on an ideal of what modern marriage is supposed to provide: intimacy, primacy and companionship, and sex. Although women and men are alike in noting these three aspects, they tend to define and value each some what differently, as we have seen, which suggests that women and men construct marriage in quite distinctive ways. The ideology of the companionate marriage is, in fact, two ideologies—his and hers—with specific visions forming the basis each gender uses to explain what went wrong.

Explorations

1. This reading suggests that in terms of intimate relationships, men and women live in different realities with different values. To what extent do you think this applies to your life?

   _____

   _____

2. To the extent that men and women do have different ideologies of marriage, are these differences permanent? If not, how can the partners change?

   _____

   _____

Key Constructions

- Emotional intimacy talk
- Companionship
- Small talk
- Gendered communication
- Relational reciprocity
- Family and friendship integration
- Institutionalized roles

| READING 43 |

Fighting for (and Despite) Dear Life

One might assume that arguments and disagreements disappear when a loved one is dying. Yet, communication complexities are not necessarily simplified by this dire, immutable fact. In Reading 43, Carolyn Ellis despairs that she and her beloved, Gene, cannot seem to avoid verbal disagreements, although they both wish to do so. One hopeful part is that of taking the perspective of the other. Although not always successful, it is a helpful alternative to remaining locked within one's own (very sensible) point of view. You will also note in this excerpt the ways in which a friend can be helpful in reframing one's position about a particular issue.

Reading 43 CAROLYN ELLIS

"Mr. Weinstein's pulmonary disorder is best described as 'end-stage' in that he has a one-year prognosis. Over the next year my patient's chronic lung disease will progressively worsen and he will need specialized homecare facilities if we are to limit the number of repeat hospital admissions." Although Dr. Simpson had informed me that Gene probably would not live more than a year, the words in the letter he sends to verify to the insurance company our need for a nursing service shock both of us. "A year," Gene asks, "just a year?"

"The doctors can't predict. And," I remind him, "we asked him to do a 'worst case' to give us a chance for reimbursement." Since my rationalizations make us feel better, I ignore the voice that says this prognosis probably is optimistic.

Gene makes arrangements for a nurse four hours a day, three days a week. Mary is cheerful and gets along well with Gene. At least once a week, she accompanies him on errands and to doctor and dental appointments, and she fixes his lunch each day. Gene likes her companionship and getting out of the house. I like the rescue from weekly grocery and drugstore errands.

By end of September, life is less rosy. The insurance company refuses our nursing claim. The services the nurse provides, they argue, could be done by a nurse's aide or companion, which they, of course, don't cover. Although we can afford twelve hours of care a week at $15 per hour, what happens when we need more? Our hesitation to increase nursing hours adds to the growing tension.

On September 28, I write:

I feel back in the rut again. I felt so much love when he was in the hospital. Now we are fighting. It's over control again. Whenever he has been sick and gets better, we argue. He feels I take over, which I do when he's sick. Then he wants control again when he's better, but it's hard for me to give it back. How do we get out of this pattern?

Just today we had a fight. Gene had planned to buy me weight equipment for my birthday. We had a good time looking at the different options (although I was a little embarrassed to be with a man who had oxygen in his nose). First, Gene got upset because I considered getting equipment that cost $1400 instead of the $400 set he wanted to buy, even though I would pay the difference. He said I wouldn't use it much. I said I would. He said I had robbed him of the pleasure of buying a present for me and that it made him feel like a cheapskate. So I gave in.

He wanted to put the equipment in the garage, instead of the spare bedroom as I had planned. I said no.

He demanded that we have it delivered and set up. Since it would cost over $50, I insisted on doing it myself. When I asked my neighbor to help me carry the equipment into the house, Gene blew up. He said he didn't want that kind of obligation to Bob. I exploded. "This is between Bob and me," I screamed. He said I should have conferred with him before asking Bob. I told him that I was an individual and could make decisions without him.

So what started as a treat ended in argument. I didn't understand it. Only later did I write:

> This was a much bigger deal to Gene. This event was a tiny part of my very busy life. It was a large part of his not so busy life. That puts it into perspective for me. I wish it would for him too.
>
> He feels that giving me gifts is a way of doing things for me since he has greater financial resources. I had partly robbed him of that by wanting equipment costing more than he wanted to pay. Gene's male ego was hurt when I asked another man to help me do what he couldn't. He wanted to compensate by paying for the equipment to be delivered and I wouldn't let him.

Gene felt good for a couple of weeks and then, suddenly, his condition changed drastically. Except for the time in the hospital, he was worse than ever. Decreasing the massive doses of steroids had left him weak, frail, and unable to move around. After our rising expectations, the drop was a huge disappointment. As usual, we took our time facing the problem. The increased tension and worn-thin patience were most apparent when we tried to leave the house.

Getting ready to go out to dinner has zapped most of our energy: his, to get himself ready; mine, to deal with all the preparations—fill the oxygen tank, make sure the wheelchair battery is charged, find the pill box under the seat, remember the antacid. Oh, no, the oxygen tank won't shut off. Get the hair drier and an extension cord. When we finally are ready to go, Gene spills urine on me from the bottle we carry in the van.

Now, I have another task—clean up the piss. I have taught all day and have looked forward to a nice dinner. "I'm sorry," I say, knowing I appear upset. "I'm not mad at you. I just get tired of the disasters."

He replies sadly, "Yeah, me too. And I always cause them." My heart goes out to him; at the same time, I can't get rid of my anger. I think of all the accidents of the last few days, like yesterday when he backed into a neighbor's car and caused $140 worth of damages.

By the time I calm down, I must deal with getting into the restaurant; the battery on the Amigo is loose; the lift gets snarled up; Gene can't breathe. Finally, my frustration starts to dissolve and Gene tries to be gay. But when the food is served, Gene's shaky hands spill a glass of wine into my plate and over my white pants. The waiter moves us to another table and gets another entree. "I can't believe you did that," I say to Gene's silence. "This is too hard." I feel sorry for both of us when I realize that any possibility for gaiety has ended, but I need to be angry now. If I cap it, the pain, the frustration, the fear, everything will explode. We realize then that our reprieve is over. Solemnly, we finish dinner, not tasting anything, and come home.

We no longer talk enthusiastically about marriage. Instead, we say, "Well, if you want it or need it, I would do it." I have cold feet, and hope he doesn't pursue it; perhaps Gene is protecting himself or responding to the negative energy between us.

My close friend Elva asks me, "Do you feel trapped?"

"Yes, I do, but I get something from him even now. And I made the bargain. I chose this."

"That doesn't mean you don't feel trapped. You had no way of knowing what it would be like."

"Not in my wildest imagination."

What relief I feel that someone understands and doesn't blame me for making the choice, nor Gene for the situation.

A few days later I write:

> I am all bottled up. Work and worry. I don't like it. I want to be light and lively again. What to do? Therapy is not the answer. Who or what is? I'll try anything. For now I'll take a good affair. I know why I want outside sex. It is the only way I know to get emotional release.

"He's so sick," I tell my friend, Sherry, a physician. "And our battles have gotten worse. When he is irascible, I scream back at him."

Sherry is supportive and encourages me to talk, then hugs me as I cry. "It looks like he'll be around for a while," she says, "so it would be best if the two of you could make this easier."

"I know. I want to. But I'm not sure his living a long time is the best thing." Although I know I have only released a trickle from the dam, I feel relieved. Talking and crying with friends is more helpful than therapy.

"I'd like to talk even though it's midnight," I say to Gene when I arrive home. He immediately turns off the TV, and we move to the kitchen table to discuss our interpretations of recent events. The battle over the weight equipment exemplifies our battle over control. Gene finally acknowledges he is responding to his shrinking world and I admit I am acting out of fear of his deterioration; we understand now that much of the problem stems from our emotional responses to his declining health.

"I'm really needy," I say, going a step further in revealing myself. "And it's difficult to talk to you about it." This conversation shocks and hurts Gene every time it comes up.

"I want you to be able to talk to me about everything."

"You know I love you?" I ask.

"Yes, you know I love you?"

"Yes, but I can't let down with you because I don't see you as being strong now," I say with care.

"But I am."

"No, not always," I respond. "You can't be because of your body."

"I guess I understand," he says sadly, "but I wish it were different. You have to let me try."

When he complains that he has no one to talk to, I reply, "You have Joan."

"But she isn't here, and, anyway, I don't like to talk about you. I have nothing to do, no social life."

"With your health problems, it's difficult to meet people," I say. We discuss his dependence on me and my unavailability because of my job. We ask how we can make his life better. Can he deal with the smoke-filled bridge room again?

We stay up until 2:00 A.M., something I usually won't do because of work. As I fall asleep, I think about how much I organize my life around my job, and it makes me question my values. Shouldn't my relationship be more important than my work? Especially now? I cuddle up close. This quiet night suddenly contrasts with the last two weeks. Gene usually tosses and turns all night now, even sometimes sitting up in bed. Occasionally his hand involuntarily shoots up and remains suspended, as though the nerves have a mind of their own. Then his body trembles and shakes. To sleep, I have had to move to my side of the bed. I grieve that night for the loss of my comforter and sleeping companion.

Explorations

1. If you had been shopping for exercise equipment with your sick partner, as Carolyn was, how might you have communicated in order to minimize the friction?

    _____

    _____

    _____

2. All of us face angry moments in relationships. This is normal. The important question is how to deal with such clashes in a way that significant damage does not result. What can you do or say to ease the tension of accusations, insults, hurt expressions, or silences? Can you indicate three ways of dealing with these types of tensions so that you are better able to take the other's perspective?

    _____

    _____

    _____

Key Constructions

- Taking the other's perspective
- Easing tensions

Family Resilience

Traditionally we speak of specific individuals as being vulnerable or easily shaken up, or contrastingly, as robust and resilient. However, in the pages of this book we have emphasized the significance of relationship. Most all our actions, we propose, emerge from our communicative relations with others. This focus on relationship is sharpened in Reading 44 by Froma Walsh, in which she shares her experience working with families. She is struck with the capacity of families to weather the storms of stress and disappointment, and the ways in which family interaction can support and protect individual family members.

Reading 44   FROMA WALSH

Resilience—the ability to overcome life's challenges—has been a valuable concept in understanding and treating individual survivors of trauma and adversity. With the overwhelming pressures on family life today contributing to a high rate of family breakdown, we need more than ever to understand and strengthen the ways in which families can survive and thrive. Marital vows express a commitment "for better or for worse, for richer or for poorer, in sickness and in health." These vows are based in a recognition that no family is problem-free; all relationships must surmount crises over the life course. We are all aware of the high risk of divorce—nearly 50% of marriages fail. But what can we learn from the 50% of marriages that succeed? What processes enable family members to build and sustain enduring relationships through turbulent times? To cope well with an illness that can't be cured or a problem that can't be solved? To regenerate after losses through death, divorce, or other life-altering transitions (such as job loss, migration, or community disaster)? To rise above severe trauma or the barriers of poverty and discrimination? Studies of resilient individuals and well-functioning families shed light on the key processes that can strengthen couples and families to meet life's challenges.

Drawing together the fruits of over two decades of research and my own clinical experience, this reading presents a family resilience framework for therapeutic and preventive efforts with couples and families. Rather than simply providing a set of techniques to treat or change families, this strength based approach enables therapists and others (including family members themselves) to draw out the abilities and potential in every family, and to encourage the active process of self-righting and growth. As families increase their capacity to rebound from immediate crises and to weather persistent stress, they also gain vital resources to deal more effectively with future challenges. Thus, in building family resilience, every intervention is also a preventive measure.

The term "family resilience" refers to coping and adaptational processes in the family *as a functional unit*. How a family confronts and manages a disruptive experience, buffers stress, effectively reorganizes, itself and moves forward with life will influence immediate and long-term adaptation for every family member *and* for the very survival and well-being of the family unit. Views of normality and health are socially constructed, influencing clinical assessment and goals for healthy family functioning. The vision of a so-called "normal" family is largely in the eye of the beholder, filtered by professional values, personal family experience, and cultural standards. Two myths of the "normal" family have perpetuated a grim view of most families.

One myth is the belief that healthy families are problem-free. Based in the medical model, health has been defined clinically as the absence of problems. Unfortunately, this leaves us in the dark about *positive* contributions to healthy functioning. More seriously, it leads to the faulty assumption that . . . my problem is symptomatic of and caused by a dysfunctional family. This belief has tended to pathologize ordinary families attempting to cope with the stresses. No family is problem-free; slings and arrows of misfortune strike us all, in varying ways and times over each family's life course. What distinguishes healthy families is not the absence of problems, but rather their coping and problem solving abilities.

A second myth is the belief that the idealized "traditional family" is the only possible model for a healthy family. For most, this conjures up the 1950s' image of a white, affluent, nuclear family headed by a breadwinner/father and supported by a full-time homemaker/mother. In the wake of massive social and economic upheaval over recent decades, nostalgic images of a simpler past are understandable but are out of touch with the diversity of family structures, values, and challenges of our changing world. Yet families that don't conform to the "one-norm-fits-all" standard have been stigmatized and pathologized by assumptions that alternative forms inherently damage children. Families of varied configurations can be successful. It is not family *form*, but rather family *processes*, that matter most for healthy functioning and resilience.

A family resilience approach builds on these developments, enables us to shift from seeing families as damaged to understanding how they are challenged by adversity. It also corrects the faulty assumption that family health can only be found in a mythologized ideal model. Instead, this approach seeks to understand how all families, in their diversity, can survive and regenerate even with overwhelming stress. It affirms the family potential for self-repair and growth out of crisis and challenge.

A resilience-based stance in family therapy is founded on a set of convictions about family potential that shapes all intervention, even with highly vulnerable families whose lives are saturated with crisis situations. Collaboration among family members is encouraged, enabling them to build new and renewed competence, mutual support, and shared confidence that they can prevail under duress. This approach fosters an empowering family climate, reinforcing the possibilities that members can overcome seemingly insurmountable obstacles by working together, and that they will experience success as largely due to their shared efforts, resources, and abilities. Experiences of shared success enhance a family's pride and sense of efficacy, enabling more effective coping with subsequent life adaptations. A particular solution to a presenting problem may not be relevant to future problems, but the promotion of *resilient processes* can prepare families to surmount unforeseen problems and to avert crises.

Creative Brainstorming

When problems are identified, it's important to involve family members in creative brainstorming. In well-functioning families, parents act as coordinators—bringing out others' ideas, voicing their own, and encouraging choice. Family members speak up, and the contributions of all members, from eldest to youngest, are respected as valuable.

Family members are encouraged to discuss both resources and constraints, and to consider a range of options, weighing the costs and benefits for all family members. Openness to trying new solutions to meet new challenges is a hallmark of well-functioning, adaptive families. This flexible and inventive approach builds resourcefulness.

Intervention efforts with the Wolff family focused on resolving both practical and emotional aspects of the family's problems [how to care for Mrs. Wolff's mother]. Joining with Mrs. Wolff's desire to provide the best care for her mother, the therapist suggested that there might be other ways to accomplish this aim besides doing it all on her own. She encouraged the parents' collaborative brainstorming and information gathering to consider a range of home-based services and placement options for "Nanna."

Mr. Wolff's involvement, which brought needed support to his wife, was framed also as an opportunity for him to share more fully in care giving arrangements, as he wished he had done for his own mother. The therapist provided a caring context for this emotion-laden problem solving, exploring each partner's conflicted feelings and encouraging mutual empathy. A family session explored the son's mixed feelings as well his love for Nanna and sadness at her decline, along with his guilt or wishing that he hadn't had to give up his room to her. Normalizing and contextualizing the many feelings of family members as natural and common in their stressful situation were helpful in reducing blame, shame, and guilt. The therapist affirmed the family's honesty and caring intentions.

It was noted that perhaps the most important family member was missing from their problem-solving efforts—Nanna herself. Mr. and Mrs. Wolff were encouraged to include the grandmother in the planning for her care by having conversations with her at home and asking for her input to our next session. They were surprised to learn that she was acutely aware of the care giving complications, but that she had been constrained from talking about them because she felt like such a burden. She came to feel more valued when her feelings and preferences were considered in making plans.

Shared Decision Making: Negotiation, Compromise, and Reciprocity

To be successful negotiators, all family members need to learn how to talk and listen with compassion and understanding. They need to avoid and interrupt negative cycles of criticism, blame, and withdrawal—the attacks and defensiveness that corrode relationships. Those who are able to sustain happy relationships learn how to repair conversations that go badly and how to soothe each other when hurt or upset: One person might say, "This isn't working: let's try talking about this again," or "Let's both cool down and try to resolve our differences more calmly when we can hear each other." Such nurturing, monitoring, and support strengthen relationships as problems are resolved.

Explorations

1. In this reading, Froma Walsh emphasizes the importance of collaborative problem solving. Describe three additional activities you believe can make a contribution to family resilience.

   _____

   _____

   _____

2. This reading emphasizes actions that contribute to family resilience. Now consider the opposite: Describe three kinds of actions in the family that lead to the members' inability to provide support and strength to one another (risk factors or barriers toward resilience).

   _____

   _____

   _____

3. Walsh is particularly interested in the capacity of families to be resilient. However, most people belong to more than one group. They are also participants in friendships, clubs, teams, and so on.

Single out a group of which you are a part, and describe the members' capacities to support and strengthen one another.

_____

_____

_____

_____

Key Constructions

- Family resilience
- Creative brainstorming
- Shared decision making

Key Constructions for Part Four, Section C

- Blended families
- Wedding rituals
- Intercultural family communication
- Family narrative
- Self-definition
- Emotional intimacy talk
- Companionship
- Small talk
- Gendered communication
- Relational reciprocity
- Family and friendship integration
- Institutionalized roles
- Taking the other's perspective
- Easing tensions
- Family resilience
- Creative brainstorming
- Shared decision making

From Conflict to Reconciliation

It should be clear from the readings so far that conflict is almost inevitable in any important relationship. Indeed, many scholars feel that we should be suspicious of any relationship without conflict. For one, if there is no conflict it may mean suppression. One member of the relationship holds so much power that another is afraid to voice any differences. Or, in some cases a lack of conflict may indicate a lack of involvement. It is easy to agree with someone if you don't depend on them in some way. Finally, a lack of conflict can mean that a relationship is dying. In relying always on the tried-and-true conventions in a relationship, interest and enthusiasm may disappear. It is when someone says something different, unusual, and unsettling that we become engaged; our curiosity peaks, and we may find ourselves growing in interesting ways.

At the same time, few people like intense conflict, and indeed, such conflict is often the prelude to the breakdown of relationships. In Section D we focus on ways of reducing the intensity of conflict, on enabling differences to coexist, and on moving from conflict to appreciating differences.

In Reading 45 we draw from the work of two mediation specialists, Stephen W. Littlejohn and Kathy Domenici. They work with both individuals and organizations looking for ways to ease intense conflict. They draw attention to the importance of asking "systemic questions." These questions focus attention away from the content of what is said to how what we say is related to broader patterns of meaning between us. Thus, in a marriage, systemic questions might not be so concerned with "why are you so angry?" but "what impact does your expressions of anger have on your spouse . . . or on your children?" Such questions allow participants to reflect on their communication and its place within relationships. As a result, new and often more promising lines of discussion are opened.

When people are in conflict they frequently seek out others with whom to share their sense of what is real and right. This means that conflicts rapidly accelerate. We draw others into them, often to the point that we have intergroup conflicts. Conflicts between groups are especially difficult to resolve because the participants are supported in their views by so many others. That the opposition is "wrong," "immoral," or "stupid" seems so very clear when we have others who agree with us.

In Reading 46 by Carol Becker, Laura Chasin, Richard Chasin, Margaret Herzig, and Sallyann Roth, we are introduced to an important form of conflict negotiation called the Public Conversations Project. A group of family therapists have developed a powerful conversational technique for moving beyond mutual hatred. Many of the dialogic moves they use in their work can also be valuable aids in our everyday conflicts. Much has been said in earlier readings in this book about the importance of narrative in constructing our worlds. In the Public Conversations Project the participants' personal stories, or narratives, are an important part of the conflict-reducing process.

In Reading 47 Grace Feuerverger describes her work in the School for Peace, which is nestled in a small village in Israel. This school brings Israeli and Palestinian high school youth together. Because of the fierce antagonism between Israel and Palestine, and the growing number of brutal deaths that have resulted on both sides, moves toward peace are difficult. The School for Peace attempts to break through the walls of separation, to overcome hatreds and to prepare the grounds for mutual understanding. As this reading demonstrates, personal narratives are a major vehicle for "border crossings."

There are no tried-and-true formulas for reducing conflict. Like our conversations, each conflict situation is different. Continuous creativity is essential. This means thinking creatively about not only our use of language, but also what kinds of conversations might be useful.

We must consider the activities in which people are engaged together. For example, conflict specialists often rely on sports, outdoor challenges, or joint projects to enhance positive communication between opposing groups. In Reading 48, Jonathan Shailor invites us to think innovatively, by introducing the practice of empowering theater. Shailor works in prisons to give voice to inmates by inviting them to dramatize their own lives. He brings about insights and understanding through this process that may lead to more promising and less conflict-intensive futures for the participants. Finally, in Reading 49 organizational consultants, David L. Cooperrider and Diana Whitney, describe an enormously successful practice—appreciative inquiry—used to replace conflict with positive building toward a better future.

READING 45

Systemic Questions: The Importance of "Us"

Conflict essentially relies on division; that is, the presumption that there are at least two or more separate parties in contention. Given that the way in which we talk constructs the taken-for-granted world, the very conception of conflict lends itself to tensions between individuals or groups. As we speak, then, of "individuals in conflict" we create a sense of difference, distance, and alienation. Yet, by the same token we can also reduce these tendencies toward conflict by speaking about ways in which we are united, or part of the same system—not "me" versus "you" but we together within a larger array of relationships. In this excerpt, mediation specialists Stephen W. Littlejohn and Kathy Domenici talk about their use of systemic questions in conflict resolution.

Reading 45   STEPHEN W. LITTLEJOHN AND KATHY DOMENICI

Systemic questions are designed to help participants talk about relationships. Systemic questions can help build a sense that one is part of a larger system and is constructing a social reality through its interaction. Systemic questions call attention to the ways in which actions elicit other actions and how statements and behaviors are connected to other statements and behaviors. Such questions help participants see how their thoughts, actions, and statements are not isolated, but connected to what others think, do, and say. . . . These questions also tune people into the time dimension. They focus attention on the flow of events from one thing to another and the connection of events over time. We might ask, "How was it different then?" or "What changed when Betty was moved out of the work group?" In this process, people will begin to talk about how things have changed, and they can begin to imagine patterns of change that might happen in the future.

We recently mediated a dispute between a department head and a physician in a hospital. As with most mediations, this began with each party telling us the horrible things they couldn't stand about the other party, the things the other one had done that offended or hurt them in some way. We began to ask systemic questions designed to widen the circle and shift the conversation to connections within the larger system. We asked who else was involved and how they were involved. We asked how people acted and responded when others did certain things. We asked them to reflect on their own behavioral responses to the actions of the other and how the other person reacted to their reactions.

While story questions ask people to provide more detail about their own experience, perspective, or point of view, systemic questions require that disputants get out of their own heads and think about what their comments elicit in others and what others' comments elicit in them. For example, you can ask participants to reflect on what it might be like for others to be listening to what they have to say. We sometimes ask, "What have you been trying to say today that John is having a hard time hearing?" We can reverse this, of course, by asking participants to reflect on their own role as listeners: "What has John been trying to say that you are having a hard time hearing? What makes it hard for you to hear this?"

Often we use systemic questions to help participants imagine new patterns of communication. These questions sound something like this: "What would need to change for your meetings to become more productive?" "If your meetings became more productive, how would things be different?" "You have said that your meetings always turn into a shouting match. If you didn't shout at one another so much, what would the discussion be like?"

You can also use systemic questions to help clients connect feelings and opinions with overt actions or behaviors. So we might ask something like, "You have said that George is constantly disgruntled. How does he show this?" "Mary, you have told us that Betty makes you very angry. Does she usually know when you are angry, and how could she tell?" "You have said that you worry a lot about the fact that Don opposes everything you are trying to do. How can you tell when he is being oppositional?" Such questions can also ask participants to share their own reactions and responses. In a typical intervention, we might ask, "What most surprised you about Terri's story?" Or, "What is most challenging to you in this situation?"

Systemic questions can be a powerful way to (a) shift the dialogue from statements of what people want and need to a conversation about how they are relating to one another and to (b) explore new patterns of interaction that might work better for them.

Explorations

1. Take the part of a therapist working with a committed couple that has a history of relational conflict. One partner tells you all about the other partner's failings and his or her anger and frustration at being in this committed relationship. The other partner proceeds to describe how the other person is always critical and demanding and how angry and frustrating this is.

Create three different *systemic questions* designed to shift the focus from the individual to the relationship.

a. _____

b. _____

c. _____

2. Why is it beneficial to explore the verbal content of a relationship instead of just the subjective feelings of the individuals?

_____

_____

_____

Key Construction

- Systemic questions

READING 46

From Stuck Debate to New Conversation

When we think of people who have opposing positions on an issue, we typically think, "well, let's have a debate." We view a debate as a way of locating the "real truth" or the "best reasons" regarding the issues at stake. However, from a constructionist standpoint, debate seldom solves any conflict. This is because each side creates its own reality and a rationality to support that reality. Each has its own values and traditions. Rather than the real truth or best reason, we are likely to find multiple truths and many good reasons, depending on one's standpoint.

In Reading 46, a group of family therapists describe their attempt to replace debate with constructive dialogue. The Public Conversations Project (www.public conversations.org), in which the authors participated, created this particular form of dialogue. It is now used broadly and effectively in many areas of conflict.

Reading 46 CAROL BECKER, LAURA CHASIN, RICHARD CHASIN, MARGARET HERZIG, AND SALLYANN ROTH

The Public Conversations Project seeks to discover and experiment with forms of public discussion that might release hot controversies from polarized public debate so that democratic resolution can become possible. We have been especially interested in what happens to people when they engage in or witness conversations on polarized public issues. How do they speak and listen? What parts of themselves do they open or shut down?

The Dominant Discourse in Polarized Public Debate

Polarized public conversations can be described as conforming to a "dominant discourse." The dominant discourse is the most generally available and accepted way of discussing the issue in a public context. For example, the dominant discourse about the American Revolutionary War defined the war as one of colonial liberation. It is not usually described in the United States as a conspiracy of tax dodgers led by a multi-millionaire from Virginia.

Dominant discourses strongly influence which ideas, experiences, and observations are regarded as normal or eccentric, relevant or irrelevant. On a subject that has been hotly polarized for a long time, the dominant discourse often delineates the issue in a win-lose-bipolar way; it draws a line between two simple answers to a complex dilemma and induces people to take a stand on one side of that line or the other. (For example, you are either a royalist or a revolutionary.) Most people who care deeply about the issue yield to this induction.

Being aligned with one group offers benefits. It gives one a socially validated place to stand while speaking, and it offers the unswerving support of likeminded people. It also exacts costs. It portrays opponents as a single-minded and malevolent gang. In the face of such frightening and unified adversaries, one's own group must be unified, strong, and certain. To be loyal to that group, one must suppress many uncertainties, morally complicated personal experiences, inner value conflicts, and differences between oneself and one's allies. Complexity and authenticity are sacrificed to the demands of presenting a unified front to the opponent. Win-lose exchanges create losers who feel they must retaliate to regain lost respect, integrity, and security, and winners who fear to lose disputed territory won at great cost.

The dominant discourse on polarized issues is fostered and sustained by a number of forces, most obviously, the media. The drama of polarized debate seems to capture the public's interest more than stories of subtle shifts in understanding on complicated issues. As simplifications of dramatic conflicts about a controversial issue become more and more accepted by the public and the media, more complicated viewpoints seem less and less to the point, as if they are not about the issue at all.

Polarized public debates exact costs not only from those who directly participate in them, but also from those who do not. Those who are conflicted or uncertain may come to believe that their views are unwelcome in public discussions. Those who are aware of discordance between some of their personal beliefs and the political position, espoused by "like-minded" others may choose to place themselves safely on the sidelines. They may worry that if they speak about their reluctance to become politically active on one side of the battle line they will be viewed as soft, muddled, unprincipled, or even as traitors. They may stop conversing even with themselves, assuming that if there is no societal validation for their views or the experiences that have shaped their views, then their views and experiences must be worthless, dangerous, or aberrant. The political process is deprived of their voices, and their ideas and democracy suffers.

Dialogue, as we use the term, involves an exchange of perspectives, experiences, and beliefs in which people speak and listen openly and respectfully. In political debates, people speak from a position of certainty, defending their own beliefs, challenging and attacking the other side, and attempting to persuade others to their point of view. They generally speak not as individuals, but as representatives of a position defined by the dominant discourse. In dialogue, participants speak as unique individuals about their own beliefs and experiences, reveal their uncertainties as well as certainties, and try to understand one another. As people in dialogue listen openly and respectfully to each other, their relationship shifts from one of opposition to one of interest—and sometimes to one of compassion and even empathic connection. The limitations of the dominant discourse are often acknowledged and possibilities for moving beyond it may be considered. Differences among participants become less frightening and may even begin to look more like potential social resources than insurmountable social problems. Old patterns of retaliation lose their appeal as the experience of dialogue leaves people feeling listened to and respected rather than beaten and embittered, or victorious and braced for backlash. [Our first important topic was about abortion.]

Preparing Participants for a Journey into the New

In our initial phone call with participants, in the letter of invitation, and in our orienting remarks at the beginning of the session, we clearly distinguish between *dialogue*, as we understand it, and debate as typically seen on television. We aim to leave no room for misunderstanding about the nature of the event, as we want people to participate with informed consent. We want those who feel unwilling to set aside the urge to persuade, or who are uninterested in respectful exploratory exchanges with the "other side," to self-select out of the process. (Only four people, two on each "side," have declined participation for such reasons.)

There is a second reason for our fully presenting our thinking to participants. Although our structured process is totally voluntary, participants can experience it as so unnatural and anxiety provoking that they may seek refuge in the familiar. To help participants resist this retreat, we highlight the differences between the usual discourse on abortion and a new dialogue among individuals to prepare them for the challenges of their voyage into the new.

We prepare them in many ways. We outline our expectations for their session, spell out specific agreements we will propose to ensure their safety throughout the session, and indicate what they might ponder in getting ready for it. We also hold before them the image of an achievable alternative to divisive debate when we mention that past participants have been able to participate with integrity and respectful curiosity, and speak about their own views and experiences with authenticity.

The careful and patient way we convey this information to participants models the respectfulness and attentiveness that will be expected of them in the dialogue. Our early interactions with participants give them reason to believe that we will diligently assist them in maintaining their agreements and consistently support the part of them that is open to listening respectfully, speaking in new ways, and learning something new about others and about themselves.

Avoiding the Old Debate

Several features of our model constitute interventions designed to prevent the old conversation and make room for a new one. When we ask people not to reveal where they stand on the issue during dinner, we prevent participants from sizing each other up through the lenses of friend or foe. This allows them to meet as unique individuals. They sometimes make guesses about who will be on which side, and find that they are not always correct. This gives them an opportunity to notice their own stereotyping process at work.

When participants enter the dialogue room they are assigned seats next to rather than opposite people with different views. This breaks up the usual face-off of opposing sides and leads to a sequence of responses in the opening go-rounds that highlights variety and interrupts tendencies to group people into "camps."

The agreements and guidelines that we propose avoid fruitless and destructive patterns of interaction. The pass rule frees people to make inquiries, and it protects everyone from being cornered. The go-round structure and the agreement about not interrupting prevent reactivity and help listeners to set aside habits of preparing responses while others are speaking. Guidelines about speaking personally, avoiding rhetorical questions, and leaving "they" and "them" out of the room, block polemics, grandstanding and blaming.

In parting comments and follow-up calls, participants sometimes comment on the liberating effect of these constraints. One man said, "Taking the super-heat out of it at least allows you to hear the other point of view better. . . . [It] provides an opportunity to be a little more of who you are and a little less guarded." Another man said that the safety offered through the ground rules allowed him to share his uncertainties. He said, "If I were debating this issue I wouldn't have told you half these things." One woman commented at the end of her session that it was "a personal victory" that she did not feel a need to make a closing comment "meant to persuade." Another said that she is is usually vulnerable to "group think" but in this case "she really felt everything she said."

A few people have said that they noticed themselves biting their tongues. One man, in his closing remarks during the session, said that he didn't feel totally honest setting aside strong language. However, in his follow-up call, he described the tone of the exchange as "admirable" and he commended the facilitators for keeping the thing on track without making anyone feel "hamstrung or crowded." When he was asked about his parting comment during the session, he said that it had been good for him to shape his comments with our guidelines in mind. "Let's face it," he said, "arguments are a dime a dozen. This was unique."

Fostering Co-Creation of a New Conversation

We begin the process of encouraging a new conversation when we propose and reiterate the "alternative frame," i.e., when we set goals and offer guidelines for a conversation that differs fundamentally from debate. We establish a tone that is heartfelt; curious, open and respectful. We set a slow pace. By the time the floor is turned over to participants, they clearly understand how we view the old "stuck" conversation and what elements we expect may emerge in a new one: curiosity, complexity, personal narrative, and sharing of uncertainties as well as certainties. The opening questions are carefully worded and sequenced to encourage these elements. They are designed with the recognition that chronic political conflict is generally not amenable to resolution through discussions of facts; it is generally rooted in deeply personal experiences and values.

The first question is: *We would like you to say something about your own life experiences in relation to the issue of abortion. For example, something about your personal history with the issue, how you got interested in it, what your involvement has been?* This question grounds the discussion in rich personal narratives and reveals connections between strongly held beliefs and subjective experiences. For some participants, it leads to reflections on the beliefs that were "in the air" in their families. For some it elicits poignant stories about abortions, adoptions, tragedies, triumphs and complicated turns of events in the lives of individuals and families. Interest is high and curiosity is stirred; no story is predictable.

> **Prolife Woman:** *As a sophomore, my closest friend took it upon herself to be president of the prolife group on campus. . . . [She] was physically handicapped with cerebral palsy, and she was very concerned about the value our society places on handicapped individuals. She died, for reasons we still don't understand to this day, and I couldn't bear to see all that she worked so hard for go by the wayside. At this point, I had come to what I term a prolife feminist position.*

> **Prochoice Man:** *Well, I was catapulted into this many decades ago because my sister had an abortion, and it turned out that the baby's father was my father.*

And that's a hard place to begin to think about all this stuff. When I was married, my wife had three miscarriages before our son was born and I have seen what it does to a woman, even in terms of that being something she has no control over. . . . I cannot advise people about [abortion]. I have to see what their particular feeling is.

The second question, *What is at the heart of the matter for you as an individual?* gives people an opportunity to say what they need to say about their convictions but it locates the core of the issue in the heartfelt, the unique and the personal. Throughout the session, our language draws participants' attention to what they care most about.

Prochoice Woman: *I think the moral maturity of women is what's really at stake for me. Anything that legislates or removes choice from an individual woman removes respect for her as a mature, moral person who is capable of making decisions that are right for her in the context of her life and her relationships.*

Prolife Woman: *The fact that a child is wanted or not wanted by someone else—it would frighten me to think that the importance of my life is contingent upon the fact that someone wants me. I am special in myself and it doesn't matter to me whether someone wants me. My life certainly shouldn't depend on it at any stage.*

We pose the third question as follows: *Many people have within their general approach to abortion some gray areas, some dilemmas about their own beliefs, or even some conflicts within themselves. Sometimes these gray areas are revealed when people consider hard cases—circumstances in which a prolife person might want to allow an abortion, or situations in which a prochoice person might not want to permit an abortion. Or, in a very different way, sometimes an individual feels that his or her own views on abortion come into conflict with other important values and beliefs. We have found it to be productive and helpful when people share whatever dilemmas, struggles, and conflicts they have within their prevailing view. We invite you to mention any pockets of uncertainty or lesser certainty, any concerns, value conflicts, or mixed feelings you may have and wish to share.* This question brings forth differentiation among the views of those with similar positions and suggests bridges between those on different sides. It encourages participants to grapple with the complexity of their own views.

Prolife Man: *I guess the way I look at it, if you terminate that life . . . there's an evil there. If it's a case of an unwanted pregnancy, there's an evil there. If it's a byproduct of rape or incest, if you have a severely impaired baby in the process, all of those things are evils. And where the uncertainty comes in for me is [in a situation like] a 13 year old girl has just been raped by her uncle and it's basically going to destroy her life. And I can't just sit there and say, on my high moral horse, "it's the ultimate universal wrong to kill an unborn child." Because I know that there are other bad things in the world and you've got to balance them.*

Prochoice Woman: *The sanctity of life is precious to me . . . and I don't think God takes it lightly that we make a decision about choosing to end a life, for whatever reason it may be. I would like us not to make abortion something we* *can do without having to think about it. I don't think there is a right answer. Sometimes there is a less bad answer than another.*

Prolife Woman: *One time I was discussing this issue with a friend, and he said, "Obviously you never grew up an unwanted child." And he was right, they wanted me. I think of the children that suffer and think to myself, would it have been better if they had been aborted? Then I think, well, they have life. But it's really hard to watch children in pain and sometimes it's hard to be prolife, but I'm so prolife. So that's something I really struggle with.*

Prochoice Woman: *After I had my baby I realized that I would never have an abortion, personally. That changed my personal view of abortion. It bothers me that there hasn't been much dialogue within the prochoice community about how far along abortions should be allowed. To me an end point would be 5 or 6 months. That, to me, is the point where we are talking about a baby, not a fetus.*

Some prolife participants have said that their moral position about abortion conflicts with their political belief in a pluralistic society founded on the idea that different values can co-exist. A prochoice woman said that thoughts about the damage done to children by drugs and alcohol before they are born are what evoke in her compassion for the fetus. This is when she entertains the idea that the fetus may have rights. A feminist prolife woman explained her belief that legal abortions allow women to be used by men who do not have to take responsibility for their actions; abortion becomes a substitute for finding solutions to the social problems of our time. She said that a woman's choice is not a genuine choice until it is made in the context of equally viable alternatives. She indicated that she is ambivalent about prohibiting abortions in a society without adequate supports for women facing unplanned pregnancies.

During the time in which we call for questions of curiosity, we have witnessed many meaningful and interesting exchanges. A prochoice leader asked a prolife leader if he could think of any reasons for keeping abortion legal. He said that he could: women would not die from illegal abortions. A Jewish prochoice woman asked a Catholic prolife woman active in Operation Rescue to describe her views about the relationship between abortion and the soul. The prolife woman disclosed a complex belief system about what happens to the soul of an aborted baby.

Hearing about beliefs in a more complex manner than can be conveyed through slogans, hearing about ambiguities usually suppressed and finding and revealing one's own silenced complexities and dilemmas can be both humbling and empowering. At the end of one session, one woman said, "None of us knows the truth. But together we can come closer to the truth. We can be safe, liberated and accepted. We can continue struggling, even though we may never have it right." Sometimes the experience of listening and speaking in a new way in the dialogue group contains lessons for participants' personal relationships. One woman said, "I'm afraid I really don't make room for others' views if they are different from mine. I don't make room for my husband's views. I don't like that about myself;

I want to change that." Another woman commented that it is hard to share personal experiences with people who hold opposing ideological positions, "but this is, in my mind, how human community is formed and deepens. We do not change the world by staying on two sides of the fence and yelling at each other."

Explorations

1. Think about a political or religious issue you feel strongly about at this time, an issue about which there is controversy. Consider your position about this issue.

   List the issue: _____

   List two specific reasons why you feel strongly about this issue.

   a. _____

   b. _____

2. Tell a personal story about why you feel the way you do about the issue.

   _____

   _____

   _____

   _____

3. On close consideration, what would you say is "at the heart of the matter" for you?

   _____

   _____

   _____

4. Consider possible "gray areas." Can you identify any areas of uncertainty in your opinions, any areas where you remain concerned, or have mixed feelings?

   _____

   _____

   _____

5. Reread your responses to the previous exercise questions. Consider yourself as someone who holds an opposing position on this issue.

   a. Which of the previous responses is most likely to arouse you to defend your opposing position?

   _____

   _____

   _____

b. Which of the responses is most likely to invite you into a conversation where mutual understanding might result?

_____

_____

Key Constructions

- Public Conversations Project
- Dominant discourse
- Polarized debate
- Debate versus dialogue

READING 47

Education for Peace: Jewish–Arab Conflict Resolution

When conflicts between groups have been intense and long-lasting, it is enormously difficult to facilitate promising dialogue between people. The School for Peace, in a small village in Israel, takes on the challenge. In Reading 47 Grace Feuerverger describes the activities of the students within the school, and their specific use of narrative in bringing antagonists together.

Reading 47 GRACE FEUERVERGER

The School for Peace (SFP) is located in a cooperative village in Israel where Jews and Arabs live together within a social, cultural, and political framework of equality and mutual respect. They came together to build a collective vision of peace for themselves and future generations. The village, Neve Shalom/Wahat Salam (which means "oasis of peace" in Hebrew and Arabic), was founded in 1972 as an intercultural experiment, and the first families took up residence there in 1978. The SFP (established in 1980) is an outreach program that conducts educational encounters bringing Jewish and Palestinian adolescents together from all over Israel and increasingly from the West Bank.

The underlying message of the SFP is that it is of utmost importance to maintain personal, social, and national identity for both Jews and Arabs. This framework assures the legitimacy of every participant's position. Each of the peace encounters takes place over a period of 3–6 months and includes one very intensive 3–day workshop. Since 1980, tens of thousands of Jewish and Palestinian adolescents have participated in these encounters.

The participants are divided into small, mixed groups of 12–14 Jews and an equal number of Arabs from high schools all over the country. The facilitators are a permanent, professional staff of Jews and Arabs in equal numbers, and each workshop is led by two facilitators, one Jewish and the other Palestinian. Accordingly, participants always have the opportunity to speak the language they are most familiar with and to identify with the facilitator from their own cultural group. The use of both languages is an important symbol of inclusiveness and mutual respect and has the capacity to construct and convey their commitment toward peacemaking.

This educational program promotes acquaintance, understanding, and dialogue between the two peoples and is especially designed to try to reach those (both students and teachers) who have leadership positions in their schools or among their peers and who are highly motivated to attempt to deal with the Jewish–Palestinian conflict. Since 1993, the workshops have been recommended to public schools by the Israeli Ministry of Education, which provides some funding through its "Education for Democracy and Coexistence" program. Moreover, the teachers who take part in these workshops receive in-service training credits.

The philosophy behind this intervention is that relationship building and problem solving are two sides of the same coin. Indeed, the workshops embody the experiential learning model. The purpose of the workshops is to formulate new modes of relations that acknowledge the "other" in order to recognize the "self," as a means of allowing the participants to break through the impasse by being given the opportunity to mirror themselves for the first time in the eyes of the "other." This idea emphasizes knowledge of the self as a precursor to knowing the other. This key theoretical notion has transformative potential and provides a framework for examining the goals and objectives of this peace education initiative:

Briefly, the objectives of the peace encounters, as stated in the curriculum guidelines, are:

1. to deepen the participants' familiarity with themselves and with the other side.
2. to raise the participants' awareness of the complex reality of relations between the sides, and to enable them to absorb this complexity.
3. to make the participants aware of their ability to select their attitude toward the conflict, to influence their lives and their surroundings, and thus to help mitigate the conflict.
4. to bring the participants to choose non-discriminatory positions and modes of behaviour and to give legitimacy to all peoples' needs, rights, and aspirations.
5. to give the participants an opportunity to experience cooperation between the sides.

Competing Victimhoods

The workshop discussions coalesced with a consistency of themes, images, and poetic voice that could be appreciated as a unified sequence of altercations, confrontations, and negotiations. Underneath the surface of the immediate moment lurked the profound woundedness that makes reconciliation between Palestinian and Jew very problematic. Reference to the Holocaust and terrorism against Jews, as well as to the treatment of Palestinians in the occupied territories, dominated the discussions. Tempers often ran high, and words were edged with hate and frustration. This was the first time both groups could express themselves so freely to the other. An Arab participant, Ibrahim, explained the process to me in a personal interview.

> We were all ready to jump at each other's throats about our grievances. I couldn't believe how cavalier some of the Jewish participants were with regard to the terrible treatment of the Palestinians in the occupied territories. It just made me feel sick. I have relatives who were badly injured in certain fights. I do see Israelis, therefore, as aggressors. I can't help it. But I never thought of the mass murders of their people in Eastern Europe. They are more traumatized than I ever imagined. We have to learn about each other's pain and acknowledge it. It's the first time I've ever considered that.

There was a sense of authentic partnership in curriculum making within the search for inter-group coexistence. Along with their participant students, the facilitators struggled to achieve a sense of balance and meaning in the precarious juggling act of conflict resolution. However, it was hardly an easy process. For example in one session, after an especially bitter outburst from Abdul [a Palestinian] about the terrible conditions in the West Bank, Ahmed finally stepped in and shouted: "Enough already. We heard you the first time. After five times it loses its power. It's time you let others express themselves."

Many other Arab participants agreed with Ahmed as Abdul sulked in his seat. In another session Tirzah cut short Hannah, a Jewish participant [an Israeli] who commented, "An Arab will remain an Arab. I don't think they deserve all the rights." Tirzah responded very annoyed: "What do you mean by that? Do you realize that your behavior and your words are totally different? First, you said that there should be equality for both peoples. Now when it comes to specifics, you are controlling what should be given or taken away."

These comments sparked off a noisy discussion where disagreement between Jew and Jew and Arab and Arab occurred. It turned out to have a constructive effect because it broke the Jewish–Palestinian division and instead created a discussion where the participants were arguing from a more fluid individual perspective, rather than a rigid group perspective.

What emerged, as the hours passed, was the salience of the personal stories. They were sacred and had to be honored within the context of this peacemaking enterprise. The sad refrain of victimhood echoed throughout the narratives that emerged within the safety of these workshops. Sarit, a Jewish participant, commented rather emotionally in one session about her reaction to terrorist acts that happen in Israel:

> To tell the truth, I feel very ambivalent about being here. How can I trust people who want to destroy me, my people? I am terrified of Arab terrorists. And these

attacks keep happening. I feel like a betrayer to be discussing coexistence with Arabs who have wreaked so much violence on us. But I guess I was enticed by these workshops because I wanted to see my enemy close up. I feel, like everybody else in this country, battle fatigued. Can there be a way out of this awful mess? But to say that I can become friends with Arabs, I don't know. But I'm willing to listen and to see what they have to say. I was told these workshops are no-nonsense and don't pretend to solve everything. I am learning to question if we Jews have any responsibility in this conflict. I know now that not every Arab wants to blow up innocent people. And it is true that the situation in the West Bank is desperate.

Mahmoud, an Arab participant, added quietly but forcefully:

My mind races with such anger when I hear how some Israeli soldiers are treating some of the Palestinians in the territories. It scares me to think that if I were there I could be humiliated badly and also could end up in prison. What hope do these people have for the future? And how does their situation relate to my own identity? And so I want to discuss it with some Jews who are willing to listen. Does that make me a traitor?

Concerning such "border dialogues," I saw that what was crucial to the Jewish and Arab participants in the context of these workshops was that as "border crossers," they were being offered the opportunity to negotiate while maintaining and strengthening their own identities. Furthermore, through the vehicle of narrative, the students were enabled to go beyond their culturally specific lived experience.

Storytelling as an Emancipatory Act

Throughout the workshops that I observed, the facilitators constantly attempted to empower their participants to become storytellers and to guide them as they gradually began a process of uncovering and reconstructing the meaning of their cultural and national identities in the shadowy spaces of trauma and fear. The facilitators created social situations where meaningful communication was achieved by the participants as a result of personal interaction with their lived texts.

The sharing of their stories was intended as a vehicle for "border crossing" but also turned out to be an exercise in risk taking. The reason for this was that for many of the participants at the beginning of the encounter, the notion of "border crossing" was considered a betrayal to their group and thus fraught with feelings of hostility and vulnerability. Therefore critical/reflective frontiers needed to be established before any real sharing could take place.

At the School for Peace, the participants' stories opened a broader perspective to their emotional location within their lived experience of conflict and war. The stories also became an excellent vehicle to discuss issues of social injustice and human rights on a more intimate basis. The feeling of dislocation and the quest for rootedness insinuated itself into every discussion in the workshop encounters. The memory of the Holocaust was the eternal ghost that haunted the workshops. Mariam, an Arab participant, offered to the group the desolate observation that the Holocaust preempted everything:

> How can we Palestinians ever get our points across if you Jews always refer back to the Holocaust? We can't compete with such a catastrophe, and the truth is that it is not our fault at all. We're paying for something that happened far away from here. I'm sorry to sound so harsh but I don't know how to handle it. Of course next to the magnitude of the Holocaust what is going on in the occupied territories seems rather small. But it is not small to us. It is our tragedy.

Mordechai, one of the Jewish participants, responded to her:

> Do you not understand that we Jews here in Israel are still surrounded by ene-mies that want to destroy us? We're not exactly in a tranquil situation. And where do you think the survivors of the Holocaust could have gone after World War II? If there had been an Israel then, the Holocaust would never have hap-pened. It's because the Jews have been without their homeland for 2000 years that all this persecution and genocide took place.
>
> I know it's not your fault, but you must listen to me. I have a right to feel worried and scared about my future and my children's future. During the Gulf War when Saddam Hussein threatened to burn half of Israel with chemical war-fare, the Jews remembered their history of the concentration camps. You Arabs did not feel afraid. In fact, you felt kind of proud because Saddam was promis-ing a strengthening of Arab identity. The Palestinians in the territories were cel-ebrating on roof tops. Do you think that made us Jews feel confident in achiev-ing peace with the Arabs?
>
> But I agree that what is happening in the territories is a terrible thing and that is why the peace process is so important. We have to find a way to live together. That's why we're here. And I appreciate how Ahmed and Tirzah have let us speak what's really in our hearts.

Conclusion

Both Jews and Arabs in Israel are caught up in webs of hatred, fear, and mutual suspicion that are layered and multiple in their complexity. The conflict resolu-tion program, the School for Peace at Neve Shalom/Wahat-Salam, is rooted in personal and political struggles for peaceful coexistence. One of the central issues explored is the extent to which these peace workshops can be seen as an attempt to come to terms with the immense separation between both Jews and Arabs inherent in the wider society.

These encounters, in contrast to the participants' normal life contexts, open a space where dissension within reflection and protection becomes possible, and interconnections between the personal and political are honored and not shunned. The workshops provide an opportunity where the participants' stories of humiliation, vulnerability, trauma, and fear can surface in a place of safety and trust. Indeed, the underlying goal of the School for Peace is to enable the participants to transcend the tyranny of established structures and to reinvent a framework upon which their understandings, relations, and identities with one another can be built.

How do you teach conflict resolution in a situation where both peoples are right? You have to make them understand that they are both entitled to their pain but that nevertheless they must acknowledge this pain in one another. Somehow they must learn to coexist. They don't have to love each other. They just have to live and let live.

"Peace in every step." And the first one is the hardest.

Explorations

1. Antagonists seldom seek each other out to have a good heart-to-heart talk. To arrange the conditions under which they can listen with understanding to each other is difficult. What do you think are some of the key conditions that enabled the Israeli and Palestinian students to speak productively together at the School for Peace?

_____

_____

_____

_____

2. Do you think it would be possible for you to develop a productive dialogue with a "terrorist?" Could you be a "border crosser" with this particular person? Why or why not?

_____

_____

_____

_____

   a. If so, what would be some necessary conditions for you to talk and to actively listen to this person?

_____

_____

_____

Key Constructions

- Identity
- Competing victimhoods
- Storying conflict
- Border crossing

READING 48

Improvising a New Life: Interactive Theater

Criminality in society is not typically recognized as conflict. To be a criminal is to be in conflict with society's laws. Quite often, this conflict between a person and society is an outcome of a more local conflict brought on in part by anger, rage, and/or competition. The American system of justice seldom takes such conflicts into account. By and large the justice system simply operates punitively by incarcerating the criminal. One of the most creative attempts to take criminal conflict into account, and to generate more promising futures is provided by Jonathan Shailor in Reading 48. Stimulated by Latin American attempts to use theater as a means of social transformation, Shailor generates settings in which prisoners can "play out a scene from their own lives." In playing the part of themselves interacting with other major characters in their lives, they acquire new insights. They begin to locate alternative positions about what brought them into prison. In this selection we excerpt from Shailor's account of one empowering prison theater exploration.

Reading 48   JONATHAN SHAILOR

The heart of the theatre of empowerment course lies in helping the men to experience themselves as the actors and directors of their own lives. Through theatre games, exercises and scene work, the men are encouraged to develop their improvisational skills. The goal is to encourage them to extend the power, range and flexibility of their everyday performances, so that they can feel less "stuck" in their habitual patterns, and more creative and compassionate in their responses to life's challenges.

The main elements of this work consist of warm-up and energy-building exercises, theatre exercises, improvisational work, and scene work. The scene work is the culmination of the other activities, so I will focus on that here. About one third to one half of the way into a course, the men are usually ready to begin focusing on their individual histories and problems. Keying in on one inmate at a time, we spend one, two or several sessions on his story, depending upon our time constraints and how quickly the work proceeds. The initial story told by an inmate is usually self-denigrating or self-pitying. There is a sense of inevitability to the narrative, with the primary cause of the inmate's problems attributed to his own deficiencies, or the cruelty and confusion of the world. The men's narrative constructions are usually closed and self-sealing, in the sense that they seem well-prepared for any challenges to the inevitability of their characterizations. The men have difficulty imagining ways in which their world could be different.

In an effort to break through this feeling of stuckness and to help the men begin to create a greater sense of possibility, I guide them through a series of enactments based on critical events in their lives. Everyone participates, either as an actor, a witness, a commentator, or in some combination of these roles. As a group, we try to create accurate and compelling recreations, which we then re-examine from various angles. Some of the re-examination occurs in discussion, but much of it also occurs in various kinds of re-enactment. We use role reversal to help men explore the point of view of a victim (a common psychodrama technique), and "forum theatre" (created by Augusto Boal) to explore alternatives to an ongoing situation.

Interactive Theatre: A Communication Episode

In this episode from September 2001, we had just begun to explore some of the dimensions of Mick's story through scene work. Mick had been convicted six times for driving under the influence, and he was now serving a second prison sentence in relation to those convictions.

He was depressed because his wife had become seriously involved with another man, and was seeking a divorce. We began our work with a sequence of scenes designed to examine how people in Mick's life have been affected by his offense. Mick identified his wife Sally, his sons Bobby and Jason, and his Grandma as the ones who had been most affected by his actions. We created a series of tableaus with Mick at the center, and each of his family members standing a distance away, with Sally (the one most affected) closest to him, and Grandma (the one least affected) standing furthest away. Mick worked with each of the actors to help them find a pose that displayed something important about what they were feeling as a result of his offense. Ralph, the actor playing Sally, sat back in a chair with his arms partly crossed, chin in hand, a wary look on his face. Mick looked on appreciatively, saying "That's Sally."

The next step involves the creation of scenes focusing on each person's response to Mick's actions. We begin with Sally. Mick suggests that Sally's new boyfriend, Roger, is the person she would most likely be sharing her feelings with. Ralph continues in his role as Sally, and another inmate, Thomas, takes on the role of Roger. In the initial unfolding of the scene, the men focus on Roger's attempts to soothe and reassure "Sally," who appears somewhat ambivalent about his help.

I ask her what she's thinking and not saying. "She" turns to "Roger" and says, "Basically, you know, I need you, but I only need you to a certain extent. And, in a way, I don't want to run you off, but you're really crowding me, dude." Mick interprets "Roger's" actions in this way: "He's moving too quick, so to speak. [*Ralph nods in the affirmative*] [*Gaining in volume*] He's trying to, he's trying to put himself in my shoes."

At this point I ask the observers if they want to ask Roger any questions. The first question from Ralph is "What are you getting out of it?" "Roger" explains that the sex is good and that he doesn't feel any pressure to make a commitment. At this point Mick breaks in to clarify a few things: Roger gave Sally a gold bracelet and asked her to marry him during the *first week* of their relationship. Mick expresses his anger about Roger's trying to "move me out of the picture." I turn to "Roger" and ask him if he might really care for Sally. His answer: "Yeah! Yeah, I care about her. "Roger wants to know why, when this means that Roger will have to take on kids that are "a problem." "And a psychotic ex-husband," Mick reminds to us with a rueful laugh. "Roger" answers by addressing "Sally" with great feeling:

> Well, 'cause you've been through enough. And I really care about you, and I love you. And you've been through enough. This guy's put you through enough. And I want to take a chance to take care of you.

Mick is provoked by this statement, and in the ensuing discussion declares that when he is released from prison, the only person Roger will need to "protect" is himself. The discussion turns to the question of what brought Roger and Sally together. Since Roger is "bald" and "skinnier 'n shit," Mick can't imagine the source of the attraction. When Mick reveals that Roger makes over $70,000 a year, the others consider the possibility that Sally may appreciate the financial security. Mick is doubtful, and instead floats the theory that both Sally and Roger are on the "rebound" (Roger is also separated from his wife, who is an alcoholic).

Ralph returns to the idea that it may be a "sex thing," and then another inmate, Phil, seems to hit a nerve:

PHIL: I'm thinkin' more along the lines that it was a *comfort* thing. You know, if he went through a bad marriage with a alcoholic, and she jus'

MICK: [*Sharp inhalation.*]

PHIL: you know, on, on the edges of comin' out of a relationship with a alcoholic, you know, he was able to comfort her, he was able to tell her, however, they met—you know what I'm saying? once they agreed upon that they both was in the same kind a relationship, he was able to comfort her somewhat

JON: Let's try to play that angle for a minute, 'cause what we're doin' is we're, we're showing some different possibilities. And this is a chance for Mick to think about these possibilities. So, in this case, try, try this: you're both comforting each other about having gotten out of a relationship with an alcoholic—and what a relief that is. Let's hear some of that.

To help us build the scene, I ask Mick to describe some of the things he did that were "hard for Sally." Mick explained that he had two affairs, and that she was "always throwing that in my face." They also fought over his drinking.

Epilogue

I often wonder if this work is making a difference in the men's lives. Occasionally, I receive feedback that tells me we're doing something right. A case in point: Shortly after taking the course, Michael was released from prison and returned home to his family. A couple of months later, I received this letter:

> Dear Dr. Shailor:
>
> My husband, Michael, took a class that you taught while he was in the Racine Correctional Institution, last fall. I just wanted to thank you for teaching that class. I have noticed a big change in him. He is much more understanding and listens to what we have to say. He cares about us and keeps us together as a family. He credits your class and talks about it often. Thank you again.
>
> Sally Smith

And in the same envelope:

> THANK YOU VERY MUCH FOR YOUR CLASS . . . I USE YOUR WAYS OF THINKING ABOUT THE THEATRE OF EMPOWERMENT.
>
> Michael Smith

Explorations

1. Consider a recent conflict you have experienced with another person (friend, family member, romantic partner, classmate). First, briefly summarize your position in the conflict.

   _____

   _____

   _____

   _____

2. Consider the other person. What would this person say was his or her position on the same conflict?

   _____

   _____

   _____

3. Now consider the conflict from the point of view of two other people (e.g., your mother, father, grandparents, brothers/sisters, friends, coworkers), not necessarily involved. If they were observing the same conflict, what might they say about it?

a. _____

_____

b. _____

_____

4. Finally, as you have considered these various viewpoints, do you see any way in which your own view might be modified or enriched?

_____

_____

Key Constructions

- Theater of empowerment
- The ability of reframing conflict through performance

READING 49

Organizational Transformation Through Appreciative Inquiry

Conflicts are frequent in organizations—teams, clubs, businesses, and more—and if action isn't taken the group may be imperiled. To move in new directions, new ways of talking together must flourish. If there are deep conflicts within the organization, if there is widespread apathy, or if there is a strong need to change the directions of the organization, new conversations must be set in motion. One of the most exciting developments in organizational transformation over the past 20 years is represented in Reading 49 excerpted from the work of David L. Cooperrider and Diana Whitney. For them the key to transformation is the exploration of the "positive core." This idea centers on organizational members' joy, enthusiasm, or vital engagement in their activities. By telling stories together that illuminate the appreciated activities, a process is set in motion that enables the organization to move forward together.

Reading 49 DAVID L. COOPERRIDER AND DIANA WHITNEY

Appreciative Inquiry (AI) is about the co-evolutionary search for the best in people, their organizations, and the relevant world around them. In its broadest focus, it involves systematic discovery of what gives "life" to a living system when it is most alive, most effective, and most constructively capable in economic, ecological, and human terms. AI involves, in a central way, the art and practice of asking questions that strengthen a system's capacity to apprehend, anticipate, and heighten positive potential. It centrally involves the mobilization of inquiry through the crafting of the "unconditional positive question," often involving hundreds or sometimes thousands of people. In AI, the arduous task of intervention gives way to the speed of imagination and innovation; instead of negation, criticism, and spiraling diagnosis, there is discovery, dream, and design. AI focuses on what people talk about as past and present capacities: achievements, assets, unexplored potentials, innovations, strengths, elevated thoughts, opportunities, benchmarks, high point moments, lived values, traditions, strategic competencies, expressions of wisdom, insights into the deeper corporate spirit or soul, and visions of valued and possible feature. AI deliberately seeks to work from accounts of this "positive change core"—and it assumes that every living system has many untapped and rich and inspiring accounts of the positive. Link the energy of this core directly to any change agenda and changes never thought possible are suddenly and democratically mobilized.

The positive core of organizational life, we submit, is one of the greatest and largely unrecognized resources in the field of change management today. At present, we are clearly in our infancy when it comes to tools for working with it, talking about it, and designing our systems in synergistic alignment with it. But one thing is evident and clear as we reflect on the most important things we have learned with AI: human systems grow in the direction of what they persistently ask questions about. The single most prolific thing a group can do if its aims are to liberate the human spirit and consciously construct a better future is to make the positive change core the common and explicit property of all.

An AI cycle can be as rapid and informal as a conversation with a friend or colleague, or as formal as an organization wide meeting involving every stakeholder, including customers, suppliers, partners, and the like.

There are four key stages in AI *Discovery*—mobilizing a whole system inquiry into the positive change core; *Dream*—creating a clear results-oriented vision of higher purpose, i.e., What is the world calling us to become?; *Design*—creating possibility propositions of the ideal organization, an organization design which people feel is capable of magnifying the positive core and realizing the articulated new dream; and *Destiny*—strengthening the affirmative capability of the whole system enabling it to momentum around a deep purpose.

At the core of the cycle is Affirmative Topic Choice. It is the most important part of any AI. If, in fact, knowledge and organizational destiny are as intricately interwoven as we think, then isn't it possible that the seeds of change are implicit in the very first questions we ask? AI theory says "yes" and takes the idea quite seriously: It says that the questions people, groups, and organizations ask are fateful. It further asserts that conversations are among the world's paramount resources.

One great myth that continues to dampen the potential here is the understanding that first we do an analysis, and then we decide on change. Not so, says the contructionist view. Even the most innocent question evokes change—even if reactions are simply changes in awareness, dialogue, feelings of boredom, or even laughter. When we consider the possibilities in these terms, that inquiry and change are a simultaneous moment, we begin reflecting anew. It is not so much "Is my question leading to right or wrong answers? "but rather" 'What impact is my question having on our lives together . . . is it helping to generate conversations about the good, the better, the possible? . . . Is it strengthening our relationship?

Put most simply, it has been our experience that building and sustaining momentum for change requires large amounts of positive affect and social bonding—things like hope, excitement, inspiration, caring, camaraderie, sense of urgent purpose, and sheer joy in creating something meaningful together. What we have found is that the more positive the question we ask in our work, the more long lasting and successful the change effort. It does not help, we have found, to begin our inquiries from the standpoint of the world as a problem to be solved. We are more effective the longer we can retain the spirit of inquiry of the everlasting beginner. The major thing we do that makes the difference is to craft and seed, in better and more catalytic ways, the unconditional positive question.

Although the positive has not been paraded as a central concept in most approaches to organization analysis and change, it is clear we need no longer be shy about bringing this language more carefully and prominently into our work. And personally speaking, it is so much healthier. We love letting go of "fixing" the world. We love doing interviews, hundreds of them, into moments of organizational life. And we are, quite frankly, more effective the more we are able to learn, to admire, to be surprised, to be inspired alongside the people with whom we are working.

In our view, the problem solving paradigm, while once perhaps quite effective, is simply out of sync with the realities of today's virtual worlds. Problem solving approaches to change are painfully slow (always asking people to look backward to yesterday's causes); they rarely result in new vision (by definition we can describe something as a problem because we already, perhaps implicitly, assume an ideal, so we are not searching to expansive new knowledge of better ideals but searching how to close "gaps"); and in human terms problem approaches are notorious for generating defensiveness (it is not my problem but yours). Words do create worlds—even in unintended ways.

Explorations

1. Thousands of organizational specialists now use appreciative inquiry in their work with businesses, nonprofit groups, religious organizations, communities, and more. Can you think of three reasons for the success of appreciative inquiry?

    a. _____

    b. _____

    c. _____

2. The authors raise serious questions about a problem-solving approach to organizational change and conflict reduction. This same approach is very common in the way we approach our lives and our relationships. What are the limitations in using a problem-solving approach in daily relational life?

    _____

    _____

3. Share with a friend about the times you both spent together that were pleasurable and positive. Describe one of these stories.

    _____

    _____

    _____

    After sharing these stories, how did you feel about the positive experience of sharing pleasurable times together?

    _____

    _____

    _____

Key Constructions

- Appreciative inquiry
- Positive core
- Deficit discourse

Key Constructions for Part Four, Section D

- Systemic questions
- Public Conversations Project
- Dominant discourse
- Polarized debate
- Debate versus dialogue
- Identity
- Competing victimhoods
- Storying conflict
- Border crossing
- Theater of empowerment
- The ability to reframe conflict through performance
- Appreciative Inquiry
- Positive core
- Deficit discourse

PART FOUR

Suggested Readings

Friendships

Bellah, R., Madsen, R., Sullivan, W.M., Swidler, A., & Tipton, S. M., (1985). *Habits of the heart.* Berkeley: University of California Press.

Coates, J. (2003). *Men talk: Stories in the making of masculinity.* Oxford, UK: Blackwell.

Johnson, F. L. (1996). Friendships among women: Closeness in dialogue. In J. T. Wood (Ed.), *Gendered relationships.* (pp. 79–94). Mountain View, CA: Mayfield.

Josselson, R., Lieblich, A., & McAdams, D. P. (Eds.) (2007). *The Meaning of others.* Washington, DC: American Psychological Association.

Nardi, P., M., & Sherrod, D. (1994). Friendship in the lives of gay men and lesbians. *Journal of Social and Personal Relationships, 11,* 185–199.

Richardson, L., (2007). *Last writes: A daybook for a dying friend.* Walnut Creek, CA: Left Coast Press.

Rose, A., & Asher, S. (2000). Children's friendships. In C. Hendrick & S. Hendrick (Eds.), *Close relationships: A sourcebook* (pp. 47–57). Thousand Oaks, CA: Sage.

Swain, S. (1989). Covert intimacy: Closeness in men's friendships. In B. Risman & P. Schwartz (Eds.), *Gender and intimate relationships* (pp. 71–86). Belmont, CA: Wadsworth.

Tannen, D. (1990). *You just don't understand: Women and men in communication.* New York: William Marrow.

Intimate Relations

Baxter, L. A., & Braithwaite, D. O. (2002). Performing marriage: Marriage renewal rituals as cultural performance. *Southern Communication Journal, 67,* 94–109.

Leeds-Hurwitz, W. (2002). *Wedding as text.* Mahwah, NJ: Erlbaum.

Long Laws, J., & Schwartz, P. (1977). *Sexual scripts: The social construction of female sexuality.* New York: Dryden.

McNamee, S., & Gergen, K. J. (2001). *Relational responsibility.* Thousand Oaks, CA: Sage.

Rust, P. (1993). "Coming out" the age of social constructionism: Sexual identity formation among lesbian and bisexual women. *Gender and Society, 7,* 50–77.

Wood, J. T. (1993). Engendered relationships: Interactions: Interaction, caring, power and responsibility in close relationships. In S. Duck (Ed.), *Processes in close relationships: Contexts of close relationships* (Vol. 31). Thousand Oaks, CA: Sage.

Families

Anderson, H. (1997). *Conversation, language, and possibilities: A postmodern approach to therapy.* New York: HarperCollins.

Ishii-Kuntz, M. (1997). Japanese American families. In M. K. DeGenova (Ed.), *Families in cultural context: Strengths and challenges in diversity* (pp. 109–130). Mountain View, CA: Mayfield.

Jorgenson, J. (1991). Co-constructing the interviewer/co-constructing the family. In F. Steier (Ed.), *Research and reflectivity.* London: Sage.

Pelias, R. (2002). For father and son: An ethnodrama with no catharsis. In A. P. Bochner & C. Ellis (Eds.) *Families in cultural context: Strengths and challenges in diversity* (pp. 173–190). Mountain View, CA Mayfield.

Pias, S. (1997). Asian Indian families in America. In M. K. DeGenova (Ed.), *Families in cultural context: Strengths and challenges in diversity* (pp. 173–190). Mountain View, CA: Mayfield.

Strong, T. & Paré, D. (Eds.) (2004). *Further talk: Advances in the discursive therapies.* New York: Kluwer Academic/Plenum Publishers.

Conflict

Bohm, D. (1996). *On dialogue* (Lee Nichol, Ed.). New York: Routledge.

Bojer, M., Roehl, H., Knuth-Hollesen, & Mgner, C. (2008). *Mapping dialogue: Essential tools for social change.* Chagrin Falls, OH: Taos Institute Publications.

Drath, W. (2001). *The deep blue sea: Rethinking the source of leadership.* San Francisco: Jossey-Bass.

Hawes, L. C. (1999). The dialogics of conversation: Power, control and vulnerability. *Communication Theory, 9,* 229–264.

Littlejohn, S., Shailor, J., & Pearce, B. (1994). The deep structure of reality in mediation. In T. Jones J. Folger (Eds.), *New directions in mediation: Communication research and perspectives* (pp. 67–83). Thousand Oaks, CA: Sage.

Pearce, W. B., (2007). *Making Social Worlds: A Communication Perspective.* Malden, MA: Blackwell Publishers.

Pearce, W. B., & Littlejohn, S. (1997). *Moral conflict: When social worlds collide.* Thousand Oaks, CA: Sage.

Shailor, J. (1994). *Empowerment in dispute mediation.* New York: Praeger.

Spano, S. (2001). *Public dialogue and participatory democracy: The Cupertino project.* Creskill, NJ: Hampton Press.

Yankelovich, D. (1999). *The magic of dialogue: Transformation conflict into cooperation.* New York: Simon and Schuster.

Web Resources

Friendships

Friendship Movies
www.friendship.com.au/media/movies.html

Deaf Friends International-An Online worldwide deaf community
www.workersforjesus.com/dfi/front-eng.htm

Friendship developed and storied from prison
www.npr.org/templates/story/story.php?storyId=5032761

Online community for young girls
www.gurl.com/

Young girls, body image, health and advocacy
www.about-face.org/r/links/

Western history of friendship theory
www.infed.org/biblio/friendship.htm#classical

Intimate Relations

Chinese dating/ and marriage website
www.chnlove.com/help/faq.php?qid=1

Contemporary romance and dating by a "sidewalk social scientist"
www.alternativenation.net/forums/articles-features/77764-column-has-alternative-culture-killed-romance.html

Courtship, love, and Filipino culture
www.seasite.niu.edu/tagalog/love.htm

Pop culture view of wedding rituals
www.beau-coup.com/cultural-traditions-weddings.htm

Two routes to marriage: India and Indian American (NPR audio clip)
www.npr.org/templates/story/story.php?storyId=5173527

Deborah Tannen on radio and film
www9.georgetown.edu/faculty/tannend/interviews.htm

Families

Collaborative family health care organization-multidisciplinary systemic view of family health
www.cfhcc.org/

Family Institute of Cambridge—Constructionist family counseling
www.familyinstitutecamb.org/

National Family Resiliency Center
www.divorceabc.com/

National Blended Family Association
www.usabfa.org/

Systemic counseling and organizational systemic consulting website
www.kcc-international.com/index.htm

Conflict

Empowerment theatre, pedagogy theatre, theatre of oppressed
www.ptoweb.org

Appreciative Inquiry Commons homepage
http://appreciativeinquiry.case.edu/intro/whatisai.cfm

National coalition for dialogue and deliberation
www.thataway.org/

Public Conversations Project—Positive action with managing disputes
www.publicconversations.org/pcp/index.php

Public Dialogue Consortium—Systemic Conflict Negotiation Consulting Group
www.publicdialogue.org/pdc/index.html

U.S. history being presented in another country—A different cultural position
(NPR Interview)
www.npr.org/templates/story/story.php?storyId=3866153

Oasis of Peace: Neve Shalom/Wahat Salam
http://nswas.org/rubrique22.html

Bar Ilan University in Israel—university history
www.biu.ac.il/General/biu_history.html

Birzeit University in Birzeit Palestine-narrative history
www.birzeit.edu/about_bzu/p/2542

Discussion Questions and/or Short Papers

1. Consider the age old question about opposite-sex friendships:
   a. Is it possible for women and men to be close friends?
   b. How might one's committed partner view one's opposite sex friendships?
      Describe various options.

2. Many people seem to want intimacy and commitment in a relationship, but also they often want freedom and autonomy.
    a. Is it possible to have both in a single relationship?
    b. What kinds of communicative activities, if any, might make this possible? (For example, lying is one way to try to have both freedom and intimacy, but with highly destructive consequences.)
    c. To what extent is this difficulty in balancing commitment and freedom a cultural phenomenon, restricted to a particular tradition or period in history?
    d. Would you wish to see your culture change in this respect (with more or less freedom or commitment, or a different conception of relationships)?
3. Interview several people about the advantages and disadvantages of living in single-parent families, divorced families, blended families, unhappily married families, and happily married families.
    a. How do the communication patterns in these various families differ in terms of parent–child interactions?
    b. What is the tone of their speech, what are the nonverbal movements, and what is the content of the communication?
    c. Which patterns seem most positive in terms of the child's well-being?
4. Select a family or relationship conflict situation that you know about personally (e.g., a couple that has broken up; friends who are not speaking). Analyze the origins of the conflict in terms of communication patterns, including verbal and nonverbal acts.
    a. To what extend did the conflict erupt because of incompatible communication patterns?
    b. Could you recommend how these might have been changed so that the disruption in their relationship might not have occurred?
5. Interpersonal conflict is often found in blended families (e.g., communication between stepmothers and stepchildren, between ex-spouses and new spouses, and between divorced parents). Very often such conflict begins with the communication of "irritation in what another person has done" (or failed to do).
    a. In such instances, what other forms of communication could be used with more positive effects?
    b. How else might one express oneself at what seems the mistake or insensitivity of another that would not yield hostility?
    c. How might role playing be helpful in creating more harmonious communications?
    d. At the same time, if one is the target of irritated blame, one is not required or hard wired to respond with hostility. What other ways of responding might be more promising for all concerned?
6. Many people, in small and large ways, work to eliminate or reduce conflict in the world.
    a. Is it always a worthy goal to reduce conflict?
    b. Are there times when conflict may be good? How so?

7. Using Appreciative Inquiry, address a topic of importance to you in an organization or institution to which you belong. An example of a topic might be that there is a lack of commitment to the group among the members.
   a. What would be a question you might ask that could discover the positive core of the group and lead to new stories and new outcomes?
   b. How do you think this approach might be helpful in creating change? What might binder positive changes, if anything?

Crossing Boundaries

Introduction

It would be comforting to think that the study of communication would yield a set of highly reliable laws. If we could discover these laws, we could make constant predictions about people's actions. For example, we could know how to make more convincing arguments, to create harmony in groups, and how to get others to do what we want. After all, if medical science can make reasonably reliable statements about good health practices, then communication studies should ultimately tell us how to practice effective communication.

Alas, the world of communication is not like the world of neural pathways and heartbeats. The human body functions in roughly the same way across history and culture. Many of its functions operate in a complex, yet, reasonably predictable manner. In contrast, communication practices are human creations. They are akin to the games we have created, like basketball, football, tennis, Monopoly, and the like. There is no end to the number of games we can construct. To be sure, every game may have its rules, but we are also free at any time to change the rules.

Yet, even this analogy between communication and games does not tell the whole story of why communication is often unpredictable. In most games, the rules are shared by all the participants, they can be written down in a rule book, and referees can determine when there are infractions. Yet, communication practices in daily life are seldom so formal. When we communicate we typically draw from many different "language games," which may be combined in many different ways. For example, we may mix metaphors with no one to tell us we cannot do so.

According to one communication theorist, Michel Bakhtin, we are *polyvocal*. That is, we inherit from the past many different practices of speech, and when we speak we are drawing words and phrases from different cultures and historical times. The simple sentence "Thomas searched for my soul" draws from the Hebrew, Germanic, Latin, and French traditions.

Many forms of communication are specific to certain contexts. The way we speak together in class, for example, is not typically the way we communicate by e-mail. In this final part of the book (Part V) we explore communication issues in context. As you will discover, when we focus on different contexts, different questions, issues, and insights will emerge. We first turn to communication across cultures (Section A). Here we confront most directly the problems of communication created by living in a world of multiple traditions, thereby multiple meanings. We may enter a relationship with someone from another culture, skilled in our own traditions, but suddenly we find our skills are useless. Even when the other knows our language, he or she may not understand, or may laugh inappropriately, lapse into inexplicable silences, and stand too close. Sometimes we may seem to cause the other to be irritated, and we don't know why. The readings in this section are designed to sharpen sensitivity and suggest possible avenues to effectively relate to people with differing cultural views than our own.

In the final section of the book (Section B) we turn to cutting-edge problems of cultural change. Communication practices are forever in motion, and there is no more dramatic context of change than that generated by communication technology. The new communication technologies of the Internet and the cell phone, in particular, challenge our traditional ways of relating, and open exciting vistas of possibility. Our lives can be radically changed through the new communication media, and the readings in this section will open discussion on some important questions.

Communicating across Cultures

We often think of cultural differences in terms of geographic regions. In the United States we have American culture; in Italy, Italian culture; and in Japan, Japanese culture. However, the reality is that we live in a world where there is a vast movement of people across the face of the earth, and an even larger circulation of ideas, tastes, entertainments, and religions through the media. Culture bursts across geographical boundaries, and everyday life can be an adventure in communicating with people who are "different."

As you will recall from earlier readings, a constructionist view of communication places strong emphasis on "mutual coordination." Thus, trying to communicate across boundaries is not a matter of simply "decoding" the meaning of others' actions. Rather, it is a matter of coordinating actions with them. Ideally this would entail a process of mutuality, whereby both parties seek to coordinate their actions with each other. It is useful here to think of individuals who play different styles of music, let's say one classical violin and the other rock guitar.

They make different sounds, and play different genres of music, but with effort they may create new forms of music (as in jazz violin). And so it is with communication: The rules by which we function are always in motion and new creations are always possible.

Section A readings feature two major themes. The first emphasizes differences and the problems they pose for communication. The second focuses on the useful ways people bridge differences. We also wish to emphasize that communicating across cultures is not an unusual event. Every day we must locate a means of communicating with people who are different, and this welcoming challenge and opportunity only becomes more frequent in our world.

In Reading 50, the health care nurses Kathryn Kavanaugh, Kathleen Absalom, William Beil, and Lucia Schliessmann, who are not Native American, speak of their experiences in working with the Lakota Native American tribe. We see that "helping" is not an individual action, but a relational one. A person cannot help others unless they acknowledge or otherwise treat the action as helping. You cannot "give a gift" unless the recipient treats it as a gift. Although this reading addresses a particular cross-cultural communication, Reading 51 brings the challenge of cultural differences into everyday life. Sara Holbrook's poem describes what someone from the "Hippie generation" feels in confronting a young Goth woman. What can she say to help the Goth understand her life? How can the Goth recognize their similarities?

The dramatic importance of these questions becomes apparent in Reading 52 by Bojun Hu. In this selection, a college student sends an e-mail to her professor about her painful but rewarding experiences working as a counselor in a camp for children with emotional and learning disabilities. This reading demonstrates the particular difficulties encountered when communication coordination is less than mutual. It is Bojun who must continuously search for ways to bring relations into harmony. This same resistance to communication is brought into focus in Reading 53. Paul Willis furnishes us with a glimpse of the way lower-working-class British students historically joined together to resist the force of education, and any effort to break up their lower-working-class loyalties and identification with one another. They developed a special language, their own narratives, and their own interpretations of reality. All of these actions make it difficult for a teacher to "break through."

Finally, in Reading 54 we "overhear" a dialogue among five seasoned communication scholars—Mary Jane Collier, Brenda J. Allen, Benjamin J. Broome, Tricia S. Jones, and Victoria Chen. Each comes from a different cultural background. They do, however, share a common interest in building cultural alliances. In the reading they speak of their varied experiences, both in daily life and in foreign lands. We see that despite the difficulties, success in communicating across cultural divides can be achieved. And with such success we can move beyond the antagonisms so prevalent in the world today.

Connecting with the Lakota

Working with the Lakota people on their reservation presents a challenge to non-Native American nurses, who have been raised in the dominant "white" society. A cultural divide in communication must be overcome for these nurses to know the people behind the "cases," and how they can best help them. The stories of the nurses show how they grapple with cultural differences—which may arise out of seemingly "thin air." The nurses reflect on how they have been changed by their experiences with Lakota culture. Most leave the reservation with nostalgia for what they are losing as they return to the "White Man's Ways."

Reading 50 KATHRYN KAVANAUGH, KATHLEEN ABSALOM, WILLIAM BEIL, AND LUCIA SCHLIESSMANN

I can't be open to possibilities when I have preplanned outcomes and objectives. I like to be introduced by a Lakota community member, shake hands, see the expressions and feel the energy from the other person. I sit only when asked, accept the offered coffee or tea with gratitude, and wait for others to begin our conversation, which is sometimes a shared silence. The stories people tell generate questions that show my interest; everything else seems like firing questions now—too much too fast. I am learning to tolerate interruptions from children, grandchildren, siblings, neighbors, meals, Indian radio, dogs barking to be fed—or simply no one being home when they said they would be. Visits may last an hour; they may last 6 hours.

Connecting comes in many forms, all requiring investments in time, communication, and the aforementioned strenuous but ongoing negotiation between objectivity and subjectivity. Possibilities exist on many levels, allowing healthy interventions to be integrated into acceptable compromises. There is a sense of "relating to the practice that needs to happen" rather than setting out to do something in a manner more typical of biomedical contexts. One nurse provides an example with a family she encountered with several children with muscular dystrophy.

They were sleeping out of doors in the hot summertime, living in poverty, way out in the country. We talked with them and offered to refer them to the community health providers, but the family rejected the whole idea. I wanted to respect their wishes but do something for the kids, so I took them a few things, including bottles of bubbles, and showed them how to use them. They loved them and did some deep breathing in the process.

Shirley Red Wing explained that her daughter had a cough for three nights. She gave her Sudafed, but it did not help. Her son picked some bitterroot and boiled it. It had a bad taste but worked enough so she could sleep. Gum weed, bitterroot, and boiled sage are used for pain relief. Joanne Fox has arthritis and uses sage when the pain bothers her. She says the younger generation has not learned to value the herbs of their elders.

Sharon Falling Horse told about her mother picking choke cherries and said, "Oh, look at those way on top!" The best ones always seemed to be way on top of the tree where she could not reach them. Sharon's mother would say, "Well, we don't need those. The birds have to have something to eat too," an attitude that Sharon says goes back to the philosophy of balance and sharing. "The other beings need something too. We should only take what we need." Sharon says that tradition is hard to incorporate into the world we live in today. Our kids get messages from the outside and even from other Indian people about "the American dream—to get rich, to have stuff—and that goes against our ways. It is good to have things, but not in excess."

I am different in the sense that I am learning the importance of "being," as opposed to "doing." It seems, as I look back over my nursing career, that people of a culture benefit from having someone "be there" with them.

Letting Go, Letting Be

Leaving the Pine Ridge Lakota and reentering previous lives is a bittersweet process that entails loosening connections, some of which may call into question previous ways of living. Participants begin re-entering with anticipation, calling relatives and friends, thinking more about home and jobs, asking themselves and each other what changes they wanted and planned to make and defining new possibilities, alternatives, and goals. Losses also come in many forms. "I feel more comfortable and safe on the reservation; I hate to lose the security." The tension experienced upon reentering Euro-American lifeways, a "reverse culture-shock" generally described as a painful or difficult psychologic weariness after enduring intense cultural encounters, may be attributable to the value shifts that, embedded as implicit cultural assumptions, resist readjustment to the reentered culture upon return.

Being on this land with Lakota people has given me great appreciation for nature. I will continue to enjoy gardening, hiking, and biking, but will stop to appreciate the beauty of nature around me. I will take time to go somewhere to view the deep, dark background of the night sky painted with light prisms, alive with falling stars, and birds in flight. The grass whispers and the trees sway in song. How I will miss the freedom of this land!

I will be leaving tomorrow after a week of intense experiences with a special family and incredible land. Driving around the res, I chance upon fleeting sounds, wisps of light—the spirits of the place. Perhaps I have heard too many stories, or am allowing the other side of my brain to work for once, I know that what is a part of life for some of the people here would cause me great difficulty back home. I realize that during my short time here, I had my masks stripped from me. I know I need to find and put them on again. My ability to be open, ready for any interaction, needs to be regained. On the open land, I somehow send myself outward, trying to touch all life, able to sense living on every level from mere existing to whatever good or evil is. In the city I am surrounded by so much noise of humanity that I pull in and protect myself from many sensations.

The people on the Pine Ridge Reservation continue to be challenged by numerous problems, some of them indigenous to the reservation and the history of Lakota peoples, and many of them not. However changeable, poverty and harsh conditions are part of daily life. There are problems spawned by a virtual absence of jobs, a long tradition of dependence, and the limited carrying capacity of the physical environment. Historically, formal education has been congruent with neither the culture nor the needs of the people, so it tends to be devalued. But there is also simplicity and an honest vitality. Generosity is abundant. Even when people have little to spare, they expect to share, are expected to share, and do so graciously and with pride.

Explorations

1. Name four specific ways in which the Lakota "taught" the nurses different ways of communicating.

   a. _____

   b. _____

   c. _____

   d. _____

2. Can you think of two additional activities that might have been useful in increasing the nurses' capacities to generate cooperative relationships?

   _____

   _____

3. Sometimes the Lakota seemed to resist the helpful assistance of the nurses. Why do you think they did not at times take the nurses' advice, even if it were for their own good?

   _____

   _____

   _____

   _____

4. What will the nurses be losing from their experiences on the reservation when they return home?

_____

_____

_____

_____

Key Constructions

- Relating to those who have different ways of communicating
- Incorporating tradition

> ### READING 51

Speaking Across the Generations: The Hippie and the Goth

Each generation has its own ways of constructing reality, and associated ways of behaving. The forms of communication and action that unify one generation can also have the effect of distancing them from other generations. Here we share a poem by Sara Holbrook in which she finds herself, from the Hippie generation, musing about how to cross the divide in speaking with a young Goth.

Reading 51 SARA HOLBROOK

Chicks Up Front

Before and After,
we stand separate,
stuck to the same beer soaked floor,
fragranced, facing the same restroom mirror.
Adjusting loose hairs—
mine brown, hers purple.
Fumbling for lipsticks
mine pink, hers black—
a color I couldn't wear anyway
since that convention of lines gathered around my mouth last
year and won't leave.
We avoid eye contact,
both of us are afraid of being carded.

Mature, I suppose, I should speak,
but what can I say to the kind of hostility
that turns hair purple and lips black?
Excuse me, I know I never pierced my nose,
but hey, I was revolting once too.
Back. Before I joined the PTA,
when wonder bras meant, "where'd I put that."
I rebelled against the government system,
the male, female system,
the corporate system, you name it.
I marched, I chanted, I demonstrated.
And when shit got passed around,
I was there, sweetheart, and I inhaled.
Does she know that tear gas
makes your nose run worse than your eyes?
Would she believe that I was a volunteer when they called
"chicks up front," because no matter
what kind of hand-to-hand combat
the helmeted authoritarians may have been
engaged in at home,
they were still hesitant to hit girls
with batons in the streets.
"CHICKS UP FRONT!" and we marched and
we marched and we marched right back home.

Where we bore the children we were not going to bring into this
        mad world, and we
brought them home to the houses we were never going to
        wallpaper
in those Laura Ashley prints
and we took jobs with the corporate mongers
we were not going to let supervise our lives,
where we skyrocketed to
middle-management positions
accepting less money
than we were never going to take anyway
and spending it on the Barbie dolls
we were not going to buy for our daughters.

And after each party
for our comings and goings
we whisked the leftovers into dust pans,
debriefing and talking each other down
from the drugs and the men
as if they were different,

resuscitating one another as women do,
mouth to mouth.

That some of those we put up front
really did get beaten down
and others now bathe themselves daily
in Prozac to maintain former freshness.
Should I explain what tedious work it is
putting role models together,
and how strategic pieces
sometimes get sucked up by this vacuum.
And while we intended to take
one giant leap for womankind,
I wound up taking one small step, alone.

What can I say at that moment
when our eyes meet in the mirror,
which they will?

What can I say to purple hair, black lips
and a nose ring?
What can I say?
Take care.

Explorations

1. Clothing and hairstyles often indicate that one belongs to a particular group, class, or tradition.

   a. Are there any ways you can identify in which your styles discourage others from relating to you?

   _____

   _____

   _____

   b. In the poem, who is discouraged and why?

   _____

   _____

   _____

2. Do you find it difficult to relate to people in older generations?

   a. Give an example of when it is difficult to talk intergenerationally.

   _____

   _____

   _____

b. Give an example of when it is easier to share. Why the difference?

_____

_____

_____

3. If you were the author of this poem, confronted with what appeared to be a communication gulf, how might you initiate a conversation with the Goth? What kinds of questions or comments might help you both understand each other?

_____

_____

_____

Key Constructions

- Identity
- Culture and intergenerational communication

READING 52

Cultural Collisions: An E-mail from Bojun

Often we work with others who are quite different from us. Under these conditions we cannot easily rely on our conventional ways of communicating. Bojun is a student friend whose ethnic background is Chinese. She took a job in a summer camp to work with children with emotional and learning disabilities. The cultural clash is extreme. Bojun sent this e-mail account of her experiences. Frustration and tears seemed the only adequate responses until she learned how to deal with her new cultural challenges. Ultimately she found ways to communicate that lead to gratification and relief.

Reading 52 BOJUN HU

As the summer draws to an end, I just want to send a message of thanks and share something of these past weeks.

I have been at a camp for emotionally and learning disabled children for the past ten weeks or so. It's hard to describe the emotional rollercoaster ride.

With fifteen-hour days (7:30 a.m. to 10 p.m. with two hours break in between), six days a week, I was a mess the first few days and ended every day in tears: stings felt like stabs, and verbal jabs like downright insults.

There were days when kids not getting out of bed in the morning pushed me off the edge and "Get away from me, you bitch! I'm gonna punch your face in if you don't leave me alone" is, well, more than a bit too much.

But after the first few weeks of adjustments it has been much easier to devote myself entirely to these kids, trust that whatever they do they do with reasons, and allow myself to be surprised by them (during dinner today, one of my campers said to me, "we never finished our discussion during lunch. You told me that I have the right to feel unsafe. What about my right to feel safe?") The camper is a 12-year-old, great chess player, with long hair that covers his eyes most of the time. He is constantly teased by other campers for being gay and "on crack" because he responds and speaks very slowly despite his well-above-average verbal abilities and intelligence. He sits diagonally across from the 11-year-old M.J. who, according to last year's counselors, was the toughest child to interact with. M.J. had constantly cursed, ran away, and threatened others' lives. This summer, his primary challenge seems to be controlling his anger during meals and resorting to methods other than grabbing knives to threaten others and attempting to harm himself. He writes two or three rap songs daily, unfortunately at times replete with cursing and violence. During meals, his arbitrary target becomes Dylan, the long-haired boy, often threatening Dylan's life when he did not cough with hand over his mouth and head turned away. M.J. easily surrenders the weapon when asked, but the consistency with which he threatens is disheartening. One tries to offer alternative ways of using knives. How degrading it is for himself to treat others like objects and to play games like "it's under your right leg, no, the left leg." He could be such a sweet boy. It never ceased to touch me how he would pat me on the back when I cough or sneeze. The point is that today, instead of threatening to chop Dylan's fingers off one by one, M.J. says to Dylan as Dylan coughs with his head turned, "Good, now every time you do that, I'll put one of these back," and he sticks one of his knives in the drawer. Three coughs later, all the knives are back, and Dylan smiles. Here seems to be the small miracle: a few minutes later, M.J. offers Dylan an Oreo from the common bowl. This from the same boy who just hours before during lunch, screamed at the top of his lungs that he will not touch anything Dylan has touched.

It is easy to become extremely attached to my campers. I wake up and put to bed six 11- to 13-year-old boys daily and work in the reading center during the day, where I get to interact with all of the campers. Their motivations, ingenuity, and innocence are awe inspiring, funny, ludicrous, and always interesting. I had a camper last session who was a hypochondriac who insisted on finger-rubs from me because his joints are inflamed." When he fell during a dodge-ball tournament, he insisted that his arm be put in a sling despite the doctor's assurance that there's absolutely nothing wrong, not even a bruise. One of the counselors had a sling and was inquired after by many people. Seeing such, when he himself fell, one of the first things he did was point to the counselor's sling and demand, "I want that." So Martin had his sweater wrapped around his neck with his arm incapacitated for about a day before he decided that, all the heat, sweat, and physical inconvenience is not worth the little bit more of attention he was getting. He was so adorable, a headful of curly hair resting on your knees as he begs to have his back rubbed until he falls asleep every night.

I could confidently say that I've had no life, but camp life. My world has been that of singing songs, staring at "I Spy" books, reading stories, talking endlessly to kids about their choices and their troubles, and doing what they call "behavioral management" for those who curse, fight, refuse to learn, refuse to share, [are] addicted to sleep, or just need someone to care.

Two more days, and I will be home in Wisconsin again. It's been quite a summer, perhaps the most difficult I've ever experienced. Yet the rewards are simply amazing.

Best,

Bojun

Explorations

1. What were the major verbal and nonverbal forms of communication between Bojun and her campers that helped her overcome the gaps between herself and them?

_____

_____

_____

_____

2. What other ways might Bojun have responded to the situation that would have led to ever greater success?

_____

_____

_____

3. What do you think you would have done if you had Bojun's job?

_____

_____

_____

Key Constructions

- Communication with children with emotional and learning disabilities
- Adult–child communication

Resisting Education

Many parents who have little formal education and a "blue-collar" job hope that their children can have greater economic success. They place special emphasis on education as a way of moving up the economic ladder. And yet, the figures show that most children tend to end up in the same social class as their parents. Why is this so? Paul Willis takes the point of view that British teenagers learn to value the social class they are in, and they do this through communicating with one another. In maintaining their communicative bonds, they also reject the values and lessons of their teachers. Their early communication patterns heavily influence what social class they find themselves in later in life.

Reading 53   PAUL WILLIS

The difficult thing to explain about how middle-class kids get middle-class jobs is why others let them? The difficult thing to explain about how working-class kids get working-class jobs is why they let themselves? It is much too simple to say that they have no choice.

The main study was of a group of twelve non-academic working class lads attending a school we shall call Hammertown Boys. They are selected on the basis of friendship links, and membership of some kind of an oppositional culture in a working-class school. I want to suggest that "failed" working-class kids do not simply take up the work of the least successful middle-class, or where the most successful working-class kids leave off.

We shall be looking at the way in which the working-class cultural pattern of "failure" is quite different and discontinuous from other patterns.

In many respects the opposition we have been looking at can be understood as a classic example of the opposition between the formal and the informal. The school is the zone of the formal. It has a clear structure: the school building, school rules, pedagogic practice, a staff hierarchy with powers ultimately sanctioned—as we have seen in small ways—by the state, the pomp and majesty of the law, and the repressive aim of state apparatus, the police.

Counter-school culture is the zone of the informal. In working-class culture generally opposition is frequently marked by a withdrawal into the informal and expressed in its characteristic modes just beyond the reach of "the rule".

Even though there are no public rules, physical structures, recognized hierarchies or institutionalized sanctions in the counter-school culture, it cannot run on air. It must have its own material base, its own infrastructure. This is, of course, the social group. The informal group is the basic unit of this culture, the fundamental and elemental source of its resistance. It locates and makes possible all other elements of the culture, and its presence decisively distinguishes "the lads" from the "ear 'oles" [middle class "goodie-goods"].

The essence of being "one of the lads" lies within the group. It is impossible to form a distinctive culture by yourself. You cannot generate fun, atmosphere and a social identity by yourself. Joining the counter-school culture means joining a group, and enjoying it means being with the group:

[In a group discussion on being "one of the lads"]

JOEY: When you'm dossing on your own, it's no good, but when you're dossing with your mates, then you're all together, you're having a laff and it's a doss . . .

BILL: If you don't do what the others do, you feel out.

SPANKEY: I can imagine . . . you know, when I have a day off school, when you come back the next day, and something happened like in the day you've been off, you feel, "Why did I have that day off," you know, "I could have been enjoying myself." You know what I mean? You come back and they're saying, "Oorh, you should have been here yesterday," you know.

Though informal, such groups nevertheless have rules of a kind which can be described—though they are characteristically framed in contrast to what "rules" are normally taken to mean.

PW: Are there any rules between you lot?

PETE: We just break other rules.

FUZZ: We ain't got no rules between us though, have we?

WILL: We ain't got rules but we do things between us; but we do things that y'know, like er . . . say, I wouldn't knock off anybody's missus or Joey's missus, and they wouldn't do it to me, y'know what I mean? Things like that or, er . . . yer give im a fag, you expect one back, like, or summat like that.

FRED: Tain't rules, it's just an understanding really.

WILL: That's it, yes.

FRED: We're as thick as thieves, that's what they say, stick together.

Explorations

1. This reading suggests that these "lads" resist school primarily because of their own choosing. Are there any other reasons you can think of as to why they communicate in this resistive manner?

_____

_____

_____

2. This reading is about British lads who are learning from each other's communication about how to be working class. From your school life, provide an example in which certain subgroups' communication patterns resisted the normal rules of the school system.

_____

_____

_____

3. Why do you think some boys—American or British—act in a way that may limit their ability to move up the economic ladder?

_____

_____

_____

Key Constructions

- Social class and communication
- Cultural rules and patterns

READING 54

Bringing Cultures Together

As the world becomes increasingly "smaller," we face situations in which we must ally ourselves with people from other cultures. Often the circumstances for such alliances are difficult. There may be at times a history of animosities or suspicion. In Reading 54, communication scholars and practitioners talk together about their experiences in forging intercultural alliances.

Reading 54 MARY JANE COLLIER, BRENDA J. ALLEN, BENJAMIN J. BROOME, AND VICTORIA CHEN

Mary Jane Collier

My goal for this reading is to provide a new kind of forum, a cyberdialogue, in which scholar-practitioners listen to, reflect on, and engage each other's views rather than reporting a set of findings, justifying of conclusions, or advocating for a particular paradigm.

Here is a request to get the dialogue started. Describe an interaction, situation, and/or relationship in which you have experienced or observed others developing intercultural alliances.

Brenda Allen

As I thought about the question regarding intercultural alliances, two relationships immediately came to mind. Both of them originated within a department where I was a faculty member. One person was a faculty colleague; the other was a graduate student. I characterize my relationship with each as an intercultural alliance because of ways that each person and I differ. My faculty colleague is a middle-aged, white lesbian; the graduate student is a young, white, heterosexual woman.

In my alliance with each person, we address(ed) issues related to acknowledging, affirming, and valuing differences, in a variety of contexts. Anna was my colleague. She and I have since taken other jobs, so we no longer work together. However, we are friends for life and we remain in touch. She currently is employed as an EEO (equal employment opportunity) officer for the federal government, and she recently gave me a stack of information about race designations to inform a writing project I'm completing. So, our alliance continues! Anna was instrumental in helping me to understand some of the challenges that gays and lesbians routinely face. We became allies because we both were concerned about how our curriculum and our colleagues dealt with diversity issues.

Karen was a graduate student who wanted to study feminism in a program that had no feminist scholar. I agreed to direct her independent study on feminism and communication, and I am glad that I did. As a result of reading and discussing her review of related literature, my consciousness was raised, and I eventually began to self-identify as a scholar who applies feminist perspectives to research and teaching. We became allies in conducting research and developing curricula that addresses issues of power, domination, complicity, and resistance. We wrote and presented a paper at the National Communication Association conference titled "The Racial Foundation of Organizational Communication," which critiques "our field's participation in preserving the normative power of organized whiteness," and offers "specific suggestions for revising the racial subtext of our scholarship."

I've known both of these women for at least a decade. I can elaborate on either or both of these relationships, but I'll close for now with an observation. One reason that my alliances with Anna and Karen have been rewarding and enduring stems from our similarities (for instance, as women, or, for Anna and me, as Baby Boomers) as well as our differences. A second reason why I believe those alliances have succeeded and endured is that, in addition to accomplishing various goals, each relationship has allowed me to grow and to learn. I'm confident enough to say that Anna and Karen would say the same for their alliance with me.

Benjamin Broome

The most powerful case of intercultural alliance building in which I have been personally involved centers around the work of Greek Cypriot and Turkish Cypriot peace builders in the small eastern Mediterranean island of Cyprus. Members of the two ethnic communities, who have been physically separated for decades, speak different native languages (Greek and Turkish), follow different religious traditions (Christian Orthodox and Muslim), hold drastically different views of history, and are schooled from an early age to view the other community as the enemy. Ethnic division began to occur following skirmishes in 1963, when the Turkish Cypriots withdrew into enclaves. In 1974 a full-scale war broke out, resulting in the ethnic division of the island, creating hundreds of thousands of refugees and resulting in the loss of homes and businesses by nearly one-third of the population. Today there stands between the two communities a buffer zone guarded by United Nations peacekeeping forces separating heavily armed Turkish and Turkish-Cypriot forces in the north and Greek-Cypriot forces in the south. Since the cease-fire that was arranged in 1974, political negotiations have made little progress toward resolving the conflict.

In the late 1980s, members of the two communities made contact, primarily through workshops they attended abroad, and started working toward ways to promote peace in Cyprus. Because it was very difficult for them to communicate directly with one another (there are no telephone or mail links between the two sides of the buffer zone), and because authorities would not grant them permission to hold bicommunal meetings, progress was slow and there were many frustrations. In the early 1990s, a U.S.-based third party, Louise Diamond of the Institute for Multi-Track Diplomacy (IMTD), based in Washington, D.C., began visiting the island periodically and working separately with members of each community, offering training in conflict resolution. Based on the success of their work, the participants approached the Cyprus Fulbright Commission about bringing a conflict resolution specialist from the United States to work with them on a full-time basis. In September 1994 I took up this newly created position as Senior Fulbright Scholar in Cyprus.

My primary task in Cyprus centered on helping the existing group develop ways to work together productively across the physical, historical, cultural, and conflict divide that separated them. As I was to discover, there were nearly as many intragroup differences as intergroup differences. During the first 9 months, I met on a regular basis (weekly) with 15 Greek Cypriots and 15 Turkish Cypriots. Each group consisted of men and women from various sectors of society (education, business, politics, NGOs), a range of ages (approximately 25 to 55), and across the political spectrum (left-leaning to right of center). Participants spoke English as their second language, and although the group sometimes used Turkish or Greek in the monocommunal meetings, English was used in the joint meetings. We progressed through several "phases" of work, including an in-depth examination of the barriers facing the group in their efforts to develop a citizen-based peace movement in Cyprus.

In the beginning, most of our meetings were held in separate communal groups, because we could not obtain permission from the authorities to meet jointly. Later, we were able to come together on a regular basis over several months in bicommunal meetings. Discussions (in both the monocommunal and bicommunal settings) were often intense and emotional, at times inspiring and at other times extremely frustrating for everyone. The group nearly broke apart on several occasions, but the commitment and dedication of participants kept us together. The group bonded in a special way through these meetings, and they became the core group of peace builders in Cyprus, forming the nucleus around which most of the developing intercommunal activities were centered.

Over the 4-year period following the series of meetings described above, more than 2000 people became involved in bicommunal activities organized by this core group. By that point, the size of the group had become threatening to those who wanted to maintain the division on the island, and the Turkish Cypriot authorities stopped giving permission to individuals in the north to cross into the buffer zone to meet with their counterparts in the south, resulting in a "ban" on bi-communal meetings that is still in effect today. Fortunately, Internet access was just being established in Cyprus when the ban was first put in place, and many projects have gone forward with electronic communication providing the primary means for people to maintain contact and work together. In addition, a number of meetings have been held abroad, and on a limited basis, in a small, remote village located within a British-controlled military area. Thus, the work has continued to this day, although it has had to take different forms.

My stay in Cyprus lasted approximately 2 1/2 years. After the initial 9-month series of meetings with the core group, I continued my Fulbright assignment and assisted with several projects, helping to form other, more specialized groups, consisting of young business leaders, young political leaders, women activists, and university students. Since my return to the United States, I have traveled back to Cyprus numerous times, and I have organized several workshops, seminars, and other meetings outside Cyprus. The members of the core group remain my most trusted colleagues, as well as good friends. We help each other keep the faith, even during difficult times.

Victoria Chen

Ben, as I read through your case, I was wondering what you would consider the essential "conditions" that make the intercultural alliances between the Greek and Turkish Cypriot possible. What was the nature of their dialogue in the process? How did the construction of their intercultural alliance evolve over time? And would it be helpful for us to know something about how your facilitation helped make this intercultural alliance possible? I understand that it might take more time for you to reflect on your role in the two groups, but I'm curious how you presented or identified yourself as a U.S. American, and how they related to you while you were trying to make a difference by creating this inter-cultural alliance.

Explorations

1. The reading discussed promising criteria for forging intercultural alliances. List five significant factors or conditions suggested by these scholar/ practitioners that would contribute to good alliance building.

   a. _____

   _____

   b. _____

   _____

   c. _____

   _____

   d. _____

   _____

   e. _____

   _____

2. Provide two ways in which you build intercultural alliances with friends, fam-ily members, coworkers, and/or intimate partners from different cultures.

   _____

   _____

   _____

   _____

   _____

Key Constructions

- Building intercultural alliances

Key Constructions for Part Five, Section A

- Relating to those who have different ways of communicating.
- Incorporating tradition
- Identity
- Culture and intergenerational communication
- Communication with children with emotional and learning disabilities
- Adult–child communication
- Social class and communication
- Cultural rules and patterns
- Building intercultural alliances

SECTION

Communicating in the New Worlds of Technology

Much of this book has been concerned with face-to-face communication. Such concerns arise from our everyday life experiences. But everyday life has changed dramatically over the past several decades, and increasingly our communication takes place electronically. Thrust between us are computers, cell phones, fax machines, and video recording devices. As often said, we increasingly live in an electronically mediated world. Shifting the context of how we communicate raises many interesting and important questions. For example, do the new forms of communication build strong bonds, or are we moving toward weaker, or more superficial relations? Do these technologies demand simplification or "dumbing down" of what we say? Are we losing our ability for more intensive and detailed communication? On the other hand, can we now move more easily across cultural boundaries? Do we become more tolerant and empathic as a result? Do these technologies only strengthen existing ties within groups and increase prejudice and discrimination to those outside?

The readings in this section are all concerned with implications for the new communication technologies for interpersonal communication. In the first three readings, we take up the important issue of human connection. Whereas communication links may expand dramatically, it is not so clear that communication over the Internet (cyberspace) makes much difference to people. Communication can be lively, but it may also be superficial. Little important change in society may result. In Reading 55, Malcolm R. Parks and Kory Floyd ask the simple question of whether Internet discussion on newsgroups breeds more than casual conversation. Do people actually become friends who sustain their relationship outside the newsgroup? Their report suggests that even newsgroups may give rise to more significant friendship. Reading 56 by John K. Miller and Kenneth J. Gergen adds further support to this possibility. Traditionally the practice of psychotherapy has been controlled by professional therapists. Yet, many people cannot afford the help. In this reading, we look at the potentials of online communication among people confronting suicide as a vehicle for helping each other.

Although Internet communication may yield significant interchange, there are also many impediments. Among the most important is the issue of trust. Typically we don't see those with whom we communicate, and if we have never met them, we face the possibility that they are not what they seem. We may find ourselves caught between the desire to believe and doubts in the authenticity of the words before us. This is perhaps nowhere more relevant than in the increasingly popular trend toward online personals, or match-making networks. In Reading 57 Jennifer L. Gibbs, Nicole B. Ellison, and Rebecca D. Heino provide a glimpse into the honesty of self-disclosure on the Net. As they find, participants generally try to paint an honest picture of themselves, but in various ways fail to do so.

In the next anonymous reading (Reading 58) we move to the freedom of participation offered by the blog, or the personal log placed on the Web. The World Wide Web makes it easy for almost anyone to set up a Web site in which he or she can describe daily experiences. Blogs are already changing the face of news reporting because we can now have direct access to people "at the front" of world events, instead of trusting newspaper syndicates. Many people also believe the blog is encouraging more freedom in daily life. Now there are thousands of blogs in which people reveal intimate details from their daily lives. One learns of new possibilities for living, and we may cease to think of ourselves as having peculiar tastes or habits.

We complete this section with Reading 59, Joshua Meyorowitz's meditation on technology and cultural change. Painted with broad strokes is the landscape of the future. As Meyorowitz sees it, technologies of communication are radically changing our cultural ways of life. Your observations and ideas on these issues are significant as you, the reader, will participate in molding this future.

READING 55

Making Friends in Cyberspace

One of the richest questions about the impact of Internet communication has to do with friendship. As we rely increasingly on Internet communications, how are patterns of friendship changed, or not? Do we gain an increasing number of friends? Are these friends important to us, or do these relationships remain superficial? If we gain meaningful friendships at a distance, do we inflict damage on our daily relationships? Or, is there a tendency to live vicariously through online relationships, and to drop out of the responsibilities of ordinary, day-to-day relationships? There are no obvious answers to these questions. There are broad differences in how we engage in Internet relationships, and life on the Net changes as new technologies emerge. However, too seldom do we ask about the effects of new technologies on our relationships. In our focus on the capabilities of the technology—their speed and sophistication, for example—we forget to ask about how our lives will be changed. Reading 55 is an invitation to explore these matters more fully.

**Reading 55 MALCOLM R. PARKS
              AND KORY FLOYD**

From its birth as a way of linking a few university and defense laboratories in the late 1960s, the Internet has grown into a global network connecting between 30 and 40 million people. Social linkages in the form of E-mail and discussion groups appeared in the first days of the Internet and have grown explosively ever since. There are over 5,000 Internet discussion groups. Aside from its sheer size, this new social milieu commands scholarly attention because it is one of the new "collaborative mass media forms" in which messages come from a wide variety of participants with little or no centralized control. It therefore blurs the traditional boundaries between interpersonal and mass communication phenomena and raises new opportunities and risks for the way individuals relate to one another.

The purpose of this study was to examine the relational world actually being created through the Internet discussion groups. Because the development of personal relationships is a pivotal issue in the larger debate about human relations in cyberspace, this study explores how often do personal relationships form and who has them.

Computer mediated communication liberates interpersonal relations from the confines of physical locality and thus creates opportunities for new, but genuine, personal relationships and communities.

How Often Do Personal Relationships Form Online?

Our first task was to determine just how common personal relationships were in online settings. To do this, as well as to address our other research questions, Internet groups and their contributors were selected through a two stage sampling procedure. In the first stage, 24 groups were randomly selected from published lists of groups in each of four major Usenet newsgroup hierarchies: "comp," "soc," "rec," and "alt." In the second stage, 22 people were randomly chosen from lists of those who had posted messages to these groups over a several day period. Surveys were then sent to prospective participants by direct E-mail. Responses were received from 176 of the 528 (33.3%) people contacted in this manner. Respondents ranged in age from 15 to 57 years. The typical respondent was 32 years old, more likely to be male than female, and more likely to be single than married. Respondents had typically been involved with newsgroups for approximately two years and contributed to an average of five groups on a monthly basis.

Our primary finding was that personal relationships were common. When we asked if our respondents had formed any new acquaintances, friendships, or other personal relationships as a result of participating in newsgroups, nearly two thirds (60.7%) reported that they had indeed formed a personal relationship with someone they had "met" for the first time via an Internet newsgroup. Further, the likelihood of developing a personal relationship did not differ across the newsgroup hierarchies of groupings we examined. That is, personal relationships seemed equally likely to develop in all sectors we examined. They were not restricted to just a few types of newsgroups. The fact that personal relationships developed for so many of our respondents and across so many different types of newsgroups suggests that criticisms of online interaction as being impersonal and hostile are overdrawn. These findings lend more credence to images of relationships liberated than to images of relationships lost.

These findings obviously raise questions about the types of relationships that our respondents were forming. Additional analysis revealed that opposite-sex relationships (55.1%) were slightly more common than same-sex relationships (44.9%) but this difference was not statistically significant. Only a few (7.9%) were romantic. Relationships ranged in duration from less than a month to six years, but most relationships (69.9%) were less than a year old. Participants communicated regularly with their online partners. Nearly a third (29.7%) reported that they communicated with their partners at least three or four times a week, and over half (55.4%) communicated with their partners on a weekly basis.

Who Has Online Personal Relationships?

Some people may be more likely than others to develop personal relationships online. Although stereotypes of lonely, perhaps dysfunctional, people being attracted to cyberspace abound in the popular press, the fact is that we lack even the most basic information about the participants in online relationships. We compared people who did and did not have an online personal relationship in terms of their demographic characteristics and patterns of Internet involvement.

Women were significantly more likely than men to have formed a personal relationship online. While 72.2% of women had formed a personal relationship, only 54.5% of men had. Additional research will be needed to distinguish potential explanations for this difference. It may stem from motivational factors. It may simply be that a greater proportion of women are looking for friends. There may be gender differences in the willingness to label an online relationship as such. Or, women may simply be more sought after in a medium where more users are male.

People who formed personal relationships online contributed to significantly more newsgroups than did those who had not. Across the total sample, approximately 40% of the respondents had no online personal relationships, about 30% had a less developed personal relationships, and about 30% had what might legitimately be considered a highly developed personal relationship.

Relationships that began in Internet newsgroups often broadened to include interaction in other channels or settings. Although nearly all respondents used direct E-mail (98%) in addition to newsgroup postings, a surprising number also supplemented computer-mediated communication with other forms of contact. About a third had used a telephone (33.3%), the postal service (28.4%), or face-to-face communication (33.3%) to contact their online friends.

Explorations

1. The study focuses exclusively on Internet newsgroups. Do you have contrasting experiences that would broaden your understanding of how relationships develop online? If you communicate with others you have never met

face-to-face in chat rooms, list serves, collective computer game situations, or other Internet contexts, does meaningful friendship ever result? Explain how.

_____

_____

_____

2. If friendships have developed in one of these contexts, how would you explain their origin? What factors favored such developments?

_____

_____

_____

3. In what ways do you think online communication (e.g., IM-ing, text messaging, avatar communities) affects your day-to-day friendships? Consider communication both with people you know only through the Internet, and communication with your face-to-face friends.

_____

_____

_____

4. The hours consumed playing computer games and other electronic games are steadily increasing in the population (e.g., PlayStation, Game Boy, Wii. . . .). What effect, if any, do these activities have on friendship patterns? (e.g., Are friendships enriched or do they become more superficial?)? What is your experience?

_____

_____

_____

Key Constructions

- Friendships in cyberspace

READING 56

Grassroots Therapy on the Net

The mental health professions have grown by leaps and bounds over the past century. Simultaneous with this rapid spurt in growth has been an eroding of the traditional face-to-face community. With various technological developments, parents often work at considerable distance from their home, children often travel distances to school, and when physically present in the home both parents and children are elsewhere psychologically—on the phone, watching television, or surfing the Web. Having close relationships within the community once acted as buffers against distress. People could talk over their problems, seek advice, and receive the kind of support that enabled them to get through hard times. With erosion of the community, people had to seek the help and support of mental health professionals.

In recent years, however, the Internet has not only stimulated the development of new relationships, but allowed people to sustain close relationships at a distance. We confront the optimistic possibility, then, that Internet communication will begin to furnish the same kinds of support and direction once supplied by face-to-face communities. The research reported in Reading 56 explores the therapeutic potentials of a suicide support network.

**Reading 56   JOHN K. MILLER AND
KENNETH J. GERGEN**

As many cultural commentators propose, the information superhighway—most specifically, the Internet—is beginning to have revolutionary effects on cultural life, extending from families, friendships, and communities to broad systems of education, government, medicine, and more. In principle, the Internet enables anyone on the globe to communicate with anyone else about any topic or concern.

Closely related to therapeutic concerns, it is possible for users to participate in discussion groups on virtually any topic they choose, from sexual deviance and scuba diving, to art and experimental aviation. In effect, thousands of people who previously had difficulty connecting with others of similar predilection have found a new medium of convenient, inexpensive, and continuously available communication.

Of specific interest to therapists, individuals connected with each other through the Net can approximate a virtual community. The community is virtual because it does not exist in a single geographic locale, does not involve face-to-face interchange, and is often constituted by communication that does not take place in real time (but rather through messages posted at one time and answered at another). A significant number of these virtual communities are specifically concerned with issues of substantial personal significance, among them love, loss, suicide, sex, drug recovery, depression, child abuse, eating disorders, and grief.

To what degree can the vital expansion in network intimacy serve deteriorating family, friendship, and community functions? Or, in terms of professional repercussions, of what therapeutic value is communication in the virtual community?

PART FIVE

272

In the present research we recorded all entries to the AOL suicide bulletin board for an 11-month period. During this period there were 98 contributors to the bulletin board, who made a total of 232 posts to the network. While this suggests that over the 11 months the participants posted fewer than three messages each, this mean masks the general pattern of contributions. A closer analysis reveals that approximately a quarter of the participants posted 51% of all entries to the board (of which a subgroup of 10 posted 41% of all entries). In general, then, while the site is occasionally visited by a range of casual or uncommitted participants (61 participants contributed only a single message), there is a nucleus of individuals who remain within the network for an extended period and contribute with substantial frequency. Let us consider more closely the content of the network entries.

Help-Seeking Interchange

Direct requests for help were relatively infrequent—only 17 requests over the period (each made by a different person). In the simple cases, participants simply request direct advice for help (e.g., "Does anyone have experience with homeopathic remedies for depression?"). Other entries were far more intense:

> What does one do, namely me, when he has been suffering through a horrifying depression for two years, has been on every medication from Ativan or Zoloft (without success), parents/friends don't understand, is gay, has no one to love, feels sick all the time, has attempted suicide once . . . has a physician and psychiatrist who have almost given up on curing me . . . is without a shred of self-confidence, self-worth/esteem, and believes that he should have the right to die? Where is hope?

In striking contrast, self-disclosure (the revealing of personal problems in such a way that help is invited) was one of the most frequently used forms of discourse in the entire sample. Of the 564 coded actions, almost a fifth featured personal disclosures. The quality of these disclosures is scarcely captured by the categorization. Many of them were highly intimate in character and were charged with emotional energy. The following post is representative:

> I was very depressed for a couple of years. I've been on antideps for a long time, a couple of years ago I hit bottom. So I was hospitalized a bunch of times. Last fall I took a massive dose of pills and was well on my way to la-la land, but was found, cleaned out and hospitalized again. I was given ECT and that has helped me rise out of depression, yet I still want to die. . . . I just wish the ground would open up and swallow me up. I look at the undersides of eighteen wheelers and want to drive under them. I pray to be hit by lightning. I've even gone out nights to the bad sections of town hoping for a drive-by shooting. My depression is stable now, I want to die, but I don't want my husband to suffer through a suicide.

Informative Interchange

It is important to note that reactions to help-seeking postings were generally both reliable and rapid. A small but significant proportion of the responses to help-seeking included some form of information exchange. With some frequency participants asked each other questions (e.g., "How many ECTs are they giving you?"). Slightly more frequently were attempts to offer useful advice. Perhaps the aspect of this advice most important to therapeutic practice is its range. Unlike many therapeutic treatments, which tend to be rather narrow in their view of appropriate remedies, the Net provides an enormous range of advice:

> When you feel especially awful, do nothing. Be inert.
>
> Prozac or other drugs can help.
>
> Be mellow and take very good care of yourself . . . like a good day of rest and a good book.
>
> The single most helpful ideas in my life have come from intelligent exploration of my own inner pain.
>
> By the way, read about seasonal affective disorder. You may have it.
>
> Call someone, anyone just to change pace. Get out of your home to be around people. Any distraction can help.
>
> Howard call your doctor now.

One of the most touching entries in the entire sample was that of a 13-year-old participant who offered advice to a mother distraught when she found her own adolescent child was suicidal:

> I know that I really don't belong here, I am 13. But I have insight into a suicidal teenager's mind. Feel lucky that he even told you. . . . I realize that you, too, must hurt. But just him telling you is an absolutely extraordinary sign. It means that he trusts you that he wants and is counting on you to help him. The problem is what you are concerned about. Don't be. I don't know if it's something that you could egg out of him. Especially if the problem has something to do with you. (I'm not Dying to place blame, just show options.) Get him someone to talk to. He seems to have a very open communication line, seeing that he even told you. He might just go with it and get help.

In a handful of cases, participants made predictions that might be useful to the help seeker in evaluating the future. In effect, participants often treated each other much as neighbors or acquaintances, exchanging practical information on their common problems.

Supportive Interchange

Although participants in online discussions of suicide frequently exchange information and advice, there is a far greater tendency to offering various forms of support. The most frequent form of discourse in the entire sample was that of empathic understanding. The following illustrates the quality and intensity of these offerings:

> *I really do feel and share your pain.*
> *I understand where you are coming from.*
> *I celebrate with you. Happy living!!!*

Punitive Interchange

In general we found sparing use of punitive discourse in network exchanges on suicide. There were 18 instances in which participants expressed doubt in another's narrations, but these were generally mild in tenor (e.g., "I agree with you, except on one issue: You do have a choice").

There were also a handful of cases in which participants attempted to reprimand or criticize each others' actions or opinions. Often this was in response to being helped (e.g., "I do not have that choice or control!! It is taken away from me every time some bleeding heart like you comes along to try to show me the error of my ways"). Most frequently, however, such attempts seemed to be aimed at improving the other (e.g., "You're just plain lazy").

Summary of Results

To summarize the emerging picture of interchange on this "suicide network," it is useful to consider the distribution of the various conversational contributions. The vast preponderance of network interchange is in the areas of self-revelation (or help-seeking) on one hand, and empathic and encouraging responses on the other. In a broad sense, the group provided much that might otherwise be obtained from intimate friendship. The participants remained at a "safe distance" but offered valuable resources in terms of validation of experience, sympathy, acceptance, and encouragement. If there is an important secondary role played by the participants, it might be described as "neighborly"; to substantial degree, the participants asked provocative questions and gave each other broad ranging advice. Although participants occasionally attacked each other, such hostilities were seldom intense. While these forms of community resources were abundantly evident, there was far less of the type of communication more typically identified with schools of therapy. In our view, participants were more content to help each other through the dark times than propel each other to change the conditions or courses of their lives. In effect, the communiques were more sustaining than transforming.

Explorations

1. If the comments of participants on the Net were helpful to others, what do you think enabled their comments to achieve such ends? Would the

comments of anyone (novice or expert), at any time (a.m. or p.m.), in any medium (face-to-face, chat room, e-mail) be equal in their effects?

_____

_____

_____

2. Is this kind of help inadequate? What limitations or shortcomings do you see in the kind of help supplied by participants on the Net?

_____

_____

_____

3. Select three e-mail messages you have received from friends in recent weeks. Print them and highlight the sections that might suggest supportive, helpful, or nurturing behaviors.

Key Constructions

- Therapeutic online communication
- Computer-mediated communication

READING 57

Honesty in Online Personals

Many people resist forming close relationships online, and most particularly with people they have never met. There are strong reservations because of the uncertainty of others' authenticity. Are they telling the truth? Are they possibly playing out a false identity, using a different name, gender, or age? Many people have frightening stories to tell about such cases. These issues play an especially important role in online dating and mating services. Increasingly people are using such services to find others with whom to play, and possibly to settle with for life. Trust is essential under these conditions, and yet, can one afford to trust? Reading 57 raises these issues, suggesting that where meeting is likely, honesty is greatest. However, even where honesty counts there are subtle pressures to "spin the self."

Reading 57 JENNIFER L. GIBBS, NICOLE B. ELLISON, AND REBECCA D. HEINO

Online dating, or communicating with individuals via the Internet or World Wide Web for the purpose of finding romantic and/or sexual partners, constitutes an exciting new realm in which to reexamine traditional interpersonal theories of self-disclosure and relationship formation as well as more recent theories of computer-mediated communication (CMC). The online dating context presents a novel opportunity to study relationships that begin online and then move to offline, face-to-face encounters.

In our research, we find that individuals with long-term goals of establishing face-to-face (Ftf) relationships engage in higher levels of self-disclosure in that they are more honest, disclose more personal information, and make more conscious and intentional disclosures to others online. Their disclosures are not necessarily more positive than disclosures of those placing less importance on FtF goals, however. This unexpected finding may be explained by the fact that they are trying to present themselves in a realistic manner (i.e., one that includes negative as well as positive attributes) because they know such attributes will eventually be revealed in time if they develop ongoing FtF relationships.

A very high percentage (94%) of our respondents strongly disagreed that they had intentionally misrepresented themselves in their profile or online communication, and 87% strongly disagreed that misrepresenting certain things in one's profile or online communication was acceptable. However, although unlikely to admit they themselves had lied, a high proportion of respondents did feel that certain characteristics were frequently misrepresented online by others. The most common were physical appearance (86%), relationship goals (49%), age (46%), income (45%) and marital status (40%). More in-depth exploration of this issue through our qualitative analysis revealed that misrepresentation was not always intentional and occurred in three ways: through representation of an inaccurate self-concept, fudging demographic information such as age to avoid being "filtered out" in searches, and portrayal of an idealized or potential future version of the self. Despite claims of honesty, these findings speak to the pressures to present an idealized online persona, which may not be a completely honest representation of one's "true self."

Explorations

1. The research focused on communication in an online dating context. Do you have contrasting experiences that would broaden our understanding? If you communicate with others you have never met face-to-face in chat rooms, list serves, collective computer game situations, or other Internet contexts, is authenticity an issue? In what ways is it important? If it is not important, explain.

_____

_____

_____

2. Have you ever represented yourself in Internet communication in ways that were not quite honest? How do you account for such actions? What were the results?

_____

_____

_____

3. Under what conditions do you most trust on online communication?

_____

_____

Key Constructions

■ Trust and honesty on the Internet

READING 58

Blogs: The Coming of Public Diaries

Personal diaries originally came into vogue in the 18th century. Although largely personal accounts, their secrecy was secured by lock and key. They presumed an imaginary reader. With the emergence of the World Wide Web, a new phenomenon has come into being: the blog, short for web log. Tens of thousands of individuals now write diaries, but they are made available for all to see. Personal lives are exposed as never before. How are we to understand this form of communication? What are its effects on the building, maintaining, and terminating of our relationships within the culture?

To stimulate your thinking on this subject, Reading 58 is excerpted from an anonymous blogger whose intimate life seems open to all.

Reading 58   ANONYMOUS

We are very, very close to falling in love. (Or maybe it's just me.)

It's not hard to fall in love with someone who likes to snuggle with me, enjoys our conversation, has the same interests, and is delicious. When he hugged me from behind and licked my ears as we watched the movie, I thought I was going to die, I was so happy.

Of course, I'm not falling. I'm walking the line. There's no point in falling in love with someone I will never end up with. It's just asking for heartbreak, right there.

We enjoy each other for what we are—an affair. A beautiful one.

Global Orgasm Day tomorrow! And he's doing me. Don't forget to dedicate your sexual energies to world peace, everybody.

Explorations

1. What do you think of this blogger's public account of herself (or himself)?

   _____

   _____

2. Is this online journal merely entertaining, or could you be subtly affected or informed by it in some way?

   _____

   _____

3. With thousands of blogs such as this open to public viewing, what might be some repercussions on cultural life? For example, do you think such blogs invite more liberal or conservative attitudes among people?

   _____

   _____

4. What are some other possibilities?

   _____

   _____

5. Select a Web search engine (e.g., www.google.com) and survey a range of blogs. Chose two that differ in significant ways from Reading 58. Print excerpts from the blog and highlight key themes. What might be some repercussions of such blogs on cultural life?

   _____

   _____

   _____

Key Constructions

■ Blogging and public identity

The Digital Landscape

In this final reading Joshua Meyorowitz (Reading 59) scans the horizon of the future, asking us to consider the implications of the enormous expansion of communication technologies. As you read this piece, try to associate freely to the images and distinctions he makes.

Reading 59   JOSHUA MEYOROWITZ

As we rely more and more on computers, mobile phones, television, and other electronic media for information, consumption, and human interaction, fewer of our activities and smaller parts of our identities are tied to, or shaped by, specific locales or fixed roles. As we face an abundance of easily located information in cyberspace, we are more likely to abandon efforts to gather all we might want and store it in our homes and businesses. Instead, we tend to "store" many items where we found them ("bookmarking" the sites, perhaps), just as nomads leave herds of game and clusters of berry bushes in their natural habitats to be accessed when needed.

When media theorist Marshall McLuhan declared that, with electronic media, we all live in a "global village," he might actually not have reached back far enough for an appropriate analogy. Rather than moving back to a village with relatively set roles and a fixed location, we are, instead, more like global nomads. We return in some ways to the earliest form of human organization, as we spiral forward as hunters and gatherers in a digital veldt. Our migration to this new cultural milieu creates changes in appearances of the houses, offices, neighbourhoods, cities, and countries we inhabit.

Electronic information seeps through walls and leaps across vast distances. While we still often think of electronic media as simply connecting one place to another more quickly, our forms of communication have been subtly but significantly altering the environments we live in, transforming them into new social places in which we are becoming new kinds of people.

A key feature of the electronic era is that most physical, social, cultural, political, and economic boundaries have become more porous, sometimes to the point of functionally disappearing. This seemingly simple proposition has far-reaching significance and implications. The relatively segregated systems that once defined distinct roles, nations, industries, products, services, and channels of communication have been leaking into each other. While the key change is literally happening "at the margins" of all social systems, the change is not simply something happening "out there." As the margins change, the contents of all forms of human organization change. As a result, we are experiencing a dramatic shift in our senses of locale, identity, time, values, ethics, etiquette, and culture.

The increasing functional permeability of boundaries—combined with the continued physical existence of most of those same boundaries—explains the contradictory feelings we have in the early 21st century:

In our electronic landscape, we have thinner distinctions:

- between here and there
- between now and then (and yet to be)
- between public and private
- between male and female spheres.
- between child and adult realms of experience
- between leaders and average citizens
- between office and home
- between work and leisure
- between businesses and customers
- between users and producers
- between news and entertainment
- between one field or discipline and another
- between different media genres
- between simulated and real
- between copies and originals
- between direct and indirect experience
- between biology and technology
- between marginal and mainstream

Explorations

1. Select a theme, image, or distinction suggested by Meyorowitz's musings and expand on it. Do you think there are significant communication changes taking place in our culture as a result of our communication technologies? Can you elaborate and give examples of how emerging technologies will change our interpersonal communication (e.g., videoconferencing, using cell phones, texting)?

_____

_____

_____

_____

Key Constructions

- Future horizons
- Global nomads
- Permeability of boundaries
- Electronic landscape

Funny Times, May 20.

Key Constructions for Part Five, Section B

- Friendships in cyberspace
- Therapeutic online communication
- Computer-mediated communication
- Trust and honesty on the Internet
- Blogging and public identity
- Future horizons
- Global nomads
- Permeability of boundaries
- Electronic landscape

PART FIVE

Suggested Readings

Culture

Gertz, C. (1973). *The interpretation of cultures*. New York: Basic Books.

Hall, B. (2002). *Among culture: The challenge of communication*. New York: Wadsworth.

Hall, S., & Jefferson, T. (Eds.). (1976). *Resistance through rituals*. New York: Hutchinson.

Jandt, F. E. (2001). *Intercultural communication*. Thousand Oaks, CA: Sage.

Katz, J. (2006). *Magic in the air: Mobile communication and the transformation of social life*. New Brunswick, NJ: Transaction Publishers.

Leeds-Hurwitz, W. (2005). *From generation to generation: Maintaining cultural identity over time*. Creskill, NJ: Hampton Press.

Rodriguez, A. (2001). *Diversity as liberation: Vol. 2. Introducing a new understanding of diversity*. Cresskill, NJ: Hampton Press.

Sugiman, T., Gergen, K. J., Wagner, W., & Y. Yamada (Eds.) (2008). *Meaning in action: Constructions, narratives, and representations*. New York: Springer.

Technology

Gergen, K. J. (1991). *The saturated self: Dilemmas of identity in contemporary life*. New York: Basic Books.

Graham, B. (1999). Why I weblog: A rumination on where the hell I'm going with this website. In J. Rodzvill (Ed.), *We've got blogs: How weblogs are changing our culture* (pp. 34–42). Cambridge, MA: Perseus.

Markham, A. N. (1988). *Life online: Researching real experience in virtual space*. New York: Altamira Press.

Nakamura, L. (2002). *Cybertypes: Race, ethnicity, and identity on the Internet*. New York: Routledge.

Turkle, S. (1997). *Life on the screen*. New York: Simon and Schuster.

Wood, A. F., & Smith, M. J. (2001). *Online communication: Linking technology, identity and culture*. Mahwah, NJ: Erlbaum.

Web Resources

Culture

Blogs about cultural differences
http://wordpress.com/tag/cultural-difference/

Association for Cypriot: Turkish and Greek affairs
www.peace-cyprus.org/ACGTA/

Working class literature, films and values resource website
http://members.aol.com/_ht_a/lsmithdog/bottomdog/webdoc4.htm

Cuban American (Miami) culture
http://icuban.com/about.html

Fundamentals of Goth culture
www.sfgoth.com/primer/

Lao cultural rites, rituals, and communication patterns
www.seasite.niu.edu/lao/undp/socialconvention.htm

Community development and collaboration
www.imaginechicago.org

Los Angeles Chinese Cultural Center-Site—Chinese business relationships
http://chinese-school.netfirms.com/guanxi.html

Navajo student living between worlds—NPR interview (audio clip)
www.npr.org/templates/story/story.php?storyId=6845552

Website of Dr. Michelle Fine – subcultural action research
http://web.gc.cuny.edu/Psychology/socpersonality/MFine.htm

Technology
Computer-mediated journals and projects-online links
http://jcmc.indiana.edu/citesite.html

Howard Rheingold high interactive website
www.rheingold.com/

MySpace.com—An online youth/young adult community
www.myspace.com/

Gender differences in using the Net; NPR interview (audio clip)
www.npr.org/templates/story/story.php?storyId=5080998

Wellness Community—Virtual tour and online cancer support groups
www.thewellnesscommunity.org/support/house.php

Virtual society information booth—listing of new technologies
www.sonycsl.co.jp/project/VS/

Sim Games
http://thesims2.ea.com/index.php

Discussion Questions and/or Short Papers

1. Communication with people who differ from us in cultural background (including ethnicity, religion, race, geographic home) can be difficult. At the same time, most of us have had very positive experiences with others who are different. We find that friendship is easy and we prize these relationships.
   a. Describe one such relationship in your own life, and try to account for why it was a success.
      1) What factors enabled you to overcome what many see as barriers to communicating across cultures?
   b. Given your experience, what are the implications for bringing world cultures together?
      1) Do you think a "world community" is possible? Why or why not? Explain.
2. New communication technologies are continuously in the making, and are now central to the landscape of everyday life. However, new forms of communication technology bring with them changes in how we live and relate.

They invite the culture in new directions, and undermine traditions of long-standing. Choose one of the following technologies and consider the ways in which it is changing cultural life. In particular, how does it influence our interpersonal relationships—our friendships, family life, romantic life, relations in clubs, relations to people in other cultures, and the like.

a. In what ways do you consider these positive changes; in what ways are they detrimental to cultural life?
   1) E-mail
   2) The cell phone
   3) Internet exchanges of video, art, and music
   4) Text messaging

credits

the Doctor–Patient Relationship: Learning How to Talk so Your Doctor Will Listen (13–33). New York: Oxford University Press. Reading 28, pp. 139–140, Carbaugh, D. (1996). The playful self: Being a fan at college basketball games. Situating selves: The communication of social identities in American scenes (pp. 41–51). Albany, NY: State University of New York Press. Reading 29, pp. 150–151, From Best Friends: The Pleasures and Perils of Girls' and Women's Friendship by Terri Apter and Ruthellen Josselson, copyright © 1998 by Terri Apter and Ruthellen Josselson. Used by permission of Crown Publishers, a division of Random House. Reading 30, pp. 153–154, From A. L. Vangelisti, S. L. Young, K. E. Carpenter-Theune, & A. L. Alexander, (2005). Why Does It Hurt? The Perceived Causes of Hurt Feelings. Communication Research, 32(4), pp. 443–477. Reading 31, pp. 155–160, Lips, H. (1999). A New Psychology of Women: Gender, Culture and Ethnicity, © 1999, pp. 145–151, Mountain View, CA: Mayfield. Reprinted with permission of McGraw-Hill Companies, Inc. Reading 32, pp. 161–162, Coates, J. (2003) Men Talk: Stories in the Making of Masculinities, pp. 69–70. Oxford: Blackwell. Reading 33, pp. 164–166, Rawlins, W. K. (2000). Teaching as a Mode of Friendship. Communication Theory 10(1), 6–26. Reading 34, pp. 168–170, Lightfoot, C. (1997). Risk-taking as a transformative experience. In C. Lightfoot (Ed.), The culture of adolescent risk-taking (pp. 123–130). New York: Guilford Press. Reading 35, pp. 174–177, Wilmot, W. W. (1995). Relational Communication. Pp. 78–90, NY: McGraw-Hill Publishers. Reading 36, pp. 180–183, Kellet, P. & Dalton, D. (2001). Changing relationships through conflict. In P. Kellet & D. Dalton (Eds.) pp. 162–182. Managing Conflict in a Negotiated World: A Narrative Approach to Achieving Dialogue and Change, Thousand Oaks, CA: Sage Publications. Reading 37, p. 184, Schrader, S., & Dobris, C. (1994) Wedding vows. Unpublished manuscript. Reading 38, pp. 185–186, Acitelli, L. (2002). Relationship Awareness: Crossing the Bridge between Cognition and Communication. Communication Theory, 12(1). 92–112. Reading 39, pp. 187–188, Penn, P. (2001). Dancing in the dark. So Close: Poems (pp. 3–4). Fort Lee, NJ: Cavan Kerry Press. Reading 40, pp. 191–193, Beirut Letters (excerpt) by Laurel Richardson & Ernest Lockridge (2002), pp. 308–318 in Ethnographically Speaking: Autoethnography, literature, and aesthetics, edited by Arthur P. Bochner and Carolyn Ellis. Reading 41, pp. 194–195, Kirkman, M. (2003). Parents' Contributions to the Narrative Identity of Offspring of Donor-Assisted Conception, Social Science & Medicine. 57(11), 2229–2242 Reading 42, pp. 196–202, Riessman, C. K., Divorce Talk: Women and Men Make Sense of Personal Relationships. Copyright © 1990 by Rutgers, The State University. Reprinted by permission of Rutgers University Press. Reading 43, pp. 203–207, Ellis, C. (1995). Final Negotiations. Philadelphia, PA: Temple University Press. Reading 44, pp. 208–211, Walsh, F. (2006). Strengthening Family Resilience. New York: Guilford Publications, Inc.. Reading 45, pp. 215–216, Littlejohn, S. & Domenici, K. (2001). Systemic Questions. In Engaging Communication in Conflict: Systemic Practice (41–42). Thousand Oaks, CA: Sage. Reading 46, pp. 217–224, Becker, C., Chasin, L., Chasin, R., Herzig, M. & Roth, S. (1995). From Stuck Debate to New Conversation on Controversial Issues: A Report from the Public Conversations Project. Copyright © 1995, The Haworth Press, Inc., Binghamton, NY, Feminist Therapy. 7. pp. 143–163. Reprinted with permission from The Haworth Press, Inc. Reading 47, pp. 225–230, Feuerverger, G. (1997). An Educational Program for Peace: Jewish-Arab Conflict Resolution in Israel. Theory into Practice, 36 (1), 17–25. From the theme issue Teaching Conflict Resolution Preparation for Pluralism. Copyright 1997 by the College of Education, The Ohio State University. All rights reserved. Reading 48, pp. 231–234, Shailor, J. (2002). Improvising a new life: The use of interactive theatre with prison inmates. Paper presented at the 88th Annual Meeting of the National Communication Association. New Orleans, LA. Reading 49, pp. 236–237, Cooperrider, D. & Whitney, D. (2000). A positive revolution in change: Appreciative inquiry. In D.Cooperrider, P. Sorensen, D. Whitney and T.Yaeger (Eds.) Appreciative Inquiry: Foundations in Positive Organizational Development. Reading 50, pp. 249–251, Kavanaugh, K., Absalom, K., Beil, W., & Schliessman, L. (1999). Connecting and becoming culturally competent, Advances in Nursing Science, 21 (3), 9–31. Reprinted by permission. Reading 51, pp. 252–254, Holbrook, S. (2000). Chicks up front. In Gary Max Glazner (Ed.). Poetry Slam: The Competitive Art of Performance Poetry. San Francisco: Manic D. Press. pp. 148–150. Reading 52, pp. 255–257, Hu, B. Email correspondence. Reading 53, pp. 258–259, Willis, P. (1997). Learning to Labour: How Working Class Kids Get Working Class Jobs, pp 1–2, 23–24. New York, NY: Columbia University Press. Reading 54, pp. 260–264, Allen, B. J., Broome, J. B., Jones, T.S., & Chen, V. (2002). Intercultural Alliances: A Cyberdialogue Among Scholars/Practitioners. In M.J. Collier (Ed.). Intercultural Alliances: Critical Transformations. Thousand Oaks, CA: Sage. Reading 55, pp. 268–270, Parks, M.R., Floyd, K. (1996). Making friends in cyberspace. Reading 56, pp. 272–275, Miller, J., & Gergen, K. J. (1998). Life on the Line: The Therapeutic Potential of Computer Mediated Conversation. Journal of Marriage and Family Therapy, 24, 189–202. Reading 57, pp. 276–277, Gibbs, J. L., Ellison, N. B., & Heino, R. D. (2006). Self-Presentation in online personals: The role of anticipated future interaction, self-disclosure, and perceived success in internet dating. Communication Research. 33(2). 152–177. Reading 58, pp. 278–279, 58. Blogs: The Coming of Public Diaries; blog entry by anonymous. Reading 59, pp. 280–281, Meyorowitz, J. (2003). Global nomads in a digital veldt, pp. 91–102. In K. Nyiri (ed.) (2003). Mobile Democracy: Essays on Society, self, and Politics. Vienna: Passagen Verlag p. 282, Cartoon by Z-Man. (May, 2004). Used by permission: Mark Zieman at: http://home.flash.net/~zmanart/markzman@markzman.com.